Contents at a Glance

Contents

20 Dinnertime Delights   237

21 Tremendous Treats   251

Appendixes

Introduction

When you picked up this cookbook, you were probably looking for a few delicious recipes you could prepare knowing that the meals you were eating provided great nutrition. Naturally, we've included mouthwatering recipes made with *superfoods*—those foods with super health benefits. We've tried to share recipes made with foods we think you'll love, as well as to intrigue your taste buds with new flavors and combinations.

Beyond the appetizing recipes, we've shared valuable information on each of the 30 superfoods. We let you know what vitamins, minerals, antioxidants, phytochemicals, and other substances can be found in each superfood, along with how they benefit your body. Equipped with these essentials, you can cook and eat, being mindful of the health advantages of what you put in your body. You should never feel restricted in your ability to put together a tasty, nourishing meal.

Here's to your health and a super new you!

How This Book Is Organized

This book is divided into seven parts:

Part 1, "A Power-Packed Plan," provides indispensable information you need to know about eating well. You'll learn the importance of eating a varied diet, how to read a food label, and more.

Part 2, "Fantastic Fruits," presents the benefits packed into berries, cherries, oranges, and grape products, along with the luscious recipes that feature them.

Part 3, "Valiant Vegetables," is packed with nutrition information and dishes for super vegetables in green, red, and orange.

Part 4, "From the Fields and Trees," highlights the farm-grown goodness of beans, nuts, and grains.

Part 5, "From the Rivers and Ranges," offers recipes made with and the health benefits provided by salmon and turkey.

Part 6, "Tongue-Tingling Tastes," satisfies your taste buds and your cravings for knowledge about yogurt, cayenne, cinnamon, peppermint, chocolate, honey, and tea.

Part 7, "Superfood Combinations," gives you recipes for breakfast, lunch, dinner, and dessert that incorporate two, three, or more superfood ingredients.

Garnishes

You'll see many sidebars throughout the book that offer you a little something extra. Here's what to look for:

Super Knowledge

If you want to sound smart at your next party, check out these boxes, full of all kinds of tidbits from how to store foods to how to get the most nutritional oomph and more.

Kryptonite

When you see these boxes, pay attention. Some might be info on watching calories or fat intake, while others might present serious warnings to avoid possible problems.

Heroic Hints

Filled with all kinds of ways to make something easier, these boxes are a must in today's busy world. Look here for valuable information to help you eat more healthfully and work more efficiently in the kitchen.

def•i•ni•tion

When dealing with health and nutrition, all kinds of big words get tossed about. These boxes help make sense out of them, plus explain some words you might have heard but don't know exactly what they mean.

Acknowledgments

While only two names are credited on the cover of this book, we are all too aware of the contributions afforded by many others who made this book possible.

Shelly would like to thank her husband, Bob, and daughter, Bethany, for occupying themselves during her long work hours. She would also like to thank all the taste testers: Garry and Mary Ellen Goldsmith, Michael Goldsmith, Rick Goldsmith, Ron and Sandy Horky, Bob James, Bob and MaryLou James, David and Julie James, Phyllis McNell, Daniel Ondrick, Paul and Patty Ondrick, Kathy Sechrest, Matt and Barb Sechrest, Lewis and Luetta Trigg, Scott and Kari Werkhoven, Bob and Kaylene Wilson, and Jeff Wilson. It's a tasty job, but somebody has to do it.

Heidi would like to thank her husband, Sean, for all the additional help and support as she worked on this book, especially all the extra daddy-daughter play times. She'd also like to thank her mom, Sandy Swadley, for her input and support.

We extend a big thank you to Tom Stevens, our acquisitions editor at Alpha, whose guidance helped shape this book into the best it could be. We thank our development editor Christy Wagner, production editor Megan Douglass, and copy editor Emily Garner for pruning our manuscript for accuracy and readability. We would also like to thank Marilyn Allen of the Allen O'Shea Literary Agency, whose confidence in our abilities advances us on our career paths.

Special Thanks to the Technical Reviewer

The Complete Idiot's Guide to the Superfood Cookbook was reviewed by an expert who double-checked the accuracy of what you'll learn here, to help us ensure that this book gives you everything you need to know about cooking and eating superfoods. Special thanks are extended to John W. Carbone.

John is a third-year doctoral student in the Department of Nutritional Sciences at the University of Connecticut. While conducting his doctoral research, John teaches a lab course in Food Composition and Preparation and is also completing a dietetic internship, the last step on his path to becoming a certified registered dietitian.

Trademarks

Part 1

A Power-Packed Plan

Whether you're already a healthy eater or this nutritious eating stuff is all new to you, it never hurts to get some new ideas. Looking for creative ways to incorporate more healthful foods into your life? Just trying to get the hang of what healthful eating is? Or are you curious about what specifically you should be eating to optimize your health? Whatever your goal, we've got the help you need in the following pages.

Dynamic Eating

In This Chapter

- ◆ Forget about "good" and "bad"
- ◆ Variety is the spice of life
- ◆ Making it all work for you

Lately, it seems that everyone you talk to has a different idea of what "healthful eating" means. This one eats a certain way to lose weight. This one has high blood pressure. This one's trying to lower his cholesterol. But in reality, with a few exceptions, all of us can follow the same basic eating plan for a healthful life.

Super for You

What's a superfood, you might ask? Its not a bunch of fruits and vegetables running around wearing capes saving the world. They can, however, help you lead a healthier life.

A superfood is a food that provides health benefits above and beyond the basic proteins, carbohydrates, and fats. They contain substances that your body doesn't necessarily need to function—breathe, pump blood, grow, etc.—but that may help lower our risk of developing diseases like cancer and heart disease.

There's a long list of foods that we'd consider "super," but for this book, we've decided to focus on these 30:

Almonds	Flax	Salmon
Beans	Grape juice	Soy
Blueberries	Honey	Spinach
Broccoli	Oats	Strawberries
Carrots	Oranges	Sweet potatoes
Cayenne	Peanuts	Tea
Cherries	Peppermint	Tomatoes
Chocolate	Pumpkins	Turkey
Cinnamon	Red bell peppers	Walnuts
Cranberries	Red wine	Yogurt

The following pages are full of delicious recipes using each and every one of these powerful foods. In addition, each chapter highlights some of the benefits of the superfoods. For more detailed information on each of the foods see *The Pocket Idiot's Guide to Superfoods* (Alpha Books, 2007).

The Good, the Bad, and the Not-So-Ugly

So many people are hung up on the idea of "good" and "bad" foods, which is really a shame because the world of food and nutrition is nowhere near that black and white. Who decides whether a food is good or bad? Many foods could fit on both lists depending on the criteria used to rate them. For example, bananas are a great source of fiber and potassium but are higher in calories than many fruits. Ice cream contains a good amount of sugar and fat but can also be a good source of calcium. How does one go about deciding which one is good and which is bad?

Aside from the confusion of what foods are on what lists, emotional issues are attached to those terms as well. If you eat a good food you're a good person. You're doing a good job. You're a success. On the other hand, eating a bad food might make you feel like a failure if you've promised yourself you wouldn't eat it. You might feel like a bad person. But come on—we're talking about food here! Food is meant to be enjoyed; it shouldn't cause guilt trips. But that's what assigning foods into these inflexible groups can lead to.

Instead of being so rigid and designating foods into two groups—those you can eat and those you can't—consider a more flexible scale, a scale on which there are no forbidden foods. Certainly some foods rank much higher than others; nutrient-packed foods are at the top, while foods containing primarily sugar and/or unhealthy fats and little or no vitamins, minerals, or other nutrients fall to the bottom. All foods can have a place on this scale, and no emotional penalties should come from eating any of them.

As you go through your day, choose the majority of your foods, say 90 percent, from the top of the scale. This should help ensure you get an assortment of health-promoting nutrients throughout the day. And if 10 percent of the foods and drinks you choose happen to come from closer to the bottom of the scale, so be it. It's a small percentage, and they're not taking the place of your nutrient-filled foods—just accessorizing them.

Kryptonite

Many fad diets are based on eliminating entire food groups from your diet. This should be a red flag telling you the diet is no good. All food groups possess their own unique nutritional attributes and are necessary for us to be healthy. If forbidding specific foods isn't the best way to eat healthfully, you can imagine how bad forbidding entire food groups is.

Variety, Variety, Variety

As long as it's healthful, what's wrong with eating the same thing day after day? A lot! Sure it's better than eating the same nutrient-void foods day after day, but you're missing so much. Say the vegetable you choose is carrots. You're getting loads of beta-carotene and vitamin A, but what about the vitamin K you need from dark green leafy veggies, or the lycopene you get from tomato products?

You're much better off choosing a variety of foods. In this case, *variety* means a few different things. Choosing foods from all the

Heroic Hints

Check out the superfood cheat sheet in Appendix B for a complete list of all the superfoods and the major health-promoting nutrients they contain.

food groups is one type of variety. Selecting several different foods from within each food group is another type. And finally, applying these selections through the meals and snacks of each day. In other words, it's important to have different foods day after day as well as different foods from meal to meal.

Putting It All Together

So how do you know if you're choosing the right balance of foods to get all the nutrients you need? Eating a variety of foods is step number one. In addition, various health organizations have set guidelines outlining how much of each food group you need each day to meet your nutritional needs. (This is discussed more in Chapter 2.)

To help ensure you eat a diverse diet, a little planning is needed. That planning starts at the grocery store. Before you can cook foods for a meal or pack a healthful lunch or snack, you need to buy an assortment of healthful foods so they're in the house and available. That might sound simple enough, but many of us go on autopilot at the grocery store, buying the same foods and drinks trip after trip. Make yourself a list of what you want to buy and follow it when you get to the store. To take it one step further, before going to the grocery store, make a rough menu for the upcoming week and then when you're at the market, purchase what you need to prepare the different meals. This helps prevent that 5 or 6 o'clock question, "What's for dinner?"

If you feel you're lacking in one or more food groups, make an effort each week to buy at least one new food from one of your weaker food groups. Maybe try some jicama or a mango from the produce section or pick up some barley from the grain aisle. You never know where you'll find your next favorite food.

> **Heroic Hints**
>
> Planning ahead like this might seem like it would take a lot of time, but it can actually *save* you time. By buying all you need in one trip, you're not heading to the market several times a week, or calling the pizza deliveryman one too many times.

The Real Stuff

Think this all sounds too confusing? Too much work? (It's not!) Think you can do be just as healthy by popping a few vitamins every day and not worry about what you eat? Think again. Sure, a simple one-a-day vitamin and/or mineral supplement can act a bit like insurance—it's there when you need it to balance out some less-than-healthful eating habits once in a while. But mega-dosing on supplements in hopes of fixing sub-par eating habits isn't a good idea, for more reasons than one.

You've probably heard the saying about too much of a good thing. That goes for nutrients, too, at least some of them. Certain vitamins—A, D, E, and K, for example—are fat-soluble. Among other things, that means they are stored in your body's fat tissue. Consuming too much of them, which is difficult to do from foods but can easily be done by overdosing on supplements, can lead to toxic levels being built up in your body's fat. These high levels can have undesirable and sometimes danger-ous side effects.

In addition, Mother Nature knew what she was doing. The specific nutrient com-binations found in many foods work synergistically. In other words, one nutrient may enhance or improve the functions of another. Add to this the fact that some nutrients, especially the super ones discussed in this book, aren't available in supplements. Then there's the real possibility that foods may contain nutrients not yet identified and, therefore, not available in supplements yet either.

The solution? Eat a variety—there's that word again—of real foods every day to meet your nutritional needs. Don't just expect a couple pills to do the job. And don't fresh strawberries dipped in dark chocolate or sautéed red bell peppers taste a heck of a lot better than a few capsules?

The Least You Need to Know

- ◆ There are no "bad" foods.

- ◆ Choose a variety of foods each day to maximize your nutrient intake.

- ◆ From the drawing board, or grocery list in this case, to your kitchen table, it's easier than you might think to get all the good stuff you need.

Chapter 2

Understanding Nutrition

In This Chapter

- ◆ Nutrition 101
- ◆ How much should I eat?
- ◆ Understanding food labels
- ◆ Deciphering ingredient lists

As with most sciences, nutrition can be rather confusing. However, with a basic understanding of a few key matters, you should have no problem creating a health-promoting diet for yourself and your family.

Determining Your Nutrient Needs

Knowing what your body needs, nutritionally speaking, can seem impossible. There are so many things to consider—height, weight, age, and gender, to just name a few. Then add in any health conditions like heart disease or diabetes, and it can feel overwhelming. But if you're trying to figure out what you and your family's needs are, help is available.

The U.S. Department of Agriculture has created a very informative website to help you figure out exactly what your nutritional needs are. At www.mypyramid.gov, you can enter data about yourself such as height, weight and activity level, and both your calorie and food group needs will be calculated.

Heroic Hints

For specific amounts of several vitamins and minerals you and your family members need based on gender and age, check out *The Pocket Idiot's Guide to Superfoods* (Alpha Books, 2007). An appendix is included in the back of the book detailing just that. In addition, Appendix B of this book highlights several of the key nutrients found in all the superfoods.

Not quite sure if potatoes are considered a starch or a vegetable? Or wonder what one serving of pasta is exactly? Wonder no more! The website goes into great detail about what foods are included in the various food groups as well as what constitutes a serving size for several different foods within each group.

Knowing your nutritional needs allows you to choose the most appropriate foods in the right amounts to enhance your health. For example, if you determine your calorie needs to be 2,000 a day, you can use that information when choosing foods to eat, whether they be recipes from this or other cookbooks or the foods on your grocer's shelves. If you find a food you want to eat as a snack and it contains 800 calories per serving, you might want to choose another snack or eat a smaller portion to stay within your calorie needs for the day. This can be applied to any of the nutrients included in this books nutrition analyses or on food labels.

A good rule of thumb to follow when trying to decide how a food can fit into your day is to divide your needs by 4. We'll use calories as an example again, but this works for fat, fiber, etc. The 4 equals 3 meals a day plus snacks. If you divide 2,000 calories by 4, you end up with 500. That means you want to eat roughly 500 calories at each meal and you also have roughly 500 calories to divide up among all your day's snacks.

Nutrition Analysis Revealed

In the following chapters, you'll notice each recipe is accompanied by a nutrition analysis, like this:

Each serving has:

330 calories

14 g total fat

6 g saturated fat

13 g protein

40 g carbohydrate

3 g fiber

25 mg cholesterol

569 mg sodium

This analysis provides you with an assortment of information for 1 serving of the recipe. It's based only on the items in the ingredient list and does not include optional additions or other foods mentioned in serving suggestions. If the ingredient list includes an alternative for a food item, only the first food listed is included in the analysis. For example, "1 whole-wheat pizza crust or 1 regular pizza crust." In this instance, the whole-wheat crust is included in the analysis, not the regular crust. And when a range of servings is given for a recipe and/or a range of ingredient amounts, the nutrition analysis is based on the *first* amount for each.

The nutrition information is provided to help you decide how each specific food can fit into your diet based on your needs. Some foods might be great everyday foods, while others might be better as once-in-a-while foods.

> **Super Knowledge**
>
> The nutrition analyses given in this book are basically guides and are not set in stone. Slight variations in ingredients or how you prepare something could yield different results. The numbers might vary slightly from what you actually create in your kitchen, but they're certainly close enough for you to keep track of.

Navigating a Food Label

A food label lists the nutrition analysis for all the packaged food you buy. Whether it's a box of cereal, frozen vegetables, or anything else, it contains a food label. A couple key things to look for on labels include serving size and number of servings per container. The rest of the information on the label refers to one serving size, so it's important for you to know how much that is.

Here are some of the nutrients and categories you'll see on a food label:

◆ Calories

◆ Calories from fat

◆ Total fat

◆ Saturated fat

◆ Cholesterol

◆ Sodium

◆ Total carbohydrate

◆ Dietary fiber

◆ Sugars

◆ Protein

All the nutrients listed on the label are important, but some might be more important to you than others, depending on your situation. Whether your weight, blood pressure, blood sugar, or something else is an issue for you, your priorities on a label may be calories, sodium, sugar, or something else.

Here's a sample nutrition facts label for you to refer to as you read:

Nutrition Facts
Serving Size 1/2 cup Blueberries (73g)
Servings Per Container

Amount Per Serving

Calories 40   Calories from Fat 0

	% Daily Value*
Total Fat 0g	**0%**
Saturated Fat 0g	**0%**
Trans Fat 0g	
Cholesterol 0mg	**0%**
Sodium 0mg	**0%**
Total Carbohydrate 11g	**4%**
Dietary Fiber 2g	**8%**
Sugars 7g	
Protein 1g	

Vitamin A 0%	•	Vitamin C 10%
Calcium 0%	•	Iron 2%

*Percent Daily Values are based on a 2,000 calorie diet. Your daily values may be higher or lower depending on your calorie needs:

		Calories	2,000	2,500
Total Fat	Less Than		65g	80g
Saturated Fat	Less Than		20g	25g
Cholesterol	Less Than		300mg	300 mg
Sodium	Less Than		2,400mg	2,400mg
Total Carbohydrate			300g	375g
Dietary Fiber			25g	30g

Calories per gram:
Fat 9 • Carbohydrate 4 • Protein 4

The right side of the food label contains the % Daily Value information. The numbers in this column are based on a 2,000-calorie diet. A food providing 10%DV protein provides 10 percent of the protein a person who eats 2,000 calories a day needs. For a person eating fewer calories, the same amount of this food provides more than 10 percent of their needs while it provides less than 10 percent of the protein needs of a person eating more than 2,000 calories. This 2,000 calorie reference point is used for fat, saturated fat, total carbohydrate, fiber, and protein. The % Daily Value for the remainder of the nutrients included on a food label apply to everyone, as they're based on the average needs of healthy adults. Knowing how to make sense of all these numbers can help you decide how a particular food can fit into your diet.

What's in This?

The food label is an important source of information on a food's packaging, but be sure to also check out the ingredient list. According to the United States Food and Drug Administration's Nutrition Labeling and Education Act, for all foods with more than one ingredient everything in the food must be included in this list in order of amount. The more of something a food has in it, the higher it is on the list.

For example, if a label lists carrots and then water, the food is mostly carrots. If, on the other hand, some sort of sugar is listed as three of the first four ingredients, know that it's a very sugar-filled food.

Super Knowledge _____

Food manufacturers use a variety of ingredients and terms that basically all mean *sugar*. When you start to read the ingredient list, keep in mind the following words, just to name a few, all mean sugar of some sort: *sugar, corn syrup, high fructose corn syrup, dextrose, sucrose, fructose, glucose, maltose, brown sugar, fruit juice concentrate, honey, invert sugar, maple syrup.*

The Least You Need to Know

◆ With a little thought, you can easily figure out exactly what your body needs to be healthy.

◆ With nutrition facts labels and ingredient lists, you can figuring out what you're eating.

◆ Don't get deceived by fancy words. Learn what label jargon means for the best nutrition.

Part 2

Fantastic Fruits

Maybe it's the fruit lover in me, but I'm always surprised when I hear someone say they only eat fruit a couple times a week. And even then, it's often your basic apple or banana or glass of juice. These choices are perfectly fine, but there's a whole other world out there in the produce section! By choosing a variety of different fruits every day, your eating is more enjoyable, plus you also get a multitude of different nutrients.

So if you're one of those people who counts the raisins in your cookie as your weekly serving of fruit, it's time to get wild and crazy—and healthy. Try the recipes in the following chapters to add some fruit to your day. And if you already eat fruit until it's coming out your ears, here are some new ways to try it!

Chapter 3

Bountiful Berries

In This Chapter

- You can't forget about blueberries
- Cranberries won't stick it to ya
- Strawberries: take 'em to heart
- Sweet treats that are good for you, too

Blueberries, cranberries, and strawberries—who would have thought that these little berries contain more antioxidant power than most other fresh fruits? Just goes to show that great things *do* come in small packages.

Unbeatable Blueberries

Tossing a handful of frozen blueberries into your oatmeal as it cooks gets both your day and your antioxidant intake off to a great start because blueberries contain a high number of antioxidants. The main type of antioxidants in blueberries are called *anthocyanidins*.

def•i•ni•tion

Anthocyanidins are phytochemicals (compounds found in plants that provide tremendous health benefits) that work to maintain healthy blood vessels. They're also responsible for the dark red, blue, and purple coloring in some fruits and vegetables.

One of the tasks these super nutrients perform is to help improve motor skills like walking and sitting; they help with hand, finger, and toe movement as well. These abilities can become more difficult as we age, but studies suggest that just 1 cup a day of these sweet berries can help prevent that deterioration. That same amount can also help undo some age-related, short-term memory loss. So until you start eating them regularly, write them on your grocery list now so you won't forget!

Cream-of-the-Crop Cranberries

Maybe you've heard that cranberries and cranberry juice are helpful in preventing urinary tract infections. However, you might not know that cranberries are beneficial in many other ways, too.

The phytochemicals in cranberries are called *proanthocyanidins*, and one of their main benefits is preventing bacteria from sticking to places. One such place is the urinary tract—the walls of it, to be specific. If bacteria can't stick to those walls, it can't grow and cause an infection. Cranberry juice appears to reduce the amount of bacteria that adheres to your teeth, too, which can help lower your chances of developing cavities and gum disease. And last but certainly not least, there's help a bit farther down the digestive tract. The bacteria that cause stomach ulcers do so by sticking to the stomach's walls. Cranberries can help prevent that from happening, thus lowering your chance of developing a painful stomach ulcer.

Super Knowledge

Current research indicates that as little as two 8-ounce glasses of cranberry juice cocktail a day is all you need to prevent all this sticking from happening.

Impressive Strawberries

The variety of nutrients found in strawberries is amazing. One strawberry contains phytochemicals, vitamin C, potassium, folate, and more. And you only have to eat about 8 medium strawberries, or 1 cup, to get more vitamin C than what you'd get from a whole orange.

While strawberries provide many different super powers, the flavonoid *quercetin* is the real superstar of the bunch. This phytonutrient's big job is slowing down the speed at which your blood clots—preventing internal blood clots that can cause strokes or heart attacks.

def•i•ni•tion

Quercetin is a major dietary flavonoid. In addition to slowing clotting, it may help lower your risk of asthma, lung cancer, and heart disease.

Flavonoids are a group of plant pigments that also provide health benefits.

Blueberry-Speckled Oatmeal Muffins

With a hint of tangy lemon flavor, these muffins can start your day off right or curb your midday hunger more healthfully.

Yield: 1 dozen
Prep time: 15 minutes
Cook time: 15 minutes
Serving size: 1 muffin
Each serving has:
136 calories
3 g total fat
<1 g saturated fat
5 g protein
25 g carbohydrate
3 g fiber
<1 mg cholesterol
120 mg sodium

1½ cups old-fashioned rolled oats

½ cup plus 2 TB. all-purpose flour

½ cup whole-wheat flour

6 TB. ground flaxseed meal

1 TB. baking powder

1 cup fat-free milk

¼ cup honey

2 large egg whites, lightly beaten

1 tsp. finely grated lemon zest

1 tsp. vanilla extract

1 cup fresh blueberries

1. Preheat the oven to 400°F. Coat the bottoms of 2³/₄-inch (regular-size) muffin cups with nonstick cooking spray.

2. Stir together oats, all-purpose flour, whole-wheat flour, flaxseed meal, and baking powder in a large bowl.

3. Combine milk, honey, egg whites, lemon zest, and vanilla extract in a medium bowl, and whisk until well blended. Add to oat mixture, and stir just until dry ingredients are moistened.

4. Gently fold in blueberries until evenly distributed.

5. Spoon batter into the prepared cups, filling each cup ³/₄ full. Bake for 15 minutes or until muffins test done with a cake tester. Cool muffins in the pan on a wire rack for 5 minutes before removing from the cups to serve.

Variation: Substitute thawed and drained frozen blueberries or drained canned blueberries for fresh blueberries.

Super Knowledge

Thanks to the ground flax, each of these yummy muffins provides 1 gram healthful omega-3 fatty acids. Look for ground flaxseed meal in the organic section or the baking aisle of your local supermarket.

Easy Blueberry Yogurt Salad

This creamy salad with an added crunch could be a quick and attractive addition to brunch or a smart snack.

½ **cup plain fat-free yogurt**   2 **cups fresh blueberries**

1½ **tsp. honey**   ¼ **cup unsalted chopped pecans or walnuts**

Yield: 4 servings
Prep time: 2 minutes
Serving size: ¹/₂ cup
Each serving has:
114 calories
6 g total fat
<1 g saturated fat
3 g protein
16 g carbohydrate
2 g fiber
1 mg cholesterol
18 mg sodium

1. Stir together yogurt and honey in a medium bowl until blended. Stir in blueberries until evenly coated.

2. Sprinkle pecans evenly over top to serve.

Variations: This is also good with the pecans or walnuts lightly toasted. Place nuts in a small, dry, nonstick skillet, and cook over medium heat for 5 minutes or until golden, shaking the skillet occasionally to prevent burning. For a combination of superfoods, substitute sliced strawberries, orange segments, or halved cherries for a portion of the blueberries.

Super Knowledge

Feel like it's tough to get enough fruits and veggies into your day? One serving of this refreshing salad gives you one whole serving of blueberries.

Blueberry Banana Pops

For sweltering summer days, you and your kids will love these naturally fruit flavored, refreshing treats; make them in smaller portions for the littlest ones.

Yield: 4 servings
Prep time: 5 minutes
Chill time: 4 hours
Serving size: 1 pop
Each serving has:
99 calories
<1 g total fat
0 g saturated fat
3 g protein
24 g carbohydrate
2 g fiber
1 mg cholesterol
35 mg sodium

1 cup plain fat-free yogurt

1 cup fresh blueberries

2 medium very ripe bananas, peeled and broken into chunks

1. Combine yogurt, blueberries, and bananas in a blender. Cover and blend on high speed for 30 to 45 seconds or until thoroughly blended.

2. Pour ¾ cup mixture into 4 (1-cup) wax-coated paper cups or plastic cups, and insert a popsicle stick in the center of each. Freeze for at least 4 hours or until solid. To serve, run tap water over the outsides of the cups to release the pops.

Variation: Substitute thawed and drained frozen blueberries or drained canned blueberries for fresh blueberries.

 Heroic Hints _____

These frozen antioxidant-packed treats are a great substitute for store-bought, sugar-filled, nutrient-lacking popsicles.

Blueberry Delight Sauce

Spoon this not-too-sweet sauce over ice cream, frozen yogurt, or a thick slice of angel food cake for a scrumptious treat, or pour it over your morning stack of pancakes or fluffy waffles.

2 cups frozen wild blueberries	**2 TB. water**
¼ cup granulated sugar	**1 tsp. lemon juice**

1. Combine 1½ cups blueberries, sugar, water, and lemon juice in a medium saucepan. Cook over medium heat for 10 minutes or until mixture starts to thicken and bubble, stirring frequently and mashing blueberries with the back of a spoon.

2. Stir in remaining ½ cup blueberries, and cook for 5 minutes, stirring often. Remove the saucepan from the heat and cool slightly to serve, or cover and chill to serve cold.

Heroic Hints

Keeping frozen blueberries on hand makes it easy to add this superfood to your day. They're great to cook with but are also a great addition to pancake batter, muffin mix, quick breads, and more. Plus, on a busy morning, a handful or two tossed into your oatmeal as it cooks makes for a quick and flavorful power boost. This works if you cook your oatmeal in the microwave just as well as if you prepare it on the stovetop.

Yield: 4 servings
Prep time: 2 minutes
Cook time: 15 minutes
Serving size: ¼ cup
Each serving has:
65 calories
1 g total fat
0 g saturated fat
1 g protein
18 g carbohydrate
2 g fiber
0 mg cholesterol
<1 mg sodium

Cranberry-Studded Wheat Muffins

Enjoy a sweet nibble with these muffins while you boost your fiber intake—and all for under 150 calories.

Yield: 1 dozen	
Prep time: 10 minutes	
Cook time: 15 to 20 minutes	
Serving size: 1 muffin	
Each serving has:	
147 calories	
4 g total fat	
<1 g saturated fat	
5 g protein	
25 g carbohydrate	
3 g fiber	
18 mg cholesterol	
82 mg sodium	

1 cup whole-wheat flour	1 cup fat-free milk
1 cup all-purpose flour	2 TB. honey
¾ cup ground flaxseed meal	½ cup dried cranberries
2 tsp. baking powder	
1 large egg, at room temperature, or egg substitute equal to 1 egg	

1. Preheat the oven to 375°F. Coat 2³/₄-inch (regular-size) muffin cups with nonstick cooking spray.

2. Stir together whole-wheat flour, all-purpose flour, flaxseed meal, and baking powder in a medium bowl.

3. In a small bowl, beat egg. Stir in milk and honey, and pour into dry ingredients, stirring until moistened. (Batter will be stiff.) Stir in cranberries until distributed evenly.

4. Spoon batter into muffin cups, dividing evenly and roughly shaping to cups. Bake for 15 to 20 minutes or until golden brown and muffins test done with a cake tester. Remove muffins immediately and cool on a wire rack.

Kryptonite

Dried fruits are delicious and nutritious treats, but they're also a very concentrated source of calories and sugar, so don't go overboard. Keep the serving size to ¼ cup.

Cran-Raspberry Waldorf Gelatin Salad

Make this easy yet impressive gelatin salad for a crowd-pleasing carry-in dish that's tart and crunchy.

1 (0.6-oz.) pkg. sugar-free raspberry gelatin

2 cups boiling water

1 (12-oz.) pkg. frozen red raspberries

½ cup fresh or unsweetened orange juice

1 (16-oz.) can whole-berry cranberry sauce

2 cups peeled and diced eating apples

1 cup thinly sliced celery

¾ cup unsalted chopped walnuts

Yield: 15 servings
Prep time: 10 minutes
Chill time: 1½ hours
Serving size: ½ cup
Each serving has:
109 calories
4 g total fat
<1 g saturated fat
2 g protein
19 g carbohydrate
2 g fiber
0 mg cholesterol
25 mg sodium

1. Pour gelatin into a large bowl, add boiling water, and stir for 2 minutes or until gelatin is completely dissolved. Stir in frozen red raspberries and orange juice for 3 minutes or until raspberries are thawed and separated and gelatin is beginning to thicken. Chill for 30 minutes or until set.

2. Stir in cranberry sauce, apples, celery, and walnuts until evenly distributed. Chill for 1 hour or until cold. Transfer to a serving bowl, or cover and chill until serving time.

Super Knowledge

If you don't have a standard favorite eating apple, here are some good ones to try: Empire, Fuji, Gala, Golden Delicious, Granny Smith, and Red Delicious. All work well in this recipe.

Whole Orange Cranberry Relish

Spoon this tangy relish atop roasted turkey or pork, or pair it with Thanksgiving Memories Open-Faced Turkey Sandwiches (recipe in Chapter 19).

Yield: 12 servings
Prep time: 8 minutes
Cook time: 7 minutes
Serving size: ¼ cup
Each serving has:
85 calories
0 g total fat
0 g saturated fat
<1 g protein
22 g carbohydrate
2 g fiber
0 mg cholesterol
1 mg sodium

1 (12-oz.) pkg. fresh or frozen cranberries

1 medium navel orange

¾ cup honey or to taste

1. Rinse cranberries with cold water and drain. Coarsely chop cranberries and place in a medium saucepan.

2. Clean orange with a commercial vegetable and fruit wash. Remove stem as necessary and cut into wedges. Remove any seeds and chop orange. Add to cranberries.

3. Stir honey into cranberry mixture, and bring to a boil over medium-high heat. Continue boiling for 4 minutes, stirring occasionally, until orange peels are softened. Remove from heat to cool. Serve warm or cold.

Super Knowledge

Using the whole orange, peel and all, makes for faster preparation. Boiling softens the peel enough to make it easy to eat and tasty.

Asian Cranberry Chicken Wings

Impress your guests with these scrumptious, piquant starters you can make ahead and bake as company arrives.

1 (16-oz.) can whole-berry cranberry sauce

¼ cup reduced-sodium soy sauce

2 TB. light brown sugar

½ tsp. ground ginger

2 medium cloves garlic, crushed

2 lb. skinless whole chicken wings

Yield: 7 servings
Prep time: 3 minutes
Cook time: 1 hour
Serving size: 1 wing
Each serving has:
215 calories
4 g total fat
1 g saturated fat
16 g protein
29 g carbohydrate
1 g fiber
42 mg cholesterol
367 mg sodium

1. Stir together cranberry sauce, soy sauce, brown sugar, ginger, and garlic in a small saucepan. Bring just to a simmer over medium heat, reduce heat to low, and simmer for 5 minutes, stirring often. Remove from heat.

2. Cut tips from chicken wings, and arrange wings in a 13×9×2-inch glass baking dish. Pour cranberry mixture over wings, and stir to coat thoroughly. Cover and marinate in the refrigerator for 2 hours.

3. Preheat oven to 350°F. Bake chicken wings for 30 minutes, turn wings, and continue baking for 20 minutes or until done (180°F on a food thermometer). Serve hot.

Variation: You can separate the wings at the joints to make two pieces—the wing or wingette and the drumette. With the wing tips removed, the baking dish will have space for a few more pieces.

Heroic Hints

Kitchen shears make quick work of cutting the wing tips. Otherwise, turn to a sturdy knife and cutting board. All kitchen utensils and surfaces that come in contact with raw meats must be washed in hot, soapy water to avoid cross-contamination.

Strawberries and Cream Wheat Pancakes

For a filling breakfast with a fresh taste, try these hearty pancakes with a velvety topping.

Yield: 6 servings
Prep time: 5 minutes
Cook time: 6 minutes per batch
Serving size: 2 pancakes with 2³/₄ tablespoons strawberries and cream
Each serving has:
205 calories
1 g total fat
<1 g saturated fat
10 g protein
42 g carbohydrate
5 g fiber
2 mg cholesterol
493 mg sodium

2 TB. lemon juice

2 cups plus 2 TB. fat-free milk

1½ cups whole-wheat flour

½ cup all-purpose flour

1 TB. granulated sugar

½ tsp. salt

1 tsp. baking soda

1¼ cups finely chopped fresh or frozen strawberries, thawed if frozen

2 oz. fat-free cream cheese, cut into small cubes

1 TB. honey or to taste

1. Stir lemon juice into 2 cups milk and set aside.

2. Stir together whole-wheat flour, all-purpose flour, sugar, and salt in a medium bowl.

3. Stir baking soda into milk mixture, and pour into flour mixture. Combine using a wire whisk until dry ingredients are moistened.

4. Whisk in ¹/₂ cup strawberries until evenly distributed.

5. Coat a large nonstick skillet or griddle with nonstick cooking spray and heat over medium heat. Pour ¹/₄ cup batter into the skillet for each pancake, preparing pancakes in batches. Cook for 3 minutes or until tops of pancakes are bubbly and edges are dry. Turn pancakes with a spatula and cook on other side for 3 minutes or until golden brown.

6. Meanwhile, combine cream cheese and remaining 2 table-spoons milk in a small bowl. Stir with a small wire whisk until airy and nearly smooth. Stir in honey and remaining ³/₄ cup strawberries until blended. Serve, spooning cream cheese mixture over hot pancakes.

Variation: For a less hearty, more subtle wheat-flavored pancake, reduce whole-wheat flour to 1 cup and prepare as directed. (Batter will be thin.)

Kryptonite

To substitute frozen strawberries for fresh strawberries in a recipe, be sure to choose unsweetened strawberries and not the sweet syrup–packed berries.

Key West Salad

Refresh your taste buds with a lunch of juicy fruits enlivened by a honey-lime dressing.

2 tsp. lime juice

2 tsp. honey

½ tsp. extra-virgin olive oil

2 TB. unsalted cashew pieces

1½ cups mixed salad greens

1 cup hulled and halved fresh strawberries

½ cup fresh pineapple chunks

½ cup halved seedless green grapes

1 medium kiwifruit, peeled, sliced, and halved

Yield: 1 serving
Prep time: 8 minutes
Each serving has:
364 calories
11 g total fat
2 g saturated fat
7 g protein
67 g carbohydrate
9 g fiber
0 mg cholesterol
31 mg sodium

1. Whisk together lime juice, honey, and olive oil in a small bowl until well blended. Chill dressing while preparing salad.

2. Place cashew pieces in a small, dry, nonstick skillet over medium heat, and toast for 3 minutes or until golden, shaking the skillet often to prevent burning. Remove cashew pieces and set aside to cool.

3. Line a serving plate with a bed of salad greens. Scatter strawberries, pineapple, grapes, and kiwifruit over top. To serve, drizzle on honey-lime dressing and scatter cashew pieces over top.

Super Knowledge

All the fruits and greens in this salad add up to more than double your daily vitamin C needs, nearly half your folate needs, and 4 milligrams iron.

Balsamic Berries

These tangy, syrupy strawberries are luscious served plain, with a dollop of whipped topping, spooned over a slice of angel food cake, or topping a dish of frozen yogurt or ice cream.

Yield: 6 servings
Prep time: 2 minutes
Stand time: 1 hour
Serving size: 1/2 cup
Each serving has:
48 calories
<1 g total fat
0 g saturated fat
1 g protein
12 g carbohydrate
2 g fiber
0 mg cholesterol
2 mg sodium

3 cups hulled and halved fresh strawberries (quartered if large)

2 TB. honey

1 TB. balsamic vinegar

1. Place strawberries in a large bowl. Pour honey and balsamic vinegar over strawberries, and stir to coat evenly.

2. Let stand at room temperature for 1 hour until juice is extracted. Stir again before serving. Refrigerate any leftovers.

Super Knowledge

The leafy base where the stem connects to the fruit is called the hull. To hull strawberries, use a paring knife to cut around the hulls and remove the inner white cores.

Strawberry Lemonade

Serve this refreshing, sweet-tart thirst quencher when regular lemonade just won't do.

3 cups hulled whole straw-berries or unsweetened fro-zen strawberries, thawed

1 cup fresh lemon juice

½ cup plus 2 TB. honey or to taste

6 cups cold water

Yield: 9 servings
Prep time: 3 minutes
Serving size: 1 cup
Each serving has:
93 calories
0 g total fat
0 g saturated fat
1 g protein
25 g carbohydrate
1 g fiber
0 mg cholesterol
6 mg sodium

1. Place strawberries in a blender, cover, and purée for 30 seconds or until liquefied. (Strain the seeds from the strawberry purée with a fine-mesh strainer if they bother you.) Add lemon juice and honey, and blend on high speed for 30 seconds or until thoroughly blended. Pour into a large pitcher.

2. Add cold water to strawberry mixture, and stir to blend. Serve immediately over ice or chill until serving time, stirring again before serving.

Heroic Hints _____

The amount of honey needed for this recipe will vary based on the sweetness of the berries you use. Growing season and age cause differences in a berry's sweetness, so sample a berry before preparing a recipe to help you gauge how much honey or other sweetener you'll need.

Chapter 4

Tree Treats

In This Chapter

◆ The benefits of cherries

◆ Oranges: more than just vitamin C

◆ Recipes for delicious cherry and orange dishes—morning, noon, and night

We love fruit, and we try to work it into our meals and snacks whenever we can. But if you're not like us, if the only orange in your diet is orange soda, and if you count cherry gelatin as a serving of fruit, you might want to consider making a few small dietary changes and include some yummy fruit in your day. Keep reading to find out why and how to do just that.

Champion Cherries

Cherries share many of the same benefits as berries (see Chapter 3), but they also have a few unique qualities. One is their ability to lower the levels of *C-reactive protein* in the blood. The anthocyanidins found in cherries may help lower your risk of developing heart disease by dealing with the inflammatory aspect of the disease. High levels of C-reactive protein on the blood serve as a marker for inflammation and, therefore, can be a risk factor for heart disease. By helping prevent inflammation, which could lead to lower levels of this protein, cherries in your diet may help decrease your heart disease risk. They may also be beneficial with other inflammatory, thus painful, diseases include arthritis and gout.

Just about 45 cherries a day provide enough anthocyanidins to reduce the pain-causing enzymes related to arthritis and gout.

Another unique property of cherries is their ability to help regulate sleep. They do so because they contain a form of *melatonin* that is easily used by the body. Eating cherries can help restore natural sleep patterns when they get a bit out of whack.

def•i•ni•tion

> **C-reactive protein** is a protein found in the blood that rises with inflammation. **Melatonin** is a hormone involved in regulating your sleeping and waking cycles.

Zestful Oranges

Oranges' biggest claim to fame might be their vitamin C content, but they give us a lot more than that. Their deep orange color indicates the presence of a *phytochemical* you may have heard of … beta-carotene. Beta-carotene is probably one of the most talked about antioxidants around. It provides benefits throughout the body; helping keep your eyes, skin, and immune system in good working order are just a few of the jobs this power-house nutrient performs.

Oranges are also loaded with vitamin C. Vitamin C helps protect you from getting sick, but goes even beyond prevention. If and when a nasty little bug does get in, vitamin C can help shorten the length and severity of your illness. The recommended daily amount of vitamin C is 75 milligrams a day for adult women and 90 milligrams daily for adult men. Vitamin C is a water-soluble vitamin, meaning your body gets rid of any you don't use, so feel free to up your intake in times of sickness. You can safely take up to 2,000 milligrams a day. So next time you're under the weather, check out these yummy recipes to give yourself an extra dose of this germ-fighting vitamin.

def•i•ni•tion

> **Phytochemicals** are plant compounds that, although not vital for proper body function, improve health and/or decrease the risk of certain diseases.

The most recent news about oranges is with regard to the phytochemical apigenin. Oranges contain a good amount of this nutrient which is also found in parsley and onions. Apigenin is currently being studied for its role in cancer prevention. Research is still very much in the early stages however it looks promising so far.

Quinoa with Berries and Cherries

With a peppery undertone and a tart taste, this quinoa mixture deliciously accompanies pork, chicken, or fish dishes.

Yield: 4 servings
Prep time: 1 minute
Cook time: 20 to 25 minutes
Serving size: ¹/₂ cup
Each serving has:
135 calories
1 g total fat
<1 g saturated fat
4 g protein
27 g carbohydrate
4 g fiber
1 mg cholesterol
39 mg sodium

½ cup *quinoa*

1 cup fat-free, less-sodium chicken or vegetable broth

¼ cup dried cranberries

¼ cup dried sour cherries

⅛ tsp. freshly ground black pepper

1. Combine quinoa and chicken broth in a small saucepan, and bring to a boil over high heat. Reduce heat to low, cover, and simmer for 12 to 15 minutes or until grains are tender and most of liquid is absorbed.

2. Stir in cranberries, cherries, and black pepper. Cover and let stand for 3 to 5 minutes or until fruits are plumped and all liquid is absorbed. Fluff with a fork and serve immediately.

def•i•ni•tion

Quinoa (pronounced *KEEN*-wa) is a whole grain that provides a complete protein. Quinoa is gluten-free, so it's good for gluten-free/wheat-free diets.

Cherry-Apple Sauce over Pork Chops

Serve the sweeter side of pork when it's topped with a juicy, irresistible fruit sauce where the cherries provide half the fiber in each serving.

¼ tsp. dried thyme

¼ tsp. salt

¼ tsp. freshly ground black pepper

1 lb. boneless pork chops, trimmed of fat and cut into serving-size pieces

1⅓ cups apple juice

1 medium Braeburn or other cooking apple, cored and cut into very thin wedges

2 green onions, finely chopped

¼ cup dried sour cherries

2 tsp. cornstarch

2 TB. water

Yield: 4 servings
Prep time: 5 minutes
Cook time: 17 minutes
Serving size: 1 pork chop with ½ cup sauce
Each serving has:
259 calories
10 g total fat
4 g saturated fat
18 g protein
23 g carbohydrate
4 g fiber
60 mg cholesterol
215 mg sodium

1. Coat an 11-inch nonstick skillet with nonstick cooking spray and heat over medium heat.

2. Stir together thyme, salt, and black pepper in a small bowl. Rub onto both sides of pork chops. Add chops to the skillet and cook for 6 minutes on each side or until done (160°F on a food thermometer). Remove chops from the skillet and keep warm.

3. Add apple juice, apple wedges, green onions, and cherries to the skillet and stir, scraping up browned bits from pork chops. Simmer for 3 minutes or until apples are tender.

4. Whisk together cornstarch and water in a small bowl until smooth and blended. Stir into the skillet, and simmer for 2 minutes or until sauce is clear and thickened. Spoon cherry-apple sauce over pork chops to serve.

Super Knowledge

Good cooking apples include the Gala, Golden Delicious, Granny Smith, Jonagold, Jonathan, and Winesap. Any of these will work in place of the Braeburn called for in this recipe.

Cherry and Pink Grapefruit Gelatin Mold

This sweet-tart salad starts a luncheon off right with its colorful presentation, and you'll like its quick-to-fix recipe.

Yield: 10 servings
Prep time: 5 minutes
Chill time: 3 hours
Serving size: 3-inch slice
Each serving has:
53 calories
<1 g total fat
0 g saturated fat
1 g protein
14 g carbohydrate
1 g fiber
0 mg cholesterol
17 mg sodium

1 (15.25-oz.) can pitted dark sweet cherries in heavy syrup, drained and rinsed

1 (15-oz.) can ruby red grapefruit sections in light syrup, drained and rinsed

1 cup boiling water

1 (0.3-oz.) pkg. sugar-free lime gelatin

1 cup diet ginger ale, chilled

Lettuce leaves (optional)

1. Coat a 6-cup ring mold with nonstick cooking spray. Alternately layer cherries and grapefruit sections in the mold.

2. In a medium bowl, stir together boiling water and gelatin until dissolved. Slowly stir in ginger ale. (Mixture will foam a little.) Pour into the mold, and cover and chill for 3 hours or until firm.

3. Invert the mold on a serving plate lined with lettuce leaves (if using). Cut into slices to serve.

Heroic Hints

A gelatin salad *should* gently slide out of a nonstick mold, but for those times when it doesn't, set the mold into a bit of warm water (without getting the gelatin wet). After a minute or two, the gelatin should be loosened enough to release.

Cheery Cherry Chocolate Parfaits

Simple, easy to make, and oh so good, these parfaits make a great everyday dessert where velvety pudding swathes sweet cherries.

1 (4-serving-size) pkg. sugar-free instant chocolate pudding mix

2 cups fat-free milk

2 cups frozen pitted dark sweet cherries, thawed and drained

Yield: 4 servings
Prep time: 5 minutes
Chill time: 5 minutes
Serving size: 1 parfait
Each serving has:
173 calories
1 g total fat
0 g saturated fat
5 g protein
38 g carbohydrate
2 g fiber
2 mg cholesterol
1,106 mg sodium

1. Prepare pudding mix with milk according to the package directions.

2. Reserve a few cherries for garnishing. Layer pudding and remaining cherries alternately in 4 parfait glasses or other dessert dishes, beginning and ending with pudding. Garnish with reserved cherries. Chill for 5 minutes or until pudding is set.

Variation: Substitute Creamy Chocolate Tofu Pudding (recipe in Chapter 10) for the prepared chocolate pudding.

Super Knowledge

Cherries enjoy a short harvesting season, usually June and early July, but take advantage of that time and choose big, smooth, dark-skinned Bing cherries to eat out of hand or use in desserts such as this one calling for dark sweet cherries. Just be sure to pit fresh cherries before serving, as a pit can be quite an unpleasant surprise. A cherry pitter allows you to keep the cherry whole while removing the pit. Place a single cherry in the bowl of the cherry pitter and push the rod through the fruit to dislodge its pit. Easy!

Sweet-Spot Tuna Salad

This combination is brighter than your typical tuna salad—great for perking you up at lunchtime.

Yield: 7 servings
Prep time: 15 minutes
Chill time: 4 hours
Serving size: 1 cup
Each serving has:
200 calories
4 g total fat
<1 g saturated fat
12 g protein
33 g carbohydrate
4 g fiber
11 mg cholesterol
189 mg sodium

2 cups uncooked whole-wheat elbow macaroni

1 (7.06-oz.) pkg. light tuna in water

2 TB. lemon juice

1 TB. chopped fresh chives

⅛ tsp. freshly ground black pepper

1 medium navel orange, peeled and finely chopped

⅓ cup finely chopped sweet gherkins

⅓ cup raisins

¼ cup reduced-fat mayonnaise

1. Cook macaroni according to the package directions and drain. Rinse with cold water and transfer to a medium bowl.

2. Add tuna, lemon juice, chives, black pepper, oranges, gherkins, and raisins to macaroni, and stir to break up tuna. Add mayonnaise and stir lightly to coat evenly. Cover and chill for at least 4 hours or overnight. Stir again before serving.

Heroic Hints

Vitamin C enhances the absorption of iron. Whenever possible, combine vitamin C–rich foods, like the oranges in this recipe, with iron-rich foods, like the tuna, raisins, and enriched pasta, to maximize your iron intake.

Orange-Kissed Asparagus

A harbinger of spring, asparagus is crisp, fresh, and deliciously enlivened by the citrus in this dish.

1½ lb. fresh asparagus, trimmed

2 TB. extra-virgin olive oil

1 medium clove garlic, halved

¼ cup fresh or unsweetened orange juice

1 TB. grated orange zest

⅛ tsp. salt

⅛ tsp. freshly ground black pepper

1 medium navel orange, peeled and chopped

Yield: 6 servings	
Prep time: 3 minutes	
Cook time: 6 minutes	
Serving size: 6 spears	
Each serving has:	
80 calories	
5 g total fat	
1 g saturated fat	
3 g protein	
9 g carbohydrate	
3 g fiber	
0 mg cholesterol	
63 mg sodium	

1. Place asparagus spears in an 11-inch nonstick skillet and add ½ inch water. Cover and bring to a boil over high heat. Reduce heat to medium, and cook for 4 minutes or until asparagus is crisp-tender. Drain and transfer to a serving plate.

2. Meanwhile, heat olive oil in a small skillet over medium heat. Add garlic and sauté for 1 minute or until golden; discard garlic. Turn off heat and slowly pour in orange juice. Stir in orange zest, salt, and black pepper, and stir to combine. Pour mixture over asparagus, and gently toss to coat. Scatter oranges over asparagus, and serve immediately.

Super Knowledge

Steaming or boiling food for a short period of time enables your body to absorb a larger amount of many of the nutrients found in dark green veggies, such as asparagus.

Tropical Mahi Mahi with Pineapple-Orange Salsa

Indulge in the tastes of the islands with this easy-to-prepare dish with flavor that belies its simplicity.

Yield: 4 servings
Prep time: 5 minutes
Chill time: 1 hour
Cook time: 15 to 18 minutes
Serving size: 1 fillet with ½ cup salsa
Each serving has:
211 calories
1 g total fat
<1 g saturated fat
22 g protein
30 g carbohydrate
2 g fiber
83 mg cholesterol
106 mg sodium

1 (20-oz.) can crushed pine-apple in pineapple juice

1 (10.5-oz.) can *mandarin orange* segments in mandarin orange juice

1 medium jalapeño pepper, seeded and minced

½ tsp. ground ginger

4 (4-oz.) boneless, skinless mahi mahi fillets

1. Combine pineapple and mandarin orange segments with their juices in a medium bowl. Stir in jalapeño pepper and ginger until well combined. Transfer 2 cups mixture with a minimal amount of juice to a small bowl. Cover and chill for 1 hour.

2. Place fillets in a gallon-size resealable plastic bag, laying flat on one side. Pour remaining pineapple mixture over fillets. Remove all air from the bag, close the bag, and marinate in the refrigerator for 1 hour.

3. Preheat the oven to 400°F. Coat a 9×9×2-inch glass baking dish or another large enough to comfortably hold fillets with nonstick cooking spray.

4. Remove salsa and fillets from the refrigerator. Transfer fillets to the prepared baking dish with a slotted spatula. (Discard marinade that came in contact with raw fillets.)

5. Bake fillets for 15 to 18 minutes or until fish flakes easily with a fork or reads 145°F on a food thermometer. Serve fillets immediately, each topped with salsa.

def•i•ni•tion

Mandarin oranges, a small type of orange, contain more than twice the amount of beta-carotene as their larger family member and four times the amount of vitamin A. A clementine is a seedless variety of a mandarin orange.

Honey-Drizzled Oranges and Bananas

Simple and speedy, this syrupy fruit dish satisfies your sweet tooth without the excessive fat and calories often served after dinner.

1 medium navel orange, peeled and cut into ¼-in. slices

2 medium bananas, peeled and cut into ¾-in. slices

3 TB. honey

2 TB. unsalted finely chopped walnuts

Yield: 4 servings
Prep time: 3 minutes
Cook time: 3 to 5 minutes
Serving size: ½ cup
Each serving has:
142 calories
3 g total fat
<1 g saturated fat
2 g protein
32 g carbohydrate
4 g fiber
0 mg cholesterol
1 mg sodium

1. Preheat the broiler.

2. Arrange orange slices and banana slices in an 8-inch round glass baking dish or other heatproof dish. Drizzle honey evenly over oranges and bananas, and scatter walnuts across top.

3. Broil on uppermost oven shelf closest to the heat source for 3 to 5 minutes or until top is bubbly. (Watch closely to keep from burning.) Serve hot.

 Heroic Hints _____

Easily pour honey from your measuring spoon by first lightly coating the measuring spoon with nonstick cooking spray.

Chapter 5

Great Grapes

In This Chapter

- A toast to your health
- Grape juice—great for any age
- Wine: drink it, simmer with it, or soak in it

Not hungry? That's okay. You can still get a powerful load of nutrients while just quenching your thirst with some grape juice or even red wine. Really, red wine? Yes. Read on.

Grape Juice Goodness

In the grocery store juice aisle, you might notice both purple and white grape juice on the shelves. Which should you buy? Both—as long as they're made from the right kind of grapes. When it comes to purple, be sure to get Concord grape juice. That should be listed right on the label or in the ingredient list. As for its paler cousin, stick to white grape juice made with Niagara grapes. Juices made with these two types of grapes contain the most nutritional benefits.

Concord grapes' major health offerings are for your heart. Heart attacks and strokes occur when blood clots form and stick in key arteries. Grape juice helps prevent these blood clots from forming by lowering the desire of blood platelets—which form the clots—to stick together.

In addition, Concord grape juice increases levels of *nitric oxide* (NO) in both the blood and the walls lining your arteries. Nitric oxide allows the walls of your vascular system to be more elastic. In turn, the more-elastic artery walls are able to expand to allow for a greater blood flow when needed.

def•i•ni•tion

Nitric oxide is a substance within your blood stream and vessel walls that contributes to a healthy cardiovascular system.

Super Knowledge

With the exceptions of purple Concord grape juice and grapefruit juice, 100 percent grape juice made from Niagara grapes has more antioxidant power than any other juice.

While Concord grape juice offers benefits we think about as we mature, juice made from white Niagara grapes helps us out early in life. Children's bellies are very sensitive to the balance of sugars found in fruit juices, even more so when they're suffering from any kind of gastrointestinal illness. Because white Niagara grape juice contains equal amounts of sugars, it's better tolerated and can result in less GI symptoms.

Able-Bodied Red Wine

A major nutritional player in red wine is the *phytoestrogen resveratrol*. In the body, this antioxidant acts similarly to the female hormone estrogen, providing relief from conditions such as menopause, osteoporosis, and heart disease.

Resveratrol also performs a few heart-related tasks. It can help prevent the sticking together of red blood cells, which causes blood clots that can lead to a heart attack or stroke. In addition, resveratrol helps increase nitric oxide levels in the blood. If you recall, this substance can help improve blood flow and in doing so, help lower your chances of having a heart attack or stroke.

def•i•ni•tion

Resveratrol is an antioxidant found primarily in red wine, grapes, raspberries, and peanuts. **Phytoestrogens** are substances from plants and in the body that act similarly to the hormone estrogen, which is involved in the development of sexual characteristics and menstruation as well as reproduction.

Red wine not only helps your heart, it may also offer protection from cancer. That resveratrol is the hard worker responsible for these benefits as well. By hindering the creation of new blood vessels needed to feed a tumor, resveratrol may help slow both the growth and spreading of cancer cells. In addition, it may cause some cancer cells to actually self-destruct. This has been seen in breast and skin cancer as well as leukemia cells.

Great Grape Smoothies

This blending of grape juice, raisins, and a ripe banana provides all the natural sweetness smoothies need.

Yield: 3 servings
Prep time: 3 minutes
Serving size: 1 cup
Each serving has:
134 calories
0 g total fat
0 g saturated fat
2 g protein
34 g carbohydrate
2 g fiber
1 mg cholesterol
27 mg sodium

1 cup Concord grape juice

½ cup fat-free plain yogurt

¼ cup raisins

1 medium very ripe banana, peeled and broken into chunks

12 large ice cubes

1. Combine grape juice, yogurt, raisins, and banana in a blender. Cover and blend on high speed for 30 seconds or until well blended and raisins are finely chopped.

2. Remove the cap from the blender's lid and, with the blender running, add ice cubes one at a time until well blended. Serve immediately.

Variation: For a sunny smoothie treat, substitute Niagara white grape juice and golden raisins.

Kryptonite

Check food labels carefully, and buy grape juice and other fruit juices that are 100 percent juice. Many are made with only a small percentage of real fruit juice. Reading the ingredient list tells you if sugar or other ingredients were added. Plus, the name of the drink might be a dead giveaway. The terms *cocktail, ade* (as in lemonade), or *juice drink* usually mean it's not 100 percent juice.

Vineyard Dressing

Dress your green salads with this imaginative, fresh-tasting blend that employs heart-healthy grape juice.

¼ cup extra-virgin olive oil

¼ cup Concord grape juice

2 TB. fresh lemon juice

1 tsp. grated fresh gingerroot

½ tsp. grated lemon zest

½ tsp. finely chopped fresh mint

Pinch salt

Yield: *4 servings*
Prep time: 2 minutes
Serving size: 2 table-spoons
Each serving has:
129 calories
14 g total fat
2 g saturated fat
0 g protein
3 g carbohydrate
0 g fiber
0 mg cholesterol
37 mg sodium

1. Combine olive oil, grape juice, lemon juice, gingerroot, lemon zest, mint, and salt in a small bowl. Whisk until well blended.

2. Refrigerate any leftovers, and whisk again before serving.

Heroic Hints

To prepare gingerroot, use a vegetable peeler to remove the smooth, light-colored peel. If you don't have a ginger grater, use the very fine rasps of a box grater or even fine, short strokes with a zester.

Red Wine Vinaigrette

Your favorite red wine replaces the vinegar in this sophisticated salad dressing.

Yield: 4 servings	
Prep time: 3 minutes	
Serving size: 2 table-spoons	
Each serving has:	
168 calories	
18 g total fat	
3 g saturated fat	
0 g protein	
1 g carbohydrate	
0 g fiber	
0 mg cholesterol	
73 mg sodium	

⅓ cup extra-virgin olive oil

2 TB. red wine

½ tsp. granulated sugar

⅛ tsp. dried basil

⅛ tsp. dried oregano

⅛ tsp. garlic powder

⅛ tsp. onion powder

⅛ tsp. salt

⅛ tsp. freshly ground black pepper

1. Combine olive oil, red wine, sugar, basil, oregano, garlic powder, onion powder, salt, and black pepper in a small bowl. Whisk until thoroughly blended.

2. Refrigerate any leftovers, and whisk again before serving.

Super Knowledge

This salad dressing might seem a bit high in fat, but it's mostly heart-healthy monounsaturated fat from the olive oil.

Sweet and Creamy Apple Soup

A bowl of this chunky cold soup imparts a frosty start to a warm, harvest-time meal.

4 medium Red Delicious or other cooking apples, cored and diced

2 TB. honey

1 TB. grated lemon zest

3 cups hot water

2 TB. all-purpose flour

¼ cup red wine

¼ cup apple juice

10 TB. fat-free evaporated milk

Yield: 10 servings
Prep time: 3 minutes
Cook time: 28 minutes
Chill time: 8 hours
Serving size: ¹/₂ cup
Each serving has:
70 calories
0 g total fat
0 g saturated fat
1 g protein
16 g carbohydrate
2 g fiber
0 mg cholesterol
23 mg sodium

1. Stir together apples, honey, lemon zest, and hot water in a large saucepan. Bring to a boil over high heat. Reduce heat and simmer for 20 minutes or until apples are very tender, stirring occasionally.

2. Whisk together flour, red wine, and apple juice in a small bowl until smooth. Pour into apple mixture, and gently simmer for 5 minutes. Cover and chill for at least 8 hours or overnight until cold.

3. To serve, stir 1 tablespoon evaporated milk into each serving and sprinkle a little ground nutmeg on top if desired.

Super Knowledge

Unclarified or "cloudy" apple juice, sometimes labeled "natural" apple juice, contains up to four times as much antioxidant power as the more processed, clear juice. Check the label to ensure that your juice has been pasteurized, especially if you're serving young children or others with susceptible immune systems.

Old-World Pasta Sauce

That slow-simmered, homemade goodness you think of when you think of good, old-fashioned pasta sauce? You can have that over your pasta tonight with this recipe.

Yield: 10 servings	
Prep time: 5 minutes	
Cook time: 2 hours, 16 minutes	
Serving size: ³/₄ cup	
Each serving has:	
185 calories	
8 g total fat	
2 g saturated fat	
12 g protein	
14 g carbohydrate	
1 g fiber	
29 mg cholesterol	
539 mg sodium	

2 TB. extra-virgin olive oil

1 large yellow onion, chopped

1 medium green bell pepper, ribs and seeds removed, and chopped

6 medium cloves garlic, minced

2 TB. Italian seasoning

1 lb. ground sirloin

1 (28-oz.) can diced tomatoes in sauce, undrained

2 (8-oz.) cans tomato sauce

1 (6-oz.) can tomato paste

³/₄ cup red wine

3 TB. drained pimiento-stuffed sliced green olives

3 TB. drained sliced black olives

2 TB. granular sugar

1. Heat olive oil in a large pot over medium heat. Add onion, green bell pepper, and garlic, and sauté for 2 minutes. Stir in Italian seasoning, and sauté for 6 minutes or until onion is translucent. Add ground sirloin and cook, stirring to break up meat, for 8 minutes or until browned. Drain.

2. Stir in diced tomatoes, tomato sauce, tomato paste, red wine, green olives, and black olives, and bring to a boil over medium heat. Reduce heat to low, and stir in sugar. Simmer, uncovered, for at least 2 hours, stirring occasionally. Ladle sauce over any whole-grain pasta to serve.

Heroic Hints

Break off garlic cloves from the head only as needed. Garlic heads covered in their papery skins keep for up to 2 months in a dark, cool, well-ventilated area. Use unpeeled individual cloves within a week.

Slow-Simmered Vegetable Beef Stew

A blustery winter's day requires a rib-sticking meal like a big beefy bowl of this aromatic, filling stew.

1 lb. extra-lean cubed stew beef

1 small yellow onion, chopped

3 medium carrots, peeled and cut on the diagonal into 1-in. pieces

1 small red bell pepper, ribs and seeds removed, and coarsely chopped

8 oz. sliced button mushrooms

2 medium tomatoes, cut into ½-in. wedges

1 cup red wine

1 bay leaf

¼ cup chopped fresh parsley

¼ tsp. crushed red pepper flakes

½ tsp. salt

¼ tsp. freshly ground black pepper

3 cups uncooked whole-wheat rotini pasta

1 cup frozen peas, rinsed to thaw

Yield: 5 servings
Prep time: 5 minutes
Cook time: 1 hour, 52 minutes
Serving size: 1⅔ cups
Each serving has:
516 calories
14 g total fat
5 g saturated fat
32 g protein
61 g carbohydrate
8 g fiber
61 mg cholesterol
348 mg sodium

1. Coat the bottom of a large pot with nonstick cooking spray and heat over medium heat. Add beef and cook for 5 minutes or until browned on all sides. Stir in onion, carrots, and red bell pepper, and cook for 1 minute.

2. Add mushrooms, tomatoes, red wine, bay leaf, parsley, and crushed red pepper flakes. Stir to combine, and bring to a simmer over medium heat. Cover, reduce heat to low, and simmer for 1½ hours, stirring occasionally.

3. Stir in salt, black pepper, and pasta. Cover and simmer for 15 minutes or until pasta is al dente. Stir in peas and cook for 1 minute or until heated through.

Heroic Hints

Whenever a bay leaf is called for in a recipe, be sure to remove it from the dish before serving. You don't want the bay leaf to be a sharp, crunchy surprise for anyone.

Drunken Chicken Breasts

Yes, you can serve red wine with chicken … er, that's serve chicken red wine with this easy-to-fix main dish.

Yield: 4 servings
Prep time: 3 minutes
Chill time: 8 hours
Cook time: 12 to 16 minutes
Serving size: 1 chicken breast half
Each serving has:
227 calories
15 g total fat
2 g saturated fat
17 g protein
1 g carbohydrate
<1 g fiber
47 mg cholesterol
42 mg sodium

½ **cup extra-virgin olive oil**

½ **cup red wine**

4 medium cloves garlic, minced

2 tsp. freshly ground black pepper

4 (3-oz.) boneless, skinless chicken breast halves, trimmed

1. Combine olive oil, red wine, garlic, and black pepper in a gallon-size resealable plastic bag. Add chicken breast halves, press out air, and seal the bag. Lay flat in the refrigerator and marinate for 8 hours or overnight, turning over occasionally.

2. Preheat the broiler and coat a broiler pan rack with nonstick cooking spray.

3. Place chicken breast halves on the broiler pan, and discard marinade. Broil for 6 to 8 minutes on each side or until done (170°F on a food thermometer).

Kryptonite

Never serve marinades that have come in contact with raw meats. If a marinade is to be served with a dish, keep a portion apart from the raw meat or bring it to a full boil before serving to avoid food poisoning.

Berry Grape Sauce for Angel Food Cake

This pairing of not-too-sweet sauce and fat-free angel food cake serves up a light, happy ending for any meal.

⅓ cup Concord grape juice

1 cup frozen unsweetened blackberries

1 cup frozen unsweetened whole strawberries

½ cup frozen unsweetened blueberries

1 (10.5-oz.) loaf angel food cake

Yield: 5 servings
Prep time: 2 minutes
Cook time: 20 minutes
Serving size: 1 slice angel food cake with ¼ cup sauce
Each serving has:
198 calories
1 g total fat
0 g saturated fat
4 g protein
46 g carbohydrate
3 g fiber
0 mg cholesterol
447 mg sodium

1. In a medium nonstick saucepan, cook grape juice over medium heat for 5 minutes or until boiling. Cook for 5 more minutes or until juice is reduced.

2. Stir in frozen blackberries, strawberries, and blueberries. Cook for 5 minutes or until mixture returns to a boil, stirring occasionally. Cook for 5 more minutes or until berries are thawed, breaking up strawberries near the end of cooking. Remove the saucepan from the heat to cool slightly.

3. Cut angel food cake into 5 slices. Spoon ¼ cup berry sauce over each slice. Top with a dollop of whipped cream, if desired.

 Heroic Hints

To cut delicate cakes such as angel food cake, use a serrated knife. Cut through the cake with a slight sawing motion for neat slices—no more crushed cake.

Part 3

Valiant Vegetables

Did your mom always nag you to eat your veggies? If so, I hope you listened to her. Back then she might not have known exactly why vegetables were so important, but she was right just the same in telling you to eat up. As it turns out, those brilliant green, red, and orange foods sitting alongside your chicken contain powerful cancer fighters and can help prevent heart disease, just to name a couple of their benefits.

Whether you're looking for an entrée, side dish, drink—that's right, I said drink—or dessert—that's right, I said *dessert*—you've come to the right place. The following chapters are filled with a variety of veggie-filled recipes to suit any palate.

Chapter 6

Going Green

In This Chapter

- ◆ Seeing the benefits of broccoli
- ◆ Be like Popeye—eat your spinach
- ◆ Super recipes featuring broccoli and spinach

Broccoli and spinach are two foods on many people's "don't like" list, and they definitely can be acquired tastes. Even if they aren't regular guests on your dinner table now, hopefully after reading about these green foods' benefits and browsing some delicious recipes, you'll reconsider.

Beneficial Broccoli

Among broccoli's many major benefits is an antioxidant called *lutein*, which is beneficial to eye health. Here's how it works: the eye's macula, which helps let your brain know what your eyes are seeing, contains high amounts of lutein. The macula lets you see straight ahead, so you use it for activities like driving and reading. Eating lutein-rich foods can help prevent both degeneration of and damage to the macula, thus helping prevent blindness as well as cataracts.

Broccoli also contains high amounts of a phytochemical called *sulforaphane*, which has been shown to help prevent cancer by both slowing the growth and increasing the breakdown or death of cancer cells. Early studies reveal sulforaphane may be beneficial in helping to prevent cancers of the colon, breast, and prostate. More studies are currently underway.

def•i•ni•tion

The antioxidant **lutein** does a great deal to improve and maintain eye health. It also plays a role in helping the heart and preventing cancer. **Sulforaphane** is an isothiocyanate found in broccoli and broccoli sprouts that acts as an antioxidant.

Also, kaempferol—a flavonol found in broccoli—may provide benefits for the cardiovascular system. One study showed a slightly lower risk of dying from coronary heart disease in woman eating the largest amount of broccoli compared to those eating the smallest amount.

The Strength of Spinach

Two key components in spinach are the phytochemicals *myricetin* and *zeaxanthin*. Myricetin, which is also found in blueberries, is still in the early stages of research, but it looks promising that this compound may offer health benefits that include preventing cancer and also preventing and improving both heart disease and arthritis.

def•i•ni•tion

Myricetin is a flavonoid that may help fight both inflammation and cancer. **Zeaxanthin** is a carotenoid that protects the eyes and may help prevent some cancers.

Zeaxanthin works right along with lutein, so eating adequate amounts of this nutrient from a variety of fruits and vegetables, including spinach, benefits your eyes. By keeping the macula of the eye healthy, zeaxanthin helps prevent age-related degeneration and cataracts.

Heroic Hints

If you're limiting your intake of fats and oils to help maintain your weight or health, don't go overboard by eliminating them entirely. Many of the nutrients in vegetables such as spinach and carrots are fat-soluble, which means they need some fat in order for your body to absorb them properly. So it's fine to have a small amount of healthful, unsaturated fats in your diet as long as you don't go overboard. Slice up some avocado on a spinach salad or drizzle your deep green, orange, and red veggies with a bit of olive oil.

Better-for-You Broccoli Soup

Using fat-free milk, fat-free and lower-sodium chicken broth, and light butter, a cup of this creamy, heady soup serves up less fat, calories, cholesterol, sodium—and guilt!

Yield: 4 servings
Prep time: 2 minutes
Cook time: 30 minutes
Serving size: 1 cup
Each serving has:
100 calories
3 g total fat
2 g saturated fat
7 g protein
12 g carbohydrate
1 g fiber
12 mg cholesterol
315 mg sodium

2 cups small broccoli florets

2 TB. light butter with canola oil

2 TB. all-purpose flour

1 (14-oz.) can fat-free, less-sodium chicken broth

2 cups fat-free milk

¼ tsp. salt

¼ tsp. freshly ground black pepper

1. Fill a steamer pot or a medium pot or saucepan with enough water to fall below the steamer basket when added, and bring to a boil over high heat. Add broccoli to the steamer basket or a collapsible steamer basket, place the basket in the pot, and cover. Steam broccoli over boiling water, reducing heat as necessary to just maintain a boil, for 10 minutes or until very tender.

2. Melt light butter in a medium saucepan over medium heat. Whisk in flour until blended. Add about ½ cup broth, and whisk until smooth and bubbly. Add remaining broth, milk, steamed broccoli, salt, and black pepper. Cook over medium heat for 15 minutes or until bubbly and slightly thickened, stirring occasionally. Serve hot.

Heroic Hints

Overboiling or overmicrowaving can destroy up to 97 percent of the crucial antioxidants found in broccoli and many other vegetables. Steaming, as in this recipe, is a much better option. It maximizes the nutrients' availability to your body as compared to eating the same veggies raw and minimizes nutrient losses. The broccoli steams a little longer than usual for this recipe, so watch that you don't boil away the water. Add more boiling water as necessary.

Broccoli, Olive, and Egg Salad

This unique make-ahead dish of green veggies flavored with dill will bring raves at your next potluck event.

6 cups small broccoli florets

¾ cup sliced pimiento-stuffed green olives

¼ cup chopped green onions

1 cup reduced-fat mayonnaise

1 tsp. dried dill weed

¼ tsp. salt

⅛ tsp. freshly ground black pepper

2 large eggs, hard-cooked and coarsely chopped

Yield: 10 servings
Prep time: 8 minutes
Cook time: 5 minutes
Chill time: 8 hours
Serving size: ½ cup
Each serving has:
79 calories
6 g total fat
1 g saturated fat
3 g protein
6 g carbohydrate
1 g fiber
42 mg cholesterol
500 mg sodium

1. Steam broccoli florets for 5 minutes or until softened but still crisp. Turn into a medium bowl and let cool.

2. Add green olives and green onions to broccoli.

3. Combine mayonnaise, dill weed, salt, and black pepper in a small bowl, and stir until blended. Stir into broccoli mixture until evenly coated, cover, and chill for at least 8 hours or overnight.

4. Before serving, stir in chopped eggs.

Heroic Hints

To hard-cook eggs, fill a pan large enough to hold the eggs in a single layer with cold water. Carefully add eggs, and bring to a boil over high heat. Then remove the pan from the heat, cover, and let stand for 20 minutes. Immediately rinse well under cold, running water. Refrigerate the eggs in their shells for up to 1 week if you're not using them immediately.

Asian-Accent Broccoli

Accompany your favorite Asian meals with this great-tasting, fast-fix side dish.

Yield: 6 servings
Prep time: 2 minutes
Cook time: 6 minutes
Serving size: ½ cup
Each serving has:
29 calories
1 g total fat
0 g saturated fat
3 g protein
4 g carbohydrate
3 g fiber
0 mg cholesterol
116 mg sodium

3 medium stalks broccoli, cut into florets (about 4 cups)

1 TB. reduced-sodium soy sauce

2 tsp. lemon juice

½ TB. toasted sesame seeds

1. Steam broccoli florets for 6 minutes or until crisp-tender. Transfer to a medium serving bowl.

2. Pour soy sauce and lemon juice over broccoli, and stir to coat. Sprinkle on sesame seeds, and stir to distribute evenly. Serve immediately.

Heroic Hints

Toasting sesame seeds (or nuts) is easy: place the raw sesame seeds in a small, dry, nonstick skillet over medium-low to medium heat and cook for 6 minutes or until golden brown, shaking the skillet often. Watch the sesame seeds carefully, as they are quick to burn.

Garlicky Broccoli and Pine Nut Pasta

A flavorful meatless entrée, this pasta blend can also serve as a hearty side dish for beef, poultry, or fish dishes.

3 cups uncooked whole-wheat rotini pasta

4 cups broccoli florets

2 TB. light butter with canola oil

1 TB. balsamic vinegar

¼ cup pine nuts

1 tsp. extra-virgin or light olive oil

6 medium cloves garlic, slivered

½ cup fat-free, less-sodium chicken broth

¼ tsp. salt

¼ tsp. freshly ground black pepper

½ cup shredded Parmesan cheese

Yield: 5 servings
Prep time: 5 minutes
Cook time: 17 minutes
Serving size: 1 cup
Each serving has:
361 calories
12 g total fat
4 g saturated fat
17 g protein
52 g carbohydrate
7 g fiber
15 mg cholesterol
390 mg sodium

1. Preheat the broiler. Coat a 1½-quart glass casserole dish with nonstick cooking spray.

2. Cook pasta in a large pot of boiling water over medium-high heat for 10 minutes. Add broccoli and boil for 3 minutes or until pasta is *al dente* and broccoli is crisp-tender. Drain and return pasta and broccoli to the pot. Stir in light butter and balsamic vinegar until butter is melted.

3. Meanwhile, add pine nuts to a small, dry, nonstick skillet over medium heat. Cook for 5 minutes or until pine nuts are golden brown, shaking skillet often to prevent burning. Remove pine nuts and set aside.

4. Add olive oil to the skillet and heat over medium heat. Add garlic and sauté for 3 minutes or until golden. Add broth, salt, and black pepper, and bring to a boil. Pour over pasta mixture and stir in pine nuts and ¼ cup Parmesan cheese.

5. Turn mixture into the prepared casserole dish, and sprinkle remaining ¼ cup cheese over top. Broil 4 to 6 inches from the heat source for 4 minutes or until top is browned and crisped, turning halfway through cooking time to crisp evenly.

def•i•ni•tion

Al dente is an Italian cooking term that means "against the teeth." Pasta cooked *al dente* should be slightly firm to the bite.

Sesame Beef and Broccoli Stir-Fry

This Asian-inspired, one-dish meal gets a zingy, meaty dinner on the table without delay on those hectic weeknights.

Yield: 4 servings

Prep time: 5 minutes

Cook time: 10 minutes

Serving size: 1 cup over ³/₄ cup rice

Each serving has:

508 calories

23 g total fat

7 g saturated fat

31 g protein

45 g carbohydrate

7 g fiber

68 mg cholesterol

504 mg sodium

Heroic Hints

When shopping for broccoli, look for tightly formed green or purplish florets with slender, freshly cut stalks. Avoid yellowing florets and thick, woody stems.

⅓ cup plus ¼ cup fat-free, less-sodium beef broth

3 TB. sodium-free rice vinegar

3 TB. reduced-sodium soy sauce

1 TB. dark sesame seed oil

1 TB. cornstarch

1 TB. peanut oil

1 lb. boneless sirloin beef stir-fry strips

3 medium stalks broccoli, cut into florets (about 4 cups)

2 TB. minced fresh ginger-root

4 medium cloves garlic, minced

1 TB. toasted sesame seeds

3 cups cooked long-grain brown rice

1. Combine ¹/₃ cup broth, rice vinegar, soy sauce, sesame seed oil, and cornstarch in a small bowl. Whisk until cornstarch is dissolved, and set aside.

2. Heat peanut oil over medium-high heat in a nonstick wok or a large nonstick skillet. Add steak and stir-fry for 5 minutes or until meat is browned. Using a slotted spoon, remove steak to a paper towel–lined plate. Drain the wok.

3. Pour remaining ¹/₄ cup broth into the wok and set over medium-high heat. Add broccoli and stir-fry for 2 minutes or until crisp-tender. Add steak, gingerroot, garlic, and cornstarch mixture, and stir-fry for 2 minutes or until sauce is clear and thickened. Stir in sesame seeds and cook for 1 minute more.

4. To serve, spoon atop a bed of cooked rice.

Honey-Sweetened Spinach Slaw

Tossed together before starting dinner or made ahead for a picnic, this milder salad blend is a nice change from traditional coleslaw.

4 cups shredded iceberg lettuce

2½ cups shredded fresh spinach

2 cups shredded red cabbage

1½ cups shredded green cabbage

½ cup low-fat slaw dressing

2 TB. honey

½ tsp. garlic powder

⅛ tsp. salt

⅛ tsp. freshly ground black pepper

Yield: 10 servings
Prep time: 6 minutes
Chill time: 20 to 30 minutes
Serving size: ¹/₂ cup
Each serving has:
71 calories
3 g total fat
<1 g saturated fat
1 g protein
12 g carbohydrate
1 g fiber
3 mg cholesterol
262 mg sodium

1. In a large bowl, toss together lettuce, spinach, red cabbage, and green cabbage.

2. In a separate small bowl, stir together slaw dressing, honey, garlic powder, salt, and black pepper until well blended. Pour over lettuce mixture, and stir until evenly coated. Chill for 20 to 30 minutes before serving.

Heroic Hints

To make this dish ahead, toss the vegetables in a large bowl and then cover and chill. Stir together the dressing mixture in a small bowl and then cover and chill it separately. Pour the dressing over the vegetables 20 to 30 minutes before serving time.

Quick Couscous with Spinach

In just minutes, you'll have this mild side dish, that won't overpower a meal, from the stove to the table.

Yield: 6 servings
Prep time: 2 minutes
Cook time: 8 minutes
Serving size: ¹/₂ cup
Each serving has:
70 calories
1 g total fat
<1 g saturated fat
3 g protein
12 g carbohydrate
2 g fiber
1 mg cholesterol
134 mg sodium

1 (14-oz.) can fat-free, less-sodium chicken broth

¾ cup whole-wheat couscous

1 tsp. extra-virgin or light olive oil

1 cup firmly packed fresh spinach

¼ tsp. garlic powder

¼ tsp. onion powder

1 TB. reduced-sodium soy sauce

1. Pour broth into a medium saucepan and set over high heat. When broth boils, turn off heat and stir in couscous. Cover and let stand for 5 minutes or until couscous is softened and broth is absorbed.

2. Meanwhile, heat olive oil in a medium skillet over medium heat. Stir in spinach, garlic powder, and onion powder. Cook, stirring constantly, for 2 or 3 minutes or until spinach is wilted.

3. Stir spinach mixture into couscous. Stir in soy sauce, and serve hot.

Variation: When you have more time available, heat 2 teaspoons olive oil and sauté ¹/₄ cup diced yellow onion and 1 medium clove minced garlic until softened before wilting spinach. Then prepare as directed, omitting garlic powder and onion powder. You can also add ¹/₄ cup shredded carrots to onion mixture if you like.

 Heroic Hints

Be sure to use the reduced-sodium soy sauce called for in this recipe. You'll save 130 milligrams sodium per serving.

Speedy Spinach and Bean Skillet

This spicy, low-calorie, fiber-packed accompaniment makes a great side dish at any meal.

1 tsp. extra-virgin or light olive oil

3 medium cloves garlic, minced

1 (15.5-oz.) can great northern beans, rinsed and drained

½ tsp. crushed red pepper flakes

1 (10-oz.) pkg. frozen leaf spinach, thawed and drained

¼ tsp. salt

Yield: 6 servings
Prep time: 2 minutes
Cook time: 7 minutes
Serving size: ½ cup
Each serving has:
64 calories
1 g total fat
<1 g saturated fat
5 g protein
12 g carbohydrate
5 g fiber
0 mg cholesterol
415 mg sodium

1. Heat olive oil in a medium skillet over medium heat. Sauté garlic for 1 minute or until sizzling and fragrant. Stir in beans and crushed red pepper flakes and cook for 2 minutes or until garlic is golden. Reduce heat to medium-low.

2. Stir in spinach and salt. Cook for 4 minutes, stirring to separate spinach, until heated through.

Super Knowledge

Just one serving of this quick dish provides you with well over a day's worth of vitamin K, a vitamin that plays a role in blood clotting and bone health.

Fork-Style Florentine Pizza

The superfood toppings are piled so high on this Tuscan-inspired specialty pizza you have to eat it with a fork.

Yield: 6 servings
Prep time: 5 minutes
Cook time: 18 to 20 minutes
Serving size: 1 wedge
Each serving has:
298 calories
9 g total fat
3 g saturated fat
31 g protein
27 g carbohydrate
3 g fiber
43 mg cholesterol
656 mg sodium

1 lb. 99 percent fat-free extra-lean ground turkey breast

¼ tsp. garlic powder

1 (12-in.) ready-made regular or whole-wheat thin pizza crust

¾ cup fat-free French onion sour cream dip

1 (10-oz.) pkg. frozen chopped spinach, thawed and well drained

1 large tomato, diced

1 cup 2 percent milk shredded Colby and Monterey Jack cheese

1. Preheat the oven to 425°F.

2. Coat a medium nonstick skillet with nonstick cooking spray and heat over medium heat. Add ground turkey breast and season with garlic powder. Cook, stirring to break up meat, for 8 minutes or until browned; drain.

3. Place pizza crust on a pizza pan or large baking sheet. Evenly spread dip over pizza crust, leaving about a 1-inch margin around the edge. Top with spinach, turkey, and tomato. Sprinkle cheese on top, and bake for 10 to 12 minutes or until heated through and cheese is melted. Let stand for a few minutes before cutting into wedges to serve.

 Heroic Hints

By keeping a few bags or boxes of frozen chopped spinach in the house, you can easily add this superfood to a variety of meals, including casseroles and pizzas.

Southern-Fried Spinach

The spiced egg mixture mellows out the spinach taste of this dish, making it appealing for folks who usually greet spinach with a scrunched-up nose.

1 (6-oz.) pkg. fresh baby spinach

1 large egg, at room temperature

¼ cup fat-free milk

1 clove garlic, minced

⅛ tsp. cayenne

Salt to taste (optional)

Yield: 2 servings
Prep time: 3 minutes
Cook time: 20 to 22 minutes
Serving size: ½ cup
Each serving has:
84 calories
3 g total fat
1 g saturated fat
6 g protein
11 g carbohydrate
4 g fiber
106 mg cholesterol
183 mg sodium

1. Wash spinach and drain loosely. Place spinach and the water that clings to the leaves in an 11-inch nonstick skillet. Cook over medium heat for 10 minutes, stirring occasionally, or until spinach is wilted and the skillet is nearly dry.

2. Meanwhile, combine egg, milk, garlic, cayenne, and salt (if using) in a small bowl. Whisk until well blended.

3. Reduce heat to medium-low. Pour egg mixture over spinach in the skillet. Cook, stirring frequently, for 10 to 12 minutes or until the skillet is nearly dry again. Serve hot.

Kryptonite

Be sure to reduce the cooking temperature before adding the egg mixture and to stir the spinach mixture or your egg will scramble.

Chapter 7

Robust Reds

In This Chapter

- ◆ Red bell peppers: good for you, inside and out
- ◆ Don't write off ketchup just yet
- ◆ Sauce 'em, roast 'em, or bake 'em

With their tremendous health benefits, tomatoes and red bell peppers can and should be enjoyed in all sorts of ways, not simply as colorful additions to burgers and sandwiches. In this chapter, we uncover some of their pros and give you several yummy recipes to try.

Productive Red Peppers

You've probably heard that you should increase your vitamin C intake when you're battling a cold, and that usually means taking vitamin C pills or drinking more orange juice. Here's another, perhaps better, option: toss some red bell peppers onto your salad. You'd have to eat three oranges to get the same amount of germ-fighting vitamin C as you'd get in one red bell pepper.

def•i•ni•tion _____

Collagen is a protein that plays a role in building your body's connective tissues like tendons, ligaments, skin, and bones. **Free radicals,** the natural result of the process of turning food into energy, damage your body's cells. They also come from exposure to UV radiation, smoke, and pollution.

And don't just think of vitamin C when you're sick, because it does far more than help you feel better. It's used to make *collagen*. Among other things, collagen helps your skin stay healthy. Vitamin C is also an essential nutrient when it comes to your wounds healing properly. And it plays a big role in protecting you from *free-radical* damage, too.

In addition to the health benefits they provide, red bell peppers are a perfect fit when you're watching your weight. They have little to no fat or sodium and are extremely low in calories. One-half cup has only 15 to 20 calories—that's next to nothing in the food world. So go ahead and pile them on guilt-free.

Super Knowledge _____

Did you know that red peppers are actually green peppers that ripened further on the vine? The longer ripining process effects more than just the radiant color. It allows red peppers to develop a sweeter flavor, which you may have noticed. But it also allows nutrients to develop more. Red bell peppers contain almost 8 times the powerful beta carotene as green bell peppers and 5 times the heart healthy folate of green ones.

Top-Notch Tomatoes

Lycopene is its name, and cancer-fighting is its game. Lycopene's main cancer enemy is prostate cancer, but it also may lower your risk of developing other cancers such as lung, breast, and stomach. Research suggests that eating tomatoes and tomato products regularly—some say twice a week—can both lower your risk of developing prostate cancer and help treat it by not allowing tumors to grow and spread.

def•i•ni•tion _____

Lycopene is a compound in the carotenoid group of phytochemicals that works primarily as an antioxidant. Lycopene is more easily and efficiently absorbed from cooked tomato products, such as sauces, pastes, and ketchups.

Roasted Red Pepper Sour Cream Dip

Dip into this chunky blend dotted with sweet, juicy pepper pieces with just a hint of heat.

1 (16-oz.) pkg. fat-free sour cream

½ (12-oz.) jar roasted red peppers packed in water, drained and diced

1 (4.5-oz.) can chopped green chilies, drained

1 medium clove garlic, minced

½ tsp. hot pepper sauce

Yield: *3 cups*		
Prep time: 5 minutes		
Chill time: 2 hours		
Serving size: 2 table-spoons		
Each serving has:		
28 calories		
<1 g total fat		
<1 g saturated fat		
1 g protein		
4 g carbohydrate		
<1 g fiber		
2 mg cholesterol		
119 mg sodium		

1. Stir together sour cream, roasted red peppers, green chilies, garlic, and hot pepper sauce in a medium bowl until well blended.

2. Cover and chill for at least 2 hours or until cold. Serve with tortilla chips, crackers, celery sticks, baby carrots, and more of your favorite dippers.

Heroic Hints

You can peel a garlic clove easily after gently pounding it under the flat side of a knife. Just be careful not to cut your hand!

Roasted Red Pepper and Tortellini Soup

Cheese-filled pasta floating in the intense flavor of roasted red peppers makes for a main-dish soup that will jump-start your taste buds.

Yield: 4 servings
Prep time: 3 minutes
Cook time: 12 minutes
Serving size: 1 cup
Each serving has:
371 calories
5 g total fat
2 g saturated fat
16 g protein
55 g carbohydrate
2 g fiber
26 mg cholesterol
1,701 mg sodium

1½ (12-oz.) jars roasted red peppers packed in water, drained

1 (14-oz.) can fat-free, less-sodium chicken broth

4 oz. sliced fresh mushrooms

½ tsp. dried basil

½ tsp. dried oregano

½ tsp. garlic powder

⅛ tsp. salt

⅛ tsp. freshly ground black pepper

1 (9-oz.) pkg. fresh three-cheese tortellini

1. Add roasted red peppers to a blender, cover, and blend on high for 30 seconds or until smooth. Pour into a large saucepan, and add broth, mushrooms, basil, oregano, garlic powder, salt, and black pepper. Stir and bring to a boil over high heat.

2. Stir in tortellini, reduce heat, and gently boil for 8 minutes or until tortellini is done. Serve hot.

Variation: If you can't find fresh, you can use dried cheese-filled tortellini; add them to the broth mixture and boil for the time indicated on the package directions rather than the time indicated above.

 Kryptonite _____

Roasted red peppers are often available packed in olive oil. Check the label before you buy these, unless you don't mind adding that additional fat to your recipe.

Red Pepper Cheddar Melts

Even when you're in a hurry, you have time for a hot lunch with the great taste of tender sweet peppers smothered in melted cheddar on toasty French bread.

4 tsp. extra-virgin olive oil

2 medium red bell peppers, ribs and seeds removed, and cut into thin strips

2 tsp. fresh lemon juice

4 (1-in.-thick) slices French bread, cut on the diagonal

4 thin slices sharp cheddar cheese

Yield: 4 servings
Prep time: 5 minutes
Cook time: 9 minutes
Serving size: 1 sandwich
Each serving has:
330 calories
14 g total fat
6 g saturated fat
13 g protein
40 g carbohydrate
3 g fiber
25 mg cholesterol
569 mg sodium

1. Preheat the broiler.

2. Heat 2 teaspoons olive oil in a large nonstick skillet over medium heat. Add red bell peppers and sauté for 8 minutes or until peppers are tender and beginning to char.

3. Stir together remaining 2 teaspoons olive oil and lemon juice in a small bowl until blended. Arrange bread slices on a nonstick baking sheet and brush lemon juice mixture over top of bread slices. Evenly distribute red bell peppers on bread slices. Cover each sandwich with a slice of cheese, breaking as necessary to fit.

4. Broil on the oven rack closest to the heat source for 1 minute or until cheese melts and is bubbly. Serve immediately.

Variation: Recipe can be halved, if desired.

Heroic Hints

To remove a pepper's seeds and ribs (inner white membranes), cut the pepper in half lengthwise and then cut out or break away the stem. Slice off the ribs before preparing the pepper for a recipe.

Summer Garden Flounder Packets

Accompany this spicy fish dish with a green salad for a complete meal you can have on the table in under 30 minutes.

Yield: 4 servings
Prep time: 8 minutes
Cook time: 20 minutes
Serving size: 1 packet with ¾ cup rice
Each serving has:
291 calories
5 g total fat
1 g saturated fat
20 g protein
42 g carbohydrate
5 g fiber
40 mg cholesterol
190 mg sodium

4 (3-oz.) flounder fillets

½ tsp. cayenne

2 medium red bell peppers, ribs and seeds removed, and cut into thin strips

1 medium yellow bell pepper, ribs and seeds removed, and cut into thin strips

1 small zucchini squash, thinly sliced

1 small yellow summer squash, thinly sliced

¼ cup low-fat Italian salad dressing

Salt (optional)

3 cups cooked long-grain brown rice

1. Preheat the oven to 450°F. Coat 4 large sheets (18 or more inches) of aluminum foil with nonstick cooking spray and fold up the edges to hold ingredients.

2. Place 1 fillet in the center of each foil sheet and sprinkle ⅛ teaspoon cayenne evenly over each fillet. Evenly divide red bell peppers, yellow bell pepper, zucchini squash, and yellow summer squash among the foil sheets, adding atop fillets. Pour 1 tablespoon salad dressing over each fillet, and season with salt (if using). Seal the foil packets by pulling up and double-folding all the edges to securely enclose ingredients.

3. Arrange the packets on the oven rack and bake for 20 minutes or until fish flakes easily with a fork and vegetables are tender-crisp. Carefully open each packet and arrange contents atop a bed of rice to serve.

 Super Knowledge _____

The assortment of veggies in these foil packets are loaded with nutrients, including vitamins A and C, potassium, and folate.

Asian-Glazed Chicken

The combination of crisp-tender red peppers and a sweet-spicy sauce are perfect served atop a bed of hot, cooked jasmine or brown rice.

1 lb. chicken breast cutlets

1 TB. grill seasoning such as Montreal steak seasoning

2 TB. olive oil

1 tsp. ground ginger

4 medium cloves garlic, minced

1 large red bell pepper, ribs and seeds removed, and thinly sliced

1 (7.5-oz.) jar duck sauce

Yield: 4 servings
Prep time: 15 minutes
Cook time: 10 minutes
Serving size: ³/₄ cup
Each serving has:
285 calories
10 g total fat
2 g saturated fat
24 g protein
25 g carbohydrate
1 g fiber
63 mg cholesterol
751 mg sodium

1. Slice chicken into thin strips and sprinkle with grill seasoning.

2. Heat olive oil in a large nonstick skillet until very hot. Add chicken and cook for 2 minutes, stirring constantly.

3. Add ginger, garlic, and red bell pepper, and cook and stir for 2 minutes. Stir in duck sauce to glaze mixture and toss for 1 minute. Serve hot.

Variation: If you can't find chicken cutlets, you can substitute chicken breasts that you pound very thin.

Heroic Hints

Look for grill seasoning in your grocer's spice aisle. Find duck sauce in the Asian section of the ethnic aisle.

Fast Italian Tomatoes

When you need a little more variety at dinnertime but don't have the time or energy to commit to another dish, consider preparing these Parmesan- and basil-topped tomato slices that are so fast and easy to make.

Yield: 4 servings
Prep time: 3 minutes
Cook time: 3 to 5 minutes
Serving size: 5 slices
Each serving has:
46 calories
3 g total fat
1 g saturated fat
2 g protein
2 g carbohydrate
1 g fiber
3 mg cholesterol
66 mg sodium

4 medium plum tomatoes

2 tsp. extra-virgin olive oil

2 TB. chopped fresh basil

2 TB. shredded Parmesan cheese

Salt and freshly ground black pepper (optional)

1. Preheat the broiler. Coat a medium nonstick baking sheet with nonstick cooking spray.

2. Core and cut each tomato into 5 (about $^1/_2$-inch) slices and place on the baking sheet. Brush olive oil over the top of each tomato slice. Sprinkle basil and cheese on top. Season with salt and black pepper (if using).

3. Broil on the oven rack closest to the heat source for 3 to 5 minutes or until cheese is melted and crisped, as desired. Serve immediately.

Super Knowledge

Plum tomatoes are also called Roma tomatoes. They tend to be more flavorful year-round than are many "winter tomatoes."

Couscous-Stuffed Tomatoes

Pack lemony, parsley-flecked couscous into red ripe tomatoes, and a light lunch has never been so fresh, delicious, and easy to make.

½ cup fat-free, less-sodium chicken broth or vegetable broth

⅓ cup whole-wheat couscous

1 TB. extra-virgin olive oil

1 TB. lemon juice

1 green onion, finely chopped

1 tsp. chopped fresh parsley

Pinch freshly ground black pepper

2 medium ripe tomatoes

Yield: 2 servings
Prep time: 7 minutes
Cook time: 2 minutes
Chill time: 1 hour
Serving size: 1 tomato
Each serving has:
176 calories
8 g total fat
1 g saturated fat
5 g protein
23 g carbohydrate
4 g fiber
1 mg cholesterol
43 mg sodium

1. Bring broth to a boil in a small saucepan over high heat. Stir in couscous. Turn off heat, cover, and let stand for 5 minutes or until broth is absorbed. Fluff couscous with a fork.

2. Meanwhile, stir together olive oil, lemon juice, green onion, parsley, and black pepper in a small bowl. Add couscous mixture and stir to mix. Cover and chill for at least 1 hour.

3. Core tomatoes and cut into 8 wedges without cutting through the bottoms. Fluff couscous mixture with a fork again and spoon ⅔ cup into the center of each tomato.

 Heroic Hints

To extract more juice from a lemon, roll it on the counter or another solid surface under the palm of your hand before cutting it.

Tomato-Flecked Cornbread

This dense, mild-flavored cornbread stands up to the addition of rosy-colored tomato bits.

Yield: 12 servings
Prep time: 5 minutes
Cook time: 35 minutes
Serving size: 1 (approximately 2-inch) square
Each serving has:
127 calories
1 g total fat
<1 g saturated fat
4 g protein
24 g carbohydrate
1 g fiber
36 mg cholesterol
184 mg sodium

2 TB. lemon juice

2 cups fat-free milk

2 cups yellow cornmeal

1 tsp. baking soda

¼ tsp. salt

½ cup seeded and diced fresh tomatoes

2 large eggs, at room temperature, or the equivalent amount of egg substitute

1. Preheat the oven to 350°F. Coat an 8×8×2-inch glass baking dish with nonstick cooking spray.

2. In a small bowl, stir lemon juice into milk. Set aside.

3. In a medium bowl, stir together cornmeal, baking soda, and salt. Add tomatoes, eggs, and milk mixture, and stir until moistened and well blended.

4. Pour batter into the prepared dish and bake for 35 minutes or until cornbread is golden and a cake tester or toothpick inserted into the center comes out clean.

5. Cut into squares to serve warm or at room temperature. Store any leftovers in the refrigerator.

 Heroic Hints

To seed a tomato, cut it in half crosswise and then gently squeeze each half over the sink to discharge the seeds, shaking and swiping with your finger as necessary.

Saucy Tuna Spaghetti

A surprising taste for spaghetti sauce, tuna adds an intriguing and enjoyable flavor to dinner.

1 TB. extra-virgin or light olive oil

1 medium yellow onion, finely chopped

1 (14.5-oz.) can stewed tomatoes, undrained

8 oz. uncooked whole-wheat thin spaghetti

2 TB. chopped fresh parsley or 2 tsp. dried parsley flakes

1 clove garlic, minced

⅛ tsp. salt

⅛ tsp. freshly ground black pepper

1 (7.06-oz.) pouch light tuna in water

¼ cup shredded Parmesan cheese

Yield: 4 servings
Prep time: 5 minutes
Cook time: 43 minutes
Serving size: 1 cup spaghetti with ¾ cup sauce and 1 tablespoon cheese
Each serving has:
342 calories
6 g total fat
2 g saturated fat
24 g protein
50 g carbohydrate
8 g fiber
20 mg cholesterol
589 mg sodium

1. Heat olive oil over medium heat in a small saucepan. Add onion and sauté for 8 minutes or until onion is tender and golden. Add stewed tomatoes, stirring to break up. Reduce heat to low, cover, and simmer for 30 minutes, stirring occasionally.

2. Meanwhile, cook spaghetti according to the package directions and drain.

3. Stir parsley, garlic, salt, black pepper, and tuna into tomato mixture, breaking up tuna. Cover and cook over low heat for 5 minutes or until heated through. Spoon tuna mixture over a bed of spaghetti and sprinkle Parmesan cheese over top to serve.

Super Knowledge

Using whole-wheat spaghetti in this dish contributes a whopping 7 grams fiber per serving, compared to just 2 grams you'd get from regular pasta. Whole-wheat pastas have really come a long way in terms of flavor and texture. But if you think you or your family won't like the whole-grain stuff, add it to your meals gradually. When you serve pasta dishes, start with ¼ whole-wheat and ¾ regular. Next time try ½ and ½, working up to 100 percent whole wheat.

Pizza Parlor Chicken Casserole

All your favorite pizza toppings lend their tongue-tingling tastes to this quick and easy chicken breast dish that rests deliciously atop a bed of pasta.

Yield: 4 servings
Prep time: 5 minutes
Cook time: 29 to 31 minutes
Serving size: 1 chicken breast half
Each serving has:
203 calories
3 g total fat
1 g saturated fat
29 g protein
14 g carbohydrate
3 g fiber
53 mg cholesterol
741 mg sodium

4 (3-oz.) boneless, skinless chicken breast halves, trimmed

2 cups prepared marinara sauce or other tomato pasta sauce

8 slices turkey pepperoni

½ small yellow onion, thinly sliced

½ medium green bell pepper, ribs and seeds removed, and cut into thin strips

½ small red bell pepper, ribs and seeds removed, cut into thin strips

1 cup sliced button mushrooms

1 cup fat-free or low-fat mozzarella cheese

1. Preheat the oven to 350°F. In a large nonstick skillet over medium heat, brown chicken breast halves on each side for 3 minutes or until browned.

2. Transfer chicken breast halves to a 13×9×2-inch glass baking dish. Spoon marinara sauce over top. Arrange 2 pepperoni slices on top of each chicken breast half. Scatter onion, bell peppers, and mushrooms over top. Cover and bake for 20 minutes.

3. Sprinkle mozzarella cheese over top of casserole. Bake, uncovered, for 3 to 5 minutes or until cheese is melted and chicken breast halves read 170°F on a food thermometer. Serve over whole-wheat spaghetti, if desired.

Kryptonite

Remember never to reuse a cooking utensil that has come in contact with raw or undercooked chicken. Wash the utensil in hot, soapy water before using again to prevent cross-contamination.

Chapter 8

Outstanding Oranges

In This Chapter

◆ Full-of-carotenoid carrots

◆ Pumpkins—good for more than just jack o' lanterns

◆ See how good sweet potatoes can be

In the orange vegetables category we have sweet potatoes, carrots, and pumpkins, all of which can add a nutritional boost to your meals. These outstanding oranges are great roasted, baked, grilled, and more, as you'll see by the recipes in this chapter.

Great Carrots

By now you should be able to guess that because of their bright orange color, carrots are packed with carotenoid-type antioxidants. Specifically, they are loaded with both beta- and *alpha-carotene*. Currently no official recommendation for these nutrients is on the books, but health officials have developed a daily suggested intake amount, and just 1 cup cooked carrots provides more than 250 percent of that suggested amount.

def•i•ni•tion

Alpha-carotene is a carotenoid that the body converts to vitamin A, which helps form and maintain healthy skin, teeth, and bones.

The combination of the phytochemicals, vitamins, and minerals found in carrots makes them very beneficial to you health-wise. Regularly eating carrots—and, therefore, these nutrients—has been linked to decreases in the chances of developing a variety of cancers, including bladder, cervical, prostate, colon, lung, and more.

Kryptonite

Although carrots and other beta-carotene–containing foods are good for you, don't overdo them. Your friends and family may notice something different about you if you start consuming large amounts of beta-carotene—the palms of your hands and soles of your feet may take on a slight orange tint! Don't panic though. It's not dangerous and will fade when you cut down a bit on the beta-carotene–rich foods.

Potent Pumpkins

One compound whose presence is signified by the bright orange color of pumpkins and other foods like oranges, carrots, and sweet potatoes is *beta-cryptoxanthin*.

def•i•ni•tion

Beta-cryptoxanthin is in the carotenoid family. Your body turns it into vitamin A.

This carotenoid, although not as strong as beta-carotene, functions similarly as it works to improve and maintain the health and function of your eyes, immune system, skin, and bones. It also has been shown to play some part in helping prevent arthritis.

Sweet Potato Power

Just one medium-size sweet potato gives you all the beta-carotene your body needs for a day. And oh what good it all does!

Probably one of the most beneficial roles beta-carotene plays is helping prevent age-related macular degeneration (ARMD), the leading cause of preventable blindness in the United States. Eating foods high in beta-carotene keeps your eyes healthy and maintains your vision longer.

Heroic Hints _____

There's no need to worry about getting too much beta-carotene from your diet (save for the orange tint your skin might temporarily develop). Your body changes as much of it as it needs to vitamin A, and whatever's not used is simply excreted. However, as with most vitamins and minerals, the safety of taking large quantities of supplements isn't clear so avoid mega-dosing of supplements unless otherwise advised by your doctor.

Easy Carrot Nut Muffins

Whip up these savory muffins in a matter of minutes anytime you need to tame your hunger.

Yield: 1 dozen
Prep time: 10 minutes
Cook time: 12 to 15 minutes
Serving size: 1 muffin
Each serving has:
160 calories
7 g total fat
1 g saturated fat
4 g protein
22 g carbohydrate
2 g fiber
18 mg cholesterol
252 mg sodium

2 cups reduced-fat baking mix (such as Bisquick Heart Smart all-purpose biscuit and baking mix)

½ cup chopped unsalted walnuts

6 TB. ground flaxseed meal

¾ cup fat-free milk

3 TB. honey

1 large egg, at room temperature, or the equivalent amount of egg substitute

1 cup shredded carrots

1. Preheat the oven to 400°F. Coat 2¾-inch (regular-size) muffin cups with nonstick cooking spray.

2. In a medium bowl, stir together baking mix, walnuts, and flaxseed meal. In a large bowl, combine milk, honey, and egg and blend well. Stir baking mix mixture into milk mixture just until moistened. Stir in carrots until evenly distributed.

3. Spoon batter evenly into the prepared muffin cups, filling each ¾ full. Bake for 12 to 15 minutes or until a cake tester inserted into the center of muffin comes out clean. Cool in the pan for 5 minutes before removing to cool on a wire rack.

Kryptonite

Homemade, nutrient-filled muffins make a great start to the day, as opposed to the ones you find at your local bakery—you know, the ones as big as a softball. Not only are they three or four times the size of what a muffin should be, they're loaded with fat and sugar. Just one of those giant muffins often contains more calories than three doughnuts.

Creamy Dill and Carrot Soup

This soup tastes fresh from the garden and is delicious with a
dollop of sour cream on top.

**2 cups peeled, thinly sliced
carrots**

¼ cup chopped yellow onions

**1 TB. light butter with canola
oil**

1 TB. all-purpose flour

½ tsp. dried dill weed

½ tsp. salt

½ cup water

2 cups fat-free milk

Yield: 4 servings
Prep time: 3 minutes
Cook time: 20 minutes
Serving size: 1 cup
Each serving has:
91 calories
2 g total fat
1 g saturated fat
5 g protein
15 g carbohydrate
2 g fiber
6 mg cholesterol
412 mg sodium

1. Fill a steamer pot or a medium pot or saucepan with enough
   water to fall below the steamer basket when added, and bring
   to a boil over high heat. Add carrots and onions to the steamer
   basket or a collapsible steamer basket, place the basket in the
   pot, and cover. Steam carrots and onions over boiling water,
   reducing heat as necessary to just maintain a boil, for 10
   minutes or until tender.

2. Melt butter in a medium saucepan over medium heat. Whisk
   in flour until blended. Stir in dill weed, salt, and water until
   smooth and blended. Whisk in milk and cook, stirring often,
   for 8 minutes or until bubbly and thickened. Remove from
   heat. Stir in carrot mixture.

3. Pour soup into a blender, cover, and purée for 30 seconds
   or until mixture is smooth or until it reaches the desired
   consistency. Serve hot.

Super Knowledge

Aside from being spreadable from the refrigerator, light butter with canola oil has 60 percent less cholesterol and 50
percent less fat than regular butter. A 1 tablespoon serving has
just 5 grams fat as opposed to 11 grams in butter, cutting the
calories in half from 100 to 50. Light butter with canola oil also
contains a more healthful 5 milligrams cholesterol compared to
30 milligrams in butter.

Asian Soba Noodle Salad

The bold, spicy flavor of this cold salad can take center stage at lunch or a potluck.

Yield: 7 servings
Prep time: 3 minutes
Cook time: 10 minutes
Chill time: 4 hours
Serving size: ½ cup
Each serving has:
99 calories
2 g total fat
<1 g saturated fat
3 g protein
17 g carbohydrate
1 g fiber
0 mg cholesterol
240 mg sodium

4 oz. uncooked buckwheat soba noodles

3 TB. reduced-sodium soy sauce

2 tsp. dark sesame seed oil

2 medium cloves garlic, minced

1 tsp. lemon juice

1 tsp. grated lemon zest

½ tsp. crushed red pepper flakes

2 tsp. water

1 cup shredded carrots

1 green onion, sliced on the diagonal

1¾ tsp. toasted sesame seeds

1. Cook soba noodles according to the package directions. Drain and rinse thoroughly with cold water.

2. Meanwhile, combine soy sauce, sesame seed oil, garlic, lemon juice, lemon zest, crushed red pepper flakes, and water in a medium bowl. Stir to blend and then stir in soba noodles to coat. Add carrots and green onion, and stir until coated.

3. Cover and chill for at least 4 hours or overnight. Stir again before serving, and sprinkle ¼ teaspoon sesame seeds over each serving.

 Heroic Hints _____

Look for buckwheat soba noodles in your supermarket's ethnic aisle. The popular Japanese noodles are gray-flecked beige in color and often sold in packaged bundles.

Savory Rosemary Carrots

When you want cooked carrots that aren't your typical sweet glazed variety, try this savory side dish.

1 TB. extra-virgin or light olive oil

12 medium carrots, thinly sliced on the diagonal

½ medium green bell pepper, ribs and seeds removed, and diced

1 tsp. crushed dried rosemary

¼ tsp. salt

¼ tsp. freshly ground black pepper

Yield: 6 servings
Prep time: 3 minutes
Cook time: 15 minutes
Serving size: ¹/₂ cup
Each serving has:
73 calories
3 g total fat
<1 g saturated fat
1 g protein
12 g carbohydrate
4 g fiber
0 mg cholesterol
182 mg sodium

1. Heat olive oil in a large nonstick skillet over medium heat. Add carrots and cook for 10 minutes or until crisp-tender, stirring often.

2. Add green bell pepper and cook for 5 minutes or until carrots and green bell pepper are tender, stirring frequently. Stir in rosemary, salt, and black pepper. Serve hot.

Super Knowledge

Beta-carotene–loaded carrots make this dish a nutritional knockout, providing more than a day's dose of powerhouse nutrients vitamin A and beta-carotene.

Dilled Carrot Purée over Baked Tilapia

When you need an entrée that's delectable as well as low in calories and fat, try this flavorful fish.

Yield: 4 servings
Prep time: 5 minutes
Cook time: 22 to 27 minutes
Serving size: 1 fillet with 2 tablespoons purée
Each serving has:
93 calories
1 g total fat
<1 g saturated fat
15 g protein
6 g carbohydrate
1 g fiber
35 mg cholesterol
141 mg sodium

3 medium carrots, peeled and cut into 1-in. rounds	**3 TB. fresh or unsweetened orange juice**
4 (2.5-oz.) tilapia fillets	**¼ tsp. dried dill weed**
Juice of ½ lemon	**⅛ tsp. salt**

1. Preheat the oven to 425°F. Coat a medium baking sheet with nonstick cooking spray.

2. Place carrots in a small saucepan, just cover with water, and bring to a boil over high heat. Reduce heat to medium-low, cover, and simmer for 20 to 25 minutes or until fork-tender.

3. Meanwhile, arrange tilapia on the prepared baking sheet, and squeeze lemon juice over top. Bake for 9 to 11 minutes or until fish flakes easily with a fork or registers 145°F on a food thermometer.

4. When carrots are tender, drain and pour into a blender. Cover and purée for 30 seconds or until finely chopped. Stir in orange juice, dill weed, and salt, and purée for 30 to 45 seconds more or until smooth. Spoon carrot purée over tilapia to serve.

Super Knowledge

Tilapia, along with other mild whitefish such as cod and haddock, is a great lean protein source.

Frost-on-the-Pumpkin Smoothies

Honey, banana, and cinnamon draw out the sweet side of the pumpkin in these irresistible sippers.

1 cup canned pure pumpkin, chilled

1 cup plain fat-free yogurt

½ cup fresh or unsweetened orange juice

1 very ripe medium banana, peeled and broken into chunks

2 TB. honey

¼ tsp. ground cinnamon

1 doz. large ice cubes

Yield: 4 servings
Prep time: 3 minutes
Serving size: 1 cup
Each serving has:
118 calories
<1 g total fat
0 g saturated fat
4 g protein
28 g carbohydrate
3 g fiber
1 mg cholesterol
39 mg sodium

1. Combine pumpkin, yogurt, orange juice, banana, honey, and cinnamon in a blender. Cover and blend on high speed for 30 to 45 seconds or until blended.

2. Remove the cap from the blender's lid and, with the blender running, add ice cubes one at a time until blended. Serve cold.

Heroic Hints

When shopping for canned pumpkin, be certain to buy plain pumpkin. Sweetened and spiced pumpkin purée is also available as pie filling but it's not really what you want for this recipe.

Family-Pleasing Pumpkin Bread

Spiced and moist, slices of this quick bread will be quick to disappear.

Yield: *16 servings*
Prep time: 15 minutes
Cook time: 65 minutes
Serving size: 1 slice
Each serving has:
220 calories
6 g total fat
1 g saturated fat
5 g protein
40 g carbohydrate
5 g fiber
26 mg cholesterol
172 mg sodium

1½ cups ground flaxseed meal

1 cup all-purpose flour

¾ cup whole-wheat flour

1 tsp. baking soda

½ tsp. salt

¼ tsp. baking powder

1½ tsp. ground cinnamon

½ tsp. ground nutmeg

¼ tsp. ground cloves

1½ cups honey

2 large eggs, at room temperature, or the equivalent amount of egg substitute

1 cup canned pure pumpkin

¼ cup water

1. Preheat the oven to 350°F. Coat a 9×5×3-inch loaf pan with nonstick cooking spray.

2. In a medium bowl, stir together flaxseed meal, all-purpose flour, whole-wheat flour, baking soda, salt, baking powder, cinnamon, nutmeg, and cloves.

3. Combine honey and eggs in a large bowl and stir to blend well. Stir in pumpkin and water to blend. Gradually stir in flour mixture until moistened.

4. Turn batter into the prepared loaf pan, and bake for 65 minutes or until a cake tester inserted into the middle of loaf comes out clean. Cool in the pan for 10 minutes before turning out to cool completely on a wire rack. Cut into ½-inch slices to serve.

 Heroic Hints

Accurately measure flour by lightly spooning it into a measuring cup and then scraping the back of a butter knife across the top of the cup.

Baked Pumpkin Rice Pudding

Savor the rich pumpkin taste of this warm pudding alongside the creamy coolness of vanilla ice cream for a special treat.

1 (15-oz.) can pure pumpkin

½ cup golden or dark raisins

½ cup honey

1½ tsp. ground cinnamon

½ tsp. ground ginger

⅛ tsp. ground cloves

¼ tsp. salt

1 large egg, lightly beaten, or the equivalent amount of egg substitute

1 tsp. vanilla extract

1 (12-oz.) can fat-free evaporated milk

3 cups cooked long-grain brown rice

Yield: 10 servings	
Prep time: 10 minutes	
Cook time: 35 to 40 minutes	
Serving size: ½ cup	
Each serving has:	
195 calories	
1 g total fat	
<1 g saturated fat	
6 g protein	
42 g carbohydrate	
3 g fiber	
21 mg cholesterol	
120 mg sodium	

1. Preheat the oven to 350°F. Coat a 3-quart or 13×9×2-inch glass baking dish with nonstick cooking spray.

2. Combine pumpkin, raisins, honey, cinnamon, ginger, cloves, salt, egg, and vanilla extract in a large bowl. Stir until blended. Gradually stir in evaporated milk, blending well. Stir in rice to coat evenly.

3. Turn mixture into the prepared dish, and bake for 35 to 40 minutes or until top is golden. Serve warm or cold.

Kryptonite _____

Evaporated milk and sweetened condensed milk are not interchangeable in recipes. Watch the labels carefully.

Home-Style Sweet Potato Salad

Bring a more nutrient-packed potato salad that's a bit sweeter to your next picnic get-together.

Yield: 20 servings
Prep time: 10 minutes
Cook time: 25 to 35 minutes
Serving size: ¹/₂ cup
Each serving has:
85 calories
4 g total fat
1 g saturated fat
1 g protein
12 g carbohydrate
2 g fiber
<1 mg cholesterol
121 mg sodium

6 medium sweet potatoes, peeled and cut into bite-size chunks

1 (8-oz.) can pineapple chunks in pineapple juice, drained

½ cup unsalted chopped pecans or walnuts

½ cup diced celery

1 cup reduced-fat mayonnaise

¼ cup fat-free sour cream

1. Place sweet potatoes in a large pot of cold water as you cut them. Bring to a boil over high heat. Reduce heat to medium-low and simmer for 15 to 20 minutes or until tender. Drain and rinse under cold water.

2. Combine potatoes, pineapple, pecans, and celery in a large bowl. Gently stir in mayonnaise and sour cream until evenly coated. Chill for at least 4 hours or overnight and then stir again before serving.

Heroic Hints

You can choose sweet potatoes or yams for this recipe. And unless you're in a Latin, Asian, or African marketplace, you're probably looking at an orange-fleshed, red-skinned variety of sweet potato—even though it's labeled a yam. A true yam is a tropical tuber seldom available in the United States.

Sweet Apple Casserole

Sweet potatoes and apples come together to create this sweet-tasting side dish.

2 medium sweet potatoes, scrubbed and ends trimmed

½ cup apple juice or apple cider

2 tsp. ground ginger

2 small Braeburn or other cooking apples, cored and chopped

1. Preheat the oven to 350°F. Coat a 1½-quart glass casserole dish with nonstick cooking spray.

2. Cut sweet potatoes into chunks and place in the prepared casserole dish. Stir together apple juice and ginger and pour over sweet potatoes. Cover with foil, and bake for 30 minutes.

3. Stir in apples. Re-cover with foil, and bake for 35 minutes more or until fork-tender.

 Heroic Hints _____

Store sweet potatoes in a cool, dark place and use them within a week, because they don't keep long.

Yield: 6 servings
Prep time: 7 minutes
Cook time: 65 minutes
Serving size: 1 cup
Each serving has:
63 calories
<1 g total fat
0 g saturated fat
1 g protein
15 g carbohydrate
2 g fiber
0 mg cholesterol
18 mg sodium

Sweet Potato Wedges

For a change of pace, serve this creative finger-friendly, sweeter side with burgers, hot dogs, and other sandwiches.

Yield: 4 servings
Prep time: 8 minutes
Cook time: 20 minutes
Serving size: ¹/₂ sweet potato (about 1 cup)
Each serving has:
58 calories
<1 g total fat
0 g saturated fat
1 g protein
13 g carbohydrate
2 g fiber
0 mg cholesterol
166 mg sodium

2 medium sweet potatoes

¹/₄ **tsp. salt**

¹/₈ **tsp. garlic powder**

¹/₈ **tsp. cayenne**

Nonstick cooking spray

1. Preheat the oven to 400°F with the oven rack positioned on the uppermost shelf. Coat a large baking sheet with nonstick cooking spray.

2. Scrub sweet potatoes and trim ends as needed. Cut each sweet potato in half widthwise and then cut into thin wedges about ¹/₂ inch thick. Arrange wedges in a single layer on the prepared baking sheet.

3. Stir together salt, garlic powder, and cayenne in a small bowl and then sprinkle evenly over sweet potatoes. Coat tops of sweet potato wedges liberally with nonstick cooking spray, and bake for 10 minutes. Turn potatoes and bake for 10 minutes more or until tender. Serve hot with honey for dipping, if desired.

 Heroic Hints _____

These wedges are a great alternative to french fries. In addition to being much lower in fat, one serving provides well over a day's worth of vitamin A and beta-carotene.

Skillet-Sizzled Sweet Potatoes

A savory preparation for sweet potatoes, these spicy rounds will wow 'em at dinner.

1 TB. olive oil	**½ tsp. garlic powder**
2 medium sweet potatoes, cut into thin slices	**¼ tsp. salt**
	⅛ tsp. cayenne
¾ tsp. ground cumin	**2 TB. chopped fresh cilantro**

1. Heat olive oil in a large nonstick skillet over medium heat. Stir in sweet potatoes to coat, and cook for 10 to 15 minutes or until tender, stirring frequently. Remove from heat.

2. Sprinkle cumin, garlic powder, salt, cayenne, and cilantro over sweet potatoes, and lightly stir to coat evenly. Serve hot.

Heroic Hints

Try to find fresh cilantro for this recipe because dried cilantro tends to lose much of its distinctive flavor. Look for hearty, fresh, and fragrant stems, and avoid wilted, yellowed, or slimy offerings.

Yield: 4 servings
Prep time: 2 minutes
Cook time: 10 to 15 minutes
Serving size: 1 cup
Each serving has:
84 calories
4 g total fat
0 g saturated fat
1 g protein
12 g carbohydrate
2 g fiber
0 mg cholesterol
167 mg sodium

Twice-Baked Sweet Potatoes

A little sweet, a little savory, and a lot impressive, these stuffed sweet potatoes are great for every day, as well as being special enough for guests.

Yield: 4 servings
Prep time: 6 minutes
Cook time: 40 minutes
Serving size: 1 sweet potato
Each serving has:
159 calories
4 g total fat
2 g saturated fat
4 g protein
29 g carbohydrate
4 g fiber
10 mg cholesterol
259 mg sodium

Super Knowledge

Just one Twice-Baked Sweet Potato gives you a quarter of your daily vitamin C needs.

4 medium sweet potatoes, scrubbed and trimmed

½ cup fat-free sour cream

2 TB. light butter with canola oil

2 TB. chopped fresh parsley

1 TB. finely chopped green onions

¼ tsp. salt

⅛ tsp. ground cinnamon

Pinch ground nutmeg

Pinch ground allspice

1. Prick sweet potatoes all over with the tines of a fork and arrange on a microwave-safe plate. Cook on high for 20 minutes or until fork-tender, turning sweet potatoes over halfway through cooking time.

2. Preheat the oven to 350°F.

3. Cut a thin slice off the top of each sweet potato, and scoop out pulp with a spoon, leaving a ¼-inch-thick shell. Place pulp in a medium bowl and mash with the back of a spoon until smooth.

4. Add sour cream, light butter, parsley, green onions, salt, cinnamon, nutmeg, and allspice, and stir until blended. Spoon mixture into shells and arrange on a nonstick baking sheet. Bake for 20 minutes or until browned and heated through.

Variation: You can substitute ¼ teaspoon apple pie spice if you don't have cinnamon, nutmeg, and allspice.

Pumpkin Lover's Morning Oatmeal

If autumn can't come fast enough for you, you can still enjoy
the tastes of the season by flavoring your breakfast with a hint of
pumpkin pie.

1 cup fat-free milk or soy milk

½ cup old-fashioned oats

¼ cup canned pure pumpkin

1 tsp. honey

⅛ tsp. pumpkin pie spice

Yield: 1 serving
Prep time: 3 minutes
Cook time: 7 minutes
Each serving has:
292 calories
4 g total fat
<1 g saturated fat
15 g protein
51 g carbohydrate
7 g fiber
5 mg cholesterol
106 mg sodium

1. Bring milk to a boil in a medium nonstick saucepan over high heat. Stir in oats and reduce heat to medium. Cook, stirring occasionally, for 5 minutes or until thickened.

2. Turn off heat. Stir in pumpkin, honey, and pumpkin pie spice. Remove from heat, cover, and let stand for 2 minutes. Serve hot.

Variation: To prepare in the microwave, combine milk and oats in a 3-cup or larger microwave-safe bowl. Cook on high for 2½ or 3 minutes or until thickened, watching carefully for boil-overs. Stir in pumpkin, honey, and pumpkin pie spice until blended. Cook on high for 30 seconds. Let stand for 2 minutes. Serve hot.

Heroic Hints

If you don't have pumpkin pie spice, you can use the individual ground spices that make up the pumpkin pie spice mix: cinnamon, ginger, nutmeg, cloves, and/or allspice. Use about half cinnamon and half remaining spices.

Part 4

From the Fields and Trees

Beans, soy, nuts, flax, and oats—what do they all have in common? For one thing, they're all loaded with a variety of nutrients to help you inside and out. From heart to colon to hot flashes and more, these are some serious power foods to include in your diet. And lucky for you, the following chapters give you a couple dozen ways to do so.

Chapter 9

The Best Beans

In This Chapter

- Fantastic fiber
- Cholesterol-lowering beans
- Bean recipes with some zip!

When you're watching your fat intake, try beans. They're practically fat free, and as a bonus, they're loaded with protein. And as most any vegetarian will tell you, they're often a great meat replacer. All that in such a small package!

The Benefits of Beans

Not only are beans virtually fat free, they're also cholesterol free and sodium free, which makes them an ideal food for anyone wanting to lower their risk of stroke or heart attack. But perhaps beans' most famous attribute is their fiber content. They contain both *soluble* and *insoluble fiber*, which work a bit differently from each other to accomplish two very important goals.

def•i•ni•tion

Soluble fiber is the part of plant-based foods your body can digest. It's found in oats, beans, fruits, and vegetables, and it slows the rate of food going through the intestines. **Insoluble fiber** is the part of plant-based foods the body cannot digest. It's found in wheat bran, whole grains, fruits, and vegetables, and it increases the rate of food going through the intestines.

Because soluble fiber moves more slowly through the digestive tract, it tends to pick up things along the way and carry them out of the body. One of the things it sweeps out is cholesterol. By carrying away cholesterol, the soluble fiber prevents the cholesterol from absorbing into the blood stream, which can help lower your blood cholesterol levels.

Insoluble fiber, on the other hand, moves quite a bit faster. Instead of being so particular about what moves along with it, this fiber drags everything along with it through the intestines and right on out. By helping to rid your body of waste more quickly, insoluble fiber can help prevent constipation.

The fiber in beans also helps regulate blood sugar levels. Foods that are quickly absorbed like processed breads, candy, and other simple carbohydrates tend to cause blood sugar levels to spike. Often we want this quick energy burst, but what goes up must go down and so do blood sugar levels. The rapid drop tends to make us feel sluggish and tired. High fiber foods like beans are absorbed slowly by the body leading to a slow, steady rise in blood sugar. The result is we still get the energy we need but its not followed by the slump. Regulating blood sugar levels by eating foods high in fiber, like beans, is also helpful for anyone with diabetes, hypoglycemia—periodic low blood sugar levels—and insulin resistance.

Kryptonite

When you soak and then cook dry beans, they contain no sodium. However, if you cook with canned beans, be aware that they can be loaded with sodium. Two solutions: rinse the beans well to get rid of much of the sodium or use no-salt-added or low-sodium canned beans.

The fiber in beans isn't the only substance lowering cholesterol levels. They also contain substances called *plant sterols*. These substances are so similar to cholesterol in their structure that they actually compete with it for absorption in the intestines. This competition means less cholesterol is absorbed, which means lower cholesterol levels in your blood. It's been shown that a diet that includes plant sterols and a lifestyle that includes exercise lowers both total and LDL—or bad—cholesterol and also increases levels of HDL—or good—cholesterol.

Lentil, Kale, and Rice Soup

This substantial soup is packed with flavor and just enough broth, so if you prefer soupier soups, start with more broth and water.

1 tsp. extra-virgin or light olive oil

1 medium yellow onion, chopped

1 cup dried lentils

2 cups water

¾ cup instant brown rice

4 cups packed torn fresh kale

½ tsp. salt

Yield: 7 servings	
Prep time: 3 minutes	
Cook time: 40 minutes	
Serving size: 1 cup	
Each serving has:	
169 calories	
2 g total fat	
<1 g saturated fat	
11 g protein	
29 g carbohydrate	
8 g fiber	
2 mg cholesterol	
242 mg sodium	

1. Heat olive oil in a large saucepan over medium heat. Add onion and sauté for 5 minutes or until golden brown. Add lentils, broth, and water, and bring to a boil over high heat. Reduce heat, cover, and simmer for 20 minutes or just until lentils are tender.

2. Stir in rice, kale, and salt, and return to a boil over high heat. Reduce heat to low or medium-low, cover, and simmer for 10 minutes or until rice and kale are tender. Serve hot.

Super Knowledge _____

Most beans require soaking time first, but dried lentils and split peas can be stirred right into a recipe.

Fast-Fix Refried Beans

You can pair all your Mexican-style entrées with this zesty, cheese-topped side—and with very little effort on your part.

Yield: 4 servings
Prep time: 2 minutes
Cook time: 5 minutes
Serving size: $^1\!/_2$ cup plus 2 tablespoons cheese
Each serving has:
138 calories
3 g total fat
2 g saturated fat
9 g protein
18 g carbohydrate
5 g fiber
10 mg cholesterol
697 mg sodium

1 (16-oz.) can fat-free refried beans

¼ cup salsa

2 or 3 TB. canned diced green chilies, drained

½ cup 2 percent milk shredded Mexican cheese blend

1. In a small saucepan, combine beans, salsa, and green chilies. Cover and cook over medium heat for 5 minutes or until bubbly and heated through.

2. Stir again and scatter 2 tablespoons cheese over each serving while hot to melt cheese slightly.

Heroic Hints

If beans tend to give you gas, natural dietary enzyme supplements such as Beano can help. Taken before a meal, these drug-free products help break down the indigestible carbohydrates that cause gas—before it happens.

Kidney Bean and Zucchini Skillet over Rice

If you have leftover cooked rice on hand, this tomato-based bean and veggie dish can be a boon when you have to get dinner on the table quickly.

2 tsp. olive oil

1 medium yellow onion, chopped

2 medium cloves garlic, minced

1 medium zucchini squash, chopped

½ large red bell pepper, ribs and seeds removed, and chopped

½ tsp. dried marjoram

½ tsp. salt

¼ tsp. freshly ground black pepper

1 (15-oz.) can dark red kidney beans, rinsed and drained

1 large tomato, chopped

½ cup no-salt-added tomato sauce

2 cups cooked long-grain brown rice

Yield: 4 servings
Prep time: 3 minutes
Cook time: 12 minutes
Serving size: 1 cup over ½ cup rice
Each serving has:
276 calories
3 g total fat
<1 g saturated fat
11 g protein
51 g carbohydrate
10 g fiber
0 mg cholesterol
522 mg sodium

1. Heat olive oil in a 10-inch nonstick skillet over medium heat. Add onion and sauté for 2 minutes. Stir in garlic and sauté for 2 more minutes or until onion is softened.

2. Stir in zucchini, red bell pepper, marjoram, salt, and black pepper. Cook and stir for 5 minutes or until vegetables are nearly tender.

3. Stir in kidney beans, tomato, and tomato sauce. Cover and cook for 3 minutes or until heated through and vegetables are tender. Serve hot over rice.

Super Knowledge

With 74 milligrams vitamin C, a serving of this dish supplies almost a day's worth of the powerful nutrient. In addition to its other tasks, vitamin C enhances the absorption of iron in this meal.

Black Bean Enchilada Bake

You might not expect this Tex-Mex dish to include mozzarella cheese, but its mild flavor balances the strong tastes of sharp cheddar cheese and cumin.

Yield: 6 servings
Prep time: 12 minutes
Cook time: 36 minutes
Serving size: 1 enchilada
Each serving has:
223 calories
7 g total fat
3 g saturated fat
14 g protein
35 g carbohydrate
6 g fiber
15 mg cholesterol
814 mg sodium

1 tsp. olive oil

1 medium yellow onion, diced

1 tsp. ground cumin

1 (15-oz.) can black beans, rinsed and drained

1 cup 2 percent milk shredded sharp cheddar cheese

½ cup fat-free shredded mozzarella cheese

6 (7-in.) whole-wheat tortillas, at room temperature or warmed

1 (10-oz.) can green enchilada sauce

1. Preheat the oven to 350°F. Coat a 13×9×2-inch glass baking dish with nonstick cooking spray.

2. Heat olive oil in a 10-inch nonstick skillet over medium heat. Add onion and stir to coat. Stir in cumin and cook for 5 minutes or until onion is tender and lightly golden, stirring frequently. Stir in beans until warmed through and then remove from heat.

3. Evenly divide ³/₄ cup cheddar cheese and mozzarella cheese among tortillas, piling in the center of each. Evenly divide bean mixture among tortillas. Roll up tortillas to enclose filling and arrange seam side down in the prepared baking dish. Spoon enchilada sauce evenly over top of enchiladas. Cover tightly with nonstick foil or foil coated with nonstick cooking spray, and bake for 30 minutes or until bubbly.

4. Uncover and sprinkle reserved ¹/₄ cup cheddar cheese over enchiladas. Serve hot with sour cream, if desired.

Super Knowledge

The low-fat cheese in this dish provides almost as much calcium per serving as a glass of milk.

Simple Red Beans and Rice

Thanks to precooked lean ham, you don't have to spend all day in the kitchen to enjoy the great taste of this classic dish.

1 TB. olive oil

1 medium yellow onion, finely chopped

½ medium green bell pepper, ribs and seeds removed, and finely chopped

¼ cup chopped fresh parsley

1 large clove garlic, minced

2 (16-oz.) cans red beans, rinsed and drained

1 cup finely diced fully cooked lean ham

1 (8-oz.) can tomato sauce

1 TB. Worcestershire sauce

¼ tsp. dried oregano or ¾ tsp. chopped fresh

3¾ cups cooked long-grain brown rice

Yield: 5 servings
Prep time: 5 minutes
Cook time: 15 minutes
Serving size: 1 cup beans with ¾ cup rice
Each serving has:
452 calories
8 g total fat
2 g saturated fat
24 g protein
69 g carbohydrate
13 g fiber
25 mg cholesterol
635 mg sodium

1. Heat olive oil in a 10-inch nonstick skillet over medium heat. Add onion, green bell pepper, parsley, and garlic, and sauté over medium heat for 5 minutes or until onion is softened.

2. Add red beans, ham, tomato sauce, Worcestershire sauce, and oregano, and cook for 10 minutes, stirring occasionally.

3. To serve, line serving plates with rice and spoon bean mixture over top.

Super Knowledge _____

Thanks to the red beans, a serving of this Latin-inspired meal provides half your daily fiber requirement.

Zippy Pinto Beans

An easy, hands-off side dish, these spicy baked beans add a little zest to an everyday meal.

Yield: 4 servings
Prep time: 5 minutes
Cook time: 1 hour
Serving size: ½ cup
Each serving has:
124 calories
1 g total fat
0 g saturated fat
7 g protein
21 g carbohydrate
7 g fiber
0 mg cholesterol
405 mg sodium

2 cups drained cooked or canned pinto beans

1 cube beef bouillon

1 cup boiling water

2 tsp. honey

¼ tsp. cayenne

¼ tsp. dry mustard

1. Preheat the oven to 350°F. Place pinto beans in a 1-quart glass baking dish coated with nonstick cooking spray.

2. In a small bowl, dissolve bouillon in boiling water. Stir in honey until blended. Stir in cayenne and dry mustard.

3. Pour bouillon mixture over pinto beans. Cover and bake for 1 hour. Serve hot.

Heroic Hints

Add the right amount of spice every time you cook. After scooping a spice from it's jar with a measuring spoon, use the back of a butter knife to level it off, pushing the excess back into the jar.

Supreme Soy

In This Chapter

- ◆ Heart-smart soy
- ◆ Cool down with cool soy treats
- ◆ Sweet and savory soy goodies

You've probably heard about the benefits of soy and maybe tofu in particular. But even if you don't relish the idea of biting into a chunk of bland tofu, you can otherwise incorporate soy into your diet in so many ways. This chapter presents just a few reasons why you should give soy another look.

So Much Soy

The two most note-worthy and health-promoting substances found in soy are protein and *isoflavones*. When it comes to preventing heart disease, each of these plays a part. Soy protein helps lower total cholesterol as well as LDL cholesterol, the bad stuff. In addition, the isoflavones may help raise HDL cholesterol, the good stuff.

def•i•ni•tion

Isoflavones are plant compounds that somewhat copy what the hormone estrogen does.

And soy may help those of you suffering from the annoying hot flashes of menopause. These benefits are achieved by eating the isoflavones, not just soy protein. This might not work for everyone, but it's certainly worth a try.

Super Knowledge

Foods made from whole soybeans such as tofu, soy milk, and soy flour, and of course edamame or other soybeans contain both protein and isoflavones. Foods such as soy burgers and soy dogs are made from soy protein concentrates and, due to both processing and the many nonsoy ingredients in them, don't contain much isoflavones. Soy sauce and soybean oil contain no isoflavones and little to no protein.

Marinated Tofu and Vegetable Salad

You can overcome tofu's typical blandness by marinating it in a highly seasoned, Asian-flavored sauce with lots of yummy veggies.

⅓ cup sodium-free rice vinegar

¼ cup dark sesame seed oil

3 TB. reduced-sodium soy sauce

½ TB. honey

2 medium cloves garlic, minced

1 tsp. minced fresh ginger-root

¼ tsp. crushed red pepper flakes

1 (14-oz.) pkg. extra-firm tofu, well drained and cut into 1-in. cubes

1 small red bell pepper, ribs and seeds removed, and diced

1 (4-oz.) pkg. petite mushrooms, stems trimmed and brushed clean

½ cup shredded carrots

2 green onions, finely chopped

¼ cup unsalted chopped peanuts

2 TB. chopped fresh cilantro

2 tsp. toasted sesame seeds

Yield: 5 servings
Prep time: 7 minutes
Chill time: 2 hours
Serving size: 1 cup
Each serving has:
220 calories
17 g total fat
2 g saturated fat
9 g protein
10 g carbohydrate
2 g fiber
0 mg cholesterol
383 mg sodium

1. Stir together rice vinegar, sesame seed oil, soy sauce, garlic, gingerroot, and crushed red pepper flakes in a large, shallow bowl. Add tofu, red bell pepper, mushrooms, carrots, and green onions, and stir gently. Cover and marinate in the refrigerator for at least 2 hours to blend flavors.

2. Stir again before serving cold or at room temperature topped with peanuts, cilantro, and sesame seeds.

Heroic Hints

If your mushrooms are too dirty to brush clean, try wiping them spotless with a damp paper towel. If they're still dirty, you can rinse them under running water to wash away the dirt. Don't soak mushrooms, though, as they act like sponges and absorb water. Allow rinsed mushrooms to air dry for a bit to avoid a watered-down flavor. Store fresh mushrooms in a paper bag in the refrigerator and wash them just before using.

Asian Chicken Salad with Edamame

Toss this colorful and healthful main-dish meal that mingles sweet and savory in your salad bowl for lunch or dinner.

Yield: 2 servings
Prep time: 5 minutes
Chill time: 8 hours
Cook time: 20 minutes
Serving size: 1 salad
Each serving has:
290 calories
10 g total fat
1 g saturated fat
24 g protein
28 g carbohydrate
7 g fiber
47 mg cholesterol
518 mg sodium

2 (3-oz.) boneless, skinless chicken breast halves, trimmed of fat

¾ cup low-fat sesame ginger salad dressing or your favorite Asian-flavored low-fat salad dressing

½ cup frozen edamame

½ small red bell pepper, ribs and seeds removed, and cut in short strips

4 cups lettuce and spring mix salad greens

1 (10.5-oz.) can mandarin orange segments in mandarin orange juice, drained

½ cup shredded carrots

1. Place chicken breast halves and ½ cup salad dressing in a resealable plastic bag. Press out all air, seal the bag, and marinate in the refrigerator for 8 hours or overnight.

2. Preheat the oven to 425°F. Coat a medium nonstick baking sheet with nonstick cooking spray.

3. Place chicken breast halves on the prepared baking sheet, and bake for 20 minutes or until done (170°F on a food thermometer). Discard marinade.

4. Meanwhile, cook edamame in a medium saucepan of boiling water for 1 minute. Add red bell pepper, and cook for 3 minutes more or until edamame is tender and red bell pepper is crisp-tender. Drain and rinse under cold water.

5. Arrange 2 cups salad greens on each of 2 serving plates. Divide edamame, red bell pepper, mandarin orange segments, and carrots evenly between the plates. Arrange 1 chicken breast half atop each salad, slicing if desired. Drizzle 2 tablespoons remaining salad dressing over each salad to serve.

Super Knowledge

Thanks to the greens and soybeans, one serving of this salad supplies more than half of your daily folate needs.

Coco-Orange Soy Milk Smoothies

Add a little chocolate for your sweet tooth, and you've got a smoothie sure to disappear quickly.

1 cup fat-free plain yogurt

1 cup fat-free plain soy milk

1 very ripe banana, peeled and broken into chunks

½ cup fresh or unsweetened orange juice

1 TB. unsweetened cocoa powder

1 TB. honey

12 large ice cubes

Yield: 4 servings
Prep time: 3 minutes
Serving size: 1 cup
Each serving has:
102 calories
<1 g total fat
<1 g saturated fat
5 g protein
29 g carbohydrate
1 g fiber
1 mg cholesterol
63 mg sodium

1. Combine yogurt, soy milk, banana, orange juice, cocoa powder, and honey in a blender. Cover and blend on high speed for 20 seconds or until well blended.

2. Remove the cap from the blender's lid and, with the blender running, add ice cubes one at a time until well blended. Serve immediately.

Super Knowledge

Unsweetened cocoa powder is a great way to get the benefits of chocolate—not to mention the yummy flavor—without any fat. Unsweetened cocoa is not the same as hot cocoa or hot chocolate mixes, which have sugar and other ingredients added to them. You can find unsweetened cocoa in the baking aisle of your grocery store. Natural is the most common type, but you may also find Dutch-processed or Alkalized. The two shouldn't be used interchangeably when baking.

Banana Berry Tofu Smoothies

When you want a more substantial smoothie with the healthful benefits of soy, whip up this fruity blend.

Yield: 3 servings
Prep time: 5 minutes
Serving size: 1 cup
Each serving has:
165 calories
2 g total fat
<1 g saturated fat
5 g protein
35 g carbohydrate
3 g fiber
0 mg cholesterol
24 mg sodium

6 oz. firm tofu, drained and chopped

1 cup berries (blueberries, raspberries, blackberries, halved strawberries, etc.)

1 medium very ripe banana, peeled and broken into chunks

3 TB. honey

¼ tsp. vanilla extract

12 large ice cubes

1. Combine tofu, berries, banana, honey, and vanilla extract in a blender. Cover and blend on high speed for 1 minute or until well blended.

2. Remove the cap from the blender's lid and, with the blender running, add ice cubes one at a time. Blend until smooth.

 Super Knowledge _____

Tofu is available in different textures—soft, firm, and extra-firm. Be sure to use the type of tofu called for in a recipe for the best results.

Creamy Chocolate Tofu Pudding

When the kids aren't looking, sneak a little tofu into always-popular chocolate pudding, and they won't even realize they're loving soybeans!

1 cup miniature semi-sweet chocolate chips

2 TB. water

1 (12.3-oz.) pkg. firm tofu, drained and chopped

¼ cup fat-free milk

1 TB. vanilla extract

Yield: 6 servings
Prep time: 3 minutes
Cook time: 3 minutes
Chill time: 1 hour
Serving size: ½ cup
Each serving has:
259 calories
12 g total fat
7 g saturated fat
7 g protein
29 g carbohydrate
0 g fiber
<1 mg cholesterol
26 mg sodium

1. Combine chocolate chips and water in a small, heavy saucepan, and melt chocolate chips over very low heat, stirring often until blended.

2. Combine tofu, chocolate mixture, milk, and vanilla extract in a blender. Blend on high speed for 1 minute or until well blended and smooth, scraping down the sides as necessary. Cover and chill for at least 1 hour or until cold.

Kryptonite

You can't rush melting chocolate, so keep the heat very low to prevent burning. Stirring helps, too, as the chocolate chips may appear to hold their shape until you stir them.

Chapter 11

Nutritional Nuts

In This Chapter

◆ Almonds—antioxidants galore

◆ Really? All that in a peanut? You bet!

◆ Omega-3–rich walnuts

◆ Nutty recipes for breakfast, lunch, dinner, and more

Almonds, peanuts, walnuts, and most other nuts offer tremendous health benefits. And although the fat and calories they contain can certainly add up if you eat large amounts of them, moderate amounts on a daily basis provide all the benefits without causing weight gain.

Amazing Almonds

Almonds rank pretty high up in terms of health benefits. They contain as much of the powerful antioxidants as some fruits and vegetables, including kaempferol, quercetin, and catechin, which are some of the most powerful of all. So almonds are pretty tough soldiers on your side when it comes to fighting cardiovascular and age-related diseases.

Almonds also contain a good amount of the mineral magnesium. In fact, just one small serving of almonds gives you almost a quarter of your daily needs. And what does all this magnesium do for you, you might ask? A couple things—by allowing your blood vessels to work better, magnesium helps improve blood flow and, thus, improve the circulation of oxygen and nutrients throughout the body. So go get some almonds!

Powerful Peanuts

Among the peanut's major vitamin players is *vitamin E*. Because it's *fat-soluble*, vitamin E needs fat for the body to absorb it. And handily, not only do peanuts supply vitamin E, they also contain a good dose of healthy fats that allow your body to absorb the E. Folks who eat the recommended amount of vitamin E have a much lower risk of developing Alzheimer's disease than those who eat very little of the vitamin. Vitamin E also helps your immune system perform at top-notch levels.

Fiber is another biggie when it comes to the peanut's power. In addition to helping to lower cholesterol and, therefore, risk of heart disease, fiber helps you maintain healthy blood sugar levels, which is important if you have diabetes or *hypoglycemia*.

def•i•ni•tion

Vitamin E is an essential fat-soluble vitamin involved in red blood cell development. It also protects the body from free radical damage. **Fat-soluble vitamins** are dissolvable in fat and stored in the body's fat. If you have **hypoglycemia,** you have episodes of low levels of sugar in your blood. It's the opposite of *hyperglycemia*, or high blood sugar levels, a classic sign of diabetes.

Because fiber slows the speed at which food is digested and enters the blood stream, it also helps fill you up and keeps you feeling full longer. So a fiber-rich diet can help decrease hunger and frequent snacking, thus making weight maintenance easier. Fiber can also help prevent constipation—just be sure to drink plenty of fluids throughout the day as well.

Winning Walnuts

Only a few foods are rich sources of omega-3 fatty acids, and walnuts are one of them. They contain the alphalinolenic acid (ALA) type of omega-3 fat. Omega-3 fats help reduce the ability of blood platelets to clump together forming blood clots. In doing so, these healthy fats can help lower your risk of blocked arteries, which can lead to heart attacks and strokes.

Omega-3s also help your brain cells stay healthy. Brain cells, like all other cells of the body, are made mostly of fat. Omega-3s help needed material get into the brain's cells and waste material to get out. This helps the cells and, therefore, your brain work better.

Heroic Hints

Eager to start upping your nut intake but worried you'll overdo it? As long as you stick to a moderate serving of the various nuts, or 1 ounce, you should be fine. Because nuts vary in size, the number of nuts in 1 ounce varies: 1 ounce almonds is about 23 nuts, 1 ounce peanuts is about 28, and 1 ounce walnuts is about 8 to 10.

Classic Pesto Sauce with Almonds

Enjoy the fresh taste of this pesto over your favorite hot pasta or spread it on your favorite sandwich as a condiment.

Yield: 5 servings
Prep time: 8 minutes
Cook time: 5 minutes
Serving size: 2 table-spoons
Each serving has:
202 calories
20 g total fat
3 g saturated fat
5 g protein
2 g carbohydrate
1 g fiber
5 mg cholesterol
134 mg sodium

⅓ cup unsalted sliced almonds

1 cup firmly packed fresh basil leaves

3 medium cloves garlic

⅓ cup extra-virgin olive oil

⅓ cup shredded Parmesan cheese

1. Place almonds in a small, dry, nonstick skillet over medium heat. Cook for 5 minutes or until toasted, shaking the skillet occasionally to prevent burning.

2. Combine basil and garlic in a blender. Blend on high speed for 1 minute or until finely chopped, stopping to scrape down the sides of the blender as needed. Add almonds and grind on high speed for 20 seconds or until ground, stopping to scrape down the sides of the blender as needed.

3. Remove the cap from the blender's lid and, with the blender running, drizzle in olive oil for 1 minute or until a smooth paste forms.

4. Spoon mixture into a small bowl and stir in Parmesan cheese until blended. Serve at room temperature. (Store any leftovers in the refrigerator directly covered with plastic wrap and stir again before serving.)

Super Knowledge

Directly covering the pesto sauce with plastic wrap blocks out air, helping prevent discoloration and keeping it fresher. Press the plastic wrap down to the surface of the pesto sauce in the bowl. Then, cover the bowl with a lid and refrigerate.

Roasted Asparagus, Garlic, and Almonds over Penne

Take advantage of spring's bumper crop of asparagus with this easy one-dish meal with a heady flavor that's ready in minutes.

1 lb. fresh asparagus

6 medium cloves garlic

¼ tsp. freshly ground black pepper

¼ cup extra-virgin olive oil

2 TB. 50 percent reduced-fat bacon pieces

¼ cup unsalted sliced almonds

4 cups cooked whole-wheat penne pasta

¼ cup freshly shredded Parmesan cheese

Yield: 4 servings
Prep time: 7 minutes
Cook time: 11 to 14 minutes
Serving size: 1³/₄ cups
Each serving has:
408 calories
20 g total fat
3 g saturated fat
16 g protein
45 g carbohydrate
7 g fiber
8 mg cholesterol
242 mg sodium

1. Preheat the oven to 425°F, placing oven rack at the uppermost position.

2. Trim ends of asparagus and discard. Cut asparagus spears into 2-inch pieces. Thinly slice garlic.

3. Combine asparagus pieces, garlic slices, black pepper, and olive oil on a medium nonstick baking sheet, tossing to coat evenly. Spread into a single layer and then sprinkle bacon pieces evenly over top. Bake for 8 to 10 minutes or until asparagus is tender.

4. Push aside asparagus mixture, if necessary, and add almonds to the baking sheet in a single layer. Bake for 3 or 4 minutes more or until almonds are colored, watching carefully to avoid burning.

5. Place pasta in a large serving bowl. Add asparagus mixture and toss to coat evenly. Serve immediately, garnishing each serving with 1 tablespoon Parmesan cheese.

Heroic Hints

Easily trim asparagus ends by holding one hand at the spear's end and your other hand about midway up the spear. Snap the end off where it naturally breaks.

Honey-Lime Almond Chicken Breasts

These almond-topped chicken breasts with a sweet citrus tang are easy enough for everyday and attractive enough for company fare.

Yield: 4 servings
Prep time: 7 minutes
Chill time: 1 hour
Cook time: 35 minutes
Serving size: 1 chicken breast half
Each serving has:
302 calories
14 g total fat
2 g saturated fat
19 g protein
25 g carbohydrate
1 g fiber
47 mg cholesterol
48 mg sodium

⅓ cup lemon juice

4½ TB. honey

2½ TB. lime juice

2½ TB. extra-virgin olive oil

1 tsp. grated lime zest

4 green onions, finely chopped

4 medium cloves garlic, minced

4 (3-oz.) boneless, skinless chicken breast halves, trimmed of fat

⅓ cup unsalted sliced almonds

1. Combine lemon juice, 2½ tablespoons honey, lime juice, olive oil, lime zest, green onions, and garlic in a small bowl. Stir until well blended.

2. Place chicken breast halves in a gallon-size resealable plastic bag and pour in all but ¼ cup lemon juice mixture. Press the air out of the bag and seal it, and marinate in the refrigerator for 1 hour.

3. Preheat the oven to 350°F.

4. Remove chicken from marinade, and discard marinade. Arrange chicken breast halves in a 13×9×2-inch glass baking dish.

5. Combine remaining ¼ cup lemon juice mixture and remaining 2 tablespoons honey in a small bowl. Stir until blended and spoon over chicken breast halves. Bake for 20 minutes.

6. Scatter almonds over chicken breast halves and continue baking for 15 minutes or until chicken is done (170°F on a food thermometer).

Super Knowledge

When preparing the ingredients, remember to grate the lime zest from the uncut lime *before* cutting it to juice it.

Peanut Butter Wheat Muffins

Enjoy these tender-textured muffins warm or at room temperature, plain or with a bit of cream cheese, peanut butter, or fruit spread on top.

1 cup all-purpose flour

1 cup whole-wheat flour

6 TB. ground flaxseed meal

½ TB. baking powder

½ tsp. salt

¼ cup no-salt natural creamy peanut butter

2 TB. *unsulfured molasses*

2 TB. honey

2 cups fat-free soy milk or milk

Yield: 1 dozen
Prep time: 10 minutes
Cook time: 25 to 30 minutes
Serving size: 1 muffin
Each serving has:
153 calories
5 g total fat
1 g saturated fat
5 g protein
24 g carbohydrate
3 g fiber
0 mg cholesterol
168 mg sodium

1. Preheat the oven to 350°F. Coat 2¾-inch (regular-size) muffin cups with nonstick cooking spray.

2. Stir together all-purpose flour, whole-wheat flour, flaxseed meal, baking powder, and salt in a large bowl. Add peanut butter, molasses, honey, and soy milk, and stir until dry ingredients are moistened.

3. Spoon batter into the prepared muffin cups, filling them ¾ full. Bake for 25 to 30 minutes or until a cake tester or toothpick inserted into the middle of muffins comes out clean. Let muffins cool in the pan for 5 minutes before removing to a wire rack to cool.

Variation: For a more peanut-y treat, blend equal portions fat-free cream cheese and natural peanut butter to smear on these muffins.

def•i•ni•tion

Unsulfured molasses is a sweet, syrupy byproduct of sugar refinement. Syrup processed from pure sugarcane without using sulfur dioxide has a sweeter, milder flavor. Check the label for the "unsulfured" designation.

Sweet and Creamy Peanut Butter Dip

While perhaps a surprising flavor combination, this peanut butter dip with honey and lemon juice can quickly become addictive!

Yield: 6 servings
Prep time: 3 minutes
Serving size: 2 tablespoons
Each serving has:
147 calories
7 g total fat
1 g saturated fat
3 g protein
19 g carbohydrate
1 g fiber
0 mg cholesterol
1 mg sodium

⅓ **cup no-salt natural creamy peanut butter**

⅓ **cup honey**

2 TB. lemon juice

1. Combine peanut butter, honey, and lemon juice in a small bowl, and stir until well blended.

2. Serve with your favorite dippers such as banana slices, apple slices, strawberries, celery sticks, and carrots. (Store any leftover dip in the refrigerator and stir again before serving.)

Heroic Hints

Be an advocate for your health by becoming a food label reader. Some natural peanut butters contain added salt, which you don't need. You want the jar with the simplest ingredients list: peanuts.

Thai-Style Chicken Skillet

Enjoy the spicy, tangy tastes of Thai cuisine with this single-skillet main dish sure to please adults and children alike.

1 tsp. peanut oil

1 lb. boneless, skinless chicken breasts, trimmed of fat and cut into bite-size pieces

6 medium cloves garlic, minced

1 (14-oz.) can fat-free, less-sodium chicken broth

¾ cup water

1 cup uncooked long-grain brown rice

¼ cup reduced-sodium soy sauce

1 tsp. dark sesame seed oil

¼ tsp. crushed red pepper flakes

2 TB. no-salt natural creamy peanut butter

2 tsp. lime juice

4 green onions, finely chopped

½ cup unsalted coarsely chopped peanuts

Yield: 4 servings
Prep time: 5 minutes
Cook time: 1 hour
Serving size: 1 cup
Each serving has:
502 calories
20 g total fat
3 g saturated fat
36 g protein
46 g carbohydrate
6 g fiber
65 mg cholesterol
665 mg sodium

1. Heat peanut oil in a large, deep skillet over medium heat. Add chicken and cook for 5 minutes or until chicken is browned on all sides. Drain.

2. Add garlic and cook for 1 minute or until golden. Stir in broth, water, brown rice, soy sauce, sesame seed oil, and crushed red pepper flakes. Bring to a boil over high heat. Reduce heat to low or medium-low, cover, and simmer for 45 minutes or until rice is plumped and tender. Turn off heat and let stand, covered, for 5 minutes.

3. Stir in peanut butter and lime juice until blended. Serve hot topped with green onions and peanuts.

Super Knowledge

Three-quarters of the fiber packed into this dinner, which is about 20 percent of your daily needs, comes from the brown rice and peanuts.

Double-Stuffed Walnut Celery Sticks

You can delight in a tangy, nutty crunch for a satisfying snack or add this finger food to your appetizer tray.

Yield: 1 dozen
Prep time: 10 minutes
Serving size: 2 celery sticks
Each serving has:
98 calories
7 g total fat
2 g saturated fat
7 g protein
2 g carbohydrate
1 g fiber
8 mg cholesterol
180 mg sodium

3 oz. fat-free cream cheese

½ cup reduced-fat crumbled blue cheese

¼ cup unsalted ground walnuts

⅛ tsp. cayenne

¼ cup unsalted finely diced walnuts

12 (3-in.) celery sticks

1. Combine cream cheese, blue cheese, ground walnuts, and cayenne in a small bowl, and stir until well blended. Stir in diced walnuts until evenly distributed.

2. Spoon cheese mixture into celery sticks, pushing into hollows and piling on. Serve cold or at room temperature, and store any leftovers in the refrigerator.

Variation: For a pretty party presentation, cut the ends of the celery sticks on the diagonal and dust the stuffing with paprika.

Super Knowledge

Although extremely beneficial, the fats in walnuts make them spoil quickly. Store shelled walnuts in an airtight container in the refrigerator for up to 6 months or in the freezer for up to 1 year. Walnuts in the shell keep well in a cool, dark, dry place for up to 6 months.

Wilted Kale with Walnuts

Get more greens in your diet with this quick and easy dish that serves up an earthy, cabbagelike flavor accented by nutty bites.

6 cups packed torn kale

½ cup unsalted coarsely chopped walnuts

1 TB. extra-virgin olive oil

1 tsp. lemon juice

1 medium clove garlic, minced

Yield: 6 servings
Prep time: 4 minutes
Cook time: 11 minutes
Serving size: ¹/₂ cup
Each serving has:
119 calories
9 g total fat
1 g saturated fat
5 g protein
8 g carbohydrate
2 g fiber
0 mg cholesterol
29 mg sodium

1. Wash kale in a large colander and drain loosely. Transfer kale to a large nonstick skillet with water that clings to leaves. Cook for 10 minutes or until the skillet is nearly dry, stirring often.

2. Meanwhile, place walnuts in a small, dry, nonstick skillet over medium heat. Toast walnuts for 5 minutes or until fragrant and colored, shaking the skillet occasionally to prevent burning.

3. Drizzle olive oil and lemon juice over kale, and stir in walnuts and garlic. Cook and stir for 1 minute or until garlic is golden. Serve hot.

Super Knowledge

One serving of this side dish supplies 4 to 6 times your daily need of vitamin K. People taking the blood thinners Coumadin or warfarin are often told to avoid this vitamin that helps blood clot because it could interfere with their medication. But as long as you eat about the same amount of vitamin K every day, your medication amount will be adjusted to account for that and total elimination isn't necessary.

Walnut-Crusted Catfish

Even ardent catfish detractors will devour these attractive, specially prepared fillets coated with an herbed, nutty breading that mellows the fish flavor.

Yield: 2 servings
Prep time: 7 minutes
Cook time: 10 or 11 minutes
Serving size: 1 fillet
Each serving has:
290 calories
16 g total fat
3 g saturated fat
22 g protein
16 g carbohydrate
1 g fiber
53 mg cholesterol
265 mg sodium

¼ **cup unsalted ground walnuts**

2 **TB. plain dry breadcrumbs**

¼ **tsp. dried parsley flakes**

¼ **tsp. dried basil**

⅛ **tsp. salt**

⅛ **tsp. freshly ground black pepper**

3 **TB. all-purpose flour**

3 **TB. fat-free soy milk or milk**

2 **(4-oz.) catfish fillets**

1. Preheat the oven to 425°F. Coat a medium nonstick baking sheet with nonstick cooking spray.

2. Stir together walnuts, breadcrumbs, parsley flakes, basil, salt, and black pepper in a shallow pie plate. Place flour into another shallow dish. Pour soy milk into a third shallow dish.

3. Dredge each fillet in flour, coating completely. Then dip each fillet in soy milk to moisten. Finally, dredge each fillet in walnut mixture, coating thoroughly. Place fillets on the prepared baking sheet, and bake for 10 or 11 minutes or until done (145°F on a food thermometer). Serve immediately.

 Heroic Hints

To prepare ground walnuts, place unsalted whole walnuts or pieces in a blender or food processor. Cover and chop or process for nearly a minute or until very finely chopped.

Soy Roasted Almonds

These lightly spiced almonds are good for snacking out-of-hand, adding crunch to a salad, or combining with pretzel sticks, rye crisps, and small crackers for a simple party mix.

2 cups unsalted whole almonds

1 TB. extra-virgin olive oil

½ TB. reduced-sodium soy sauce

½ TB. Worcestershire sauce

1 tsp. honey

½ tsp. garlic powder

½ tsp. onion powder

¼ tsp. cayenne

Yield: 2 cups
Prep time: 5 minutes
Cook time: 20 minutes
Serving size: ¼ cup
Each serving has:
232 calories
20 g total fat
2 g saturated fat
7 g protein
8 g carbohydrate
4 g fiber
0 mg cholesterol
45 mg sodium

1. Preheat the oven to 300°F. Line a medium (about 10×14-inch) baking sheet with parchment paper.

2. In a small bowl, combine almonds, olive oil, soy sauce, Worcestershire sauce, honey, garlic powder, onion powder, and cayenne. Stir until almonds are evenly coated.

3. Turn out almonds onto the prepared baking sheet in a single layer. Bake for 20 minutes or until toasted. Stir and return to a single layer to cool completely before storing in an airtight container.

Super Knowledge

Parchment paper is a great way to bake without the grimy cleanup. Use just the length needed to line the baking sheet to avoid contact with the oven walls or racks. But don't worry about which side should face up; they're the same.

Great Grains

In This Chapter

- Ladies, get to know flax
- Some bet-you-didn't-knows about oats
- Sweet treats and more

Great things come in small packages, and that's especially true with grains such as flax and oats. The many health benefits packed into small oats and tiny flaxseeds seems to never end. Nature really is something to put together all these healthful treats for us to enjoy.

Fabulous Flaxseed

Flax offers a bevy of benefits, involving not only women's health but also the cardiovascular system and more. Let's take a look at just what flax does for the body.

The two main substances in flax are *lignans* and an omega-3 fatty acid called alphalinolenic acid (ALA). Lignans' biggest bragging rights focus on women's health, especially potential protection from breast cancer. They do so by changing to hormonelike substances in our intestines. High levels of these substances have been suggested to lower a woman's risk of developing breast cancer.

def•i•ni•tion

Lignans are substances from plants that work both as antioxidants and *phytoestrogens*, or substances that come from plants and in the body act similarly to the hormone estrogen. **Alphalinolenic acid** is an essential fatty acid (EFA), meaning it's needed for the body to work properly and the body cannot make it on its own. This EFA is found mostly in flaxseeds, canola oil, and walnuts.

Kryptonite

The hormonal effect lignans exert have not yet been well studied on the developing fetus, infants, and young children, so women who are pregnant or breastfeeding and youngsters should avoid making flax a large part of their daily diet until more is known.

Additionally, because of the hormone effect lignans have, they help promote normal ovulation, which might help improve a woman's chances of conceiving. Lignans also lengthen the second half of the menstrual cycle, helping balance hormone levels and reducing or even preventing the not-so-enjoyable symptoms of perimenopause such as mood swings, headaches, and fluid retention.

On to ALA, which is an essential fat for your body. Among other advantages, this omega-3 fat helps decrease the kinds of inflammation associated with arthritis, asthma, and migraines.

In addition, both ALA and lignans help slow the release of C-reactive protein, or CRP. High levels of this protein are associated with high blood pressure, heart disease, and a condition called insulin resistance, which is a risk factor for type-2 diabetes. These flax components may lower your risk of these diseases as indicated by lower CRP levels.

Super Knowledge

You can buy flax in three different forms—whole seeds, ground, or oil. Ground seeds are best nutritionally. Our body doesn't digest the whole seeds so they pass right through, and the oil doesn't contain the fiber found in the seeds. To achieve benefits, the recommended daily intake is 1 or 2 tablespoons ground seeds per day or 1 teaspoon oil.

Outstanding Oats

Nutritionally speaking, oats' biggest and best achievements come from fiber. But from that one substance, we obtain *so* much help. The specific type of fiber found in oats is called *beta-glucan*, which helps lower cholesterol levels.

The body makes bile acids, which aid digestion, out of cholesterol. The gel formed by beta-glucan and water binds with the acids and carries them out of the body. In return, the body creates more bile acids, using more cholesterol, therefore lowering cholesterol levels in the blood. In addition, as with any soluble fiber, beta-glucan may lower the intestinal absorption of cholesterol from food. A good deal of scientific research has been done on this subject, and the results have all been positive, from lowering total cholesterol levels in those with high as well as normal blood cholesterol levels to decreasing bad, or LDL, cholesterol levels.

> **def•i•ni•tion**
>
> **Beta-glucan** is a soluble fiber that creates viscous, jellylike liquid when combined with water. This liquid helps sweep cholesterol out of the body.

But this beta-glucan gel does more than just deal with cholesterol. By slowing the rate at which nutrients are absorbed from food, including sugar, it helps diabetics keep their blood sugar levels and, consequently, insulin levels more even.

> **Super Knowledge**
>
> The daily recommended intake of fiber for adults is 25 to 30 grams. For kids age 2 and up, it's 5 plus their age. So a 2-year-old child would need 7 grams a day while a 13-year-old teenager would need 18 grams per day.

And by eating the recommended amount of fiber daily, you can help lower your blood pressure. People who eat the recommended amount of fiber each day are shown to be 50 percent less likely to have high blood pressure compared to those eating less than half of that. So eat your oats!

But there's more to oats than just its fantastic fiber. A recent study that followed more than 20,000 people for 20 years show that eating whole grain cereals, like oatmeal, regularly may help cut your chances of heart failure. The folks who ate a whole grain cereal just one day a week lowered their risk for heart failure by 14 percent while those who enjoyed it seven days a week doubled their savings by lowering their risk by 28 percent. And lucky for you we give you all sorts of delicious ways to add oats to your diet, and don't be surprised to find out they're not just for breakfast.

Chocolate-Covered-Banana Smoothies

Up your omega-3 intake by slurping up this sweet-treat smoothie.

Yield: 3 servings
Prep time: 5 minutes
Serving size: 1 cup
Each serving has:
164 calories
4 g total fat
<1 g saturated fat
4 g protein
32 g carbohydrate
5 g fiber
1 mg cholesterol
54 mg sodium

½ cup fat-free plain yogurt

2 very ripe medium bananas, peeled and broken into chunks

3 TB. flaxseeds

3 TB. chocolate syrup

¼ cup fat-free soy milk or milk

12 large ice cubes

1. Combine yogurt, bananas, flaxseeds, chocolate syrup, and soy milk in a blender. Cover and blend on high speed for 30 seconds or until well blended.

2. Remove the cap from the blender's lid and, with the blender running, add ice cubes one at a time until well blended. Serve immediately.

Kryptonite

Never turn on a blender without the lid in place. That includes the times you need to remove the cap to add ingredients. Sometimes the blender's contents splash up when the blender is first turned on, so start the blender with the lid on and then remove the cap from the lid for mess-free blending. To prevent accidental power-ups, keep the blender unplugged until you're ready to start it.

Chocolate-Chip Muffins

Try these tasty, sweet-studded muffins as a good way to add a few
health benefits to a treat you know they'll eat.

1 cup all-purpose flour	**1 cup fat-free milk**
¾ cup ground flaxseed meal	**¼ cup plus 1 TB. honey**
½ cup whole-wheat flour	**¾ cup miniature semi-sweet chocolate chips**
2 tsp. baking powder	**2 tsp. grated orange zest**
½ tsp. salt	
1 large egg, at room temperature, or the equivalent amount of egg substitute	

Yield: 1 dozen
Prep time: 15 minutes
Cook time: 15 minutes
Serving size: 1 muffin
Each serving has:
213 calories
8 g total fat
3 g saturated fat
5 g protein
32 g carbohydrate
3 g fiber
18 mg cholesterol
181 mg sodium

1. Preheat the oven to 375°F. Coat 2¾-inch (regular-size) muffin cups with nonstick cooking spray.

2. Stir together all-purpose flour, flaxseed meal, whole-wheat flour, baking powder, and salt in a large bowl. Add egg, milk, and honey, and stir just until blended and dry ingredients are moistened. Stir in chocolate chips and orange zest until evenly distributed.

3. Spoon batter into the prepared muffin cups, filling ⅔ full. Bake for 15 minutes or until a cake tester or toothpick inserted into the middle of muffins comes out clean. Cool in the pan for 5 minutes before removing to a wire rack to cool.

Heroic Hints

Look for ground flaxseed meal in your local supermarket's organic department and use it in all your baked goods to reduce the fat content. Replace butter, shortening, and oil at a 3:1 ratio with 1½ cups ground flaxseed meal substituted for ½ cup oil in a recipe. Check for doneness early, as the baked goods may brown more quickly.

Banana, Nut, and Flax Quick Bread

The crunchy texture of a delicious slice of nut bread can mask the addition of beneficial flaxseeds from even your most suspicious eaters.

Yield: 16 servings
Prep time: 18 minutes
Cook time: 65 to 70 minutes
Serving size: 1 slice
Each serving has:
177 calories
7 g total fat
1 g saturated fat
5 g protein
26 g carbohydrate
4 g fiber
26 mg cholesterol
170 mg sodium

1 cup ground flaxseed meal

1 cup all-purpose flour

⅔ cup whole-wheat flour

1 tsp. baking soda

½ tsp. salt

¼ tsp. baking powder

½ cup honey

2 large eggs, at room temperature, or the equivalent amount of egg substitute

3 very ripe medium bananas, peeled and broken into chunks

⅓ cup water

½ cup unsalted chopped walnuts

2 TB. flaxseeds

1. Preheat the oven to 350°F. Coat a 9×5×3-inch loaf pan with nonstick cooking spray.

2. Stir together flaxseed meal, all-purpose flour, whole-wheat flour, baking soda, salt, and baking powder in a medium bowl.

3. In a large bowl, blend together honey and eggs. Add bananas and water, and using the back of a fork, mash bananas into the mixture until nearly smooth. Gradually stir flour mixture into banana mixture until moistened. Stir in walnuts and flaxseeds until evenly distributed.

4. Turn batter into the prepared loaf pan. Bake for 65 to 70 minutes or until a cake tester or toothpick inserted into the middle of loaf comes out clean. Let cool in the pan for 5 minutes before removing to cool completely on a wire rack. Cut into ¹/₂-inch slices to serve.

Heroic Hints

Ground flaxseeds spoil quickly, so to maintain freshness, store them in an airtight container in the refrigerator or freezer. For an even longer shelf life, buy whole flaxseeds (which don't turn rancid as quickly) and grind them as you need them in a small coffee or spice grinder.

Creamy, Flax-Speckled Coleslaw

The powerful flavor of coleslaw is the perfect vehicle for adding healthful flaxseeds to your diet.

1 (16-oz.) pkg. coleslaw with carrots mix

¼ cup flaxseeds

½ cup reduced-fat mayonnaise

½ cup low-fat slaw dressing

1. Combine coleslaw mix and flaxseeds in a large bowl. Stir in mayonnaise and slaw dressing until evenly coated.

2. Cover and chill for 30 minutes. Stir again before serving.

Heroic Hints

Although this recipe yields 4 cups coleslaw, be sure to choose a *large* bowl for mixing. The raw cabbage is more substantial, as the dressed slaw wilts a bit while chilling. You'll need plenty of room for mixing.

Yield: 8 servings

Prep time: 5 minutes

Chill time: 30 minutes

Serving size: ½ cup

Each serving has:

122 calories

7 g total fat

1 g saturated fat

2 g protein

14 g carbohydrate

3 g fiber

4 mg cholesterol

414 mg sodium

Oatmeal Raisin Muffins

This version of the classic treat combines both oats and flax (plus cinnamon and honey) in one superfood muffin.

Yield: 1 dozen	

Prep time: 15 minutes

Cook time: 15 to 18 minutes

Serving size: 1 muffin

Each serving has:

168 calories

5 g total fat

1 g saturated fat

6 g protein

28 g carbohydrate

4 g fiber

18 mg cholesterol

312 mg sodium

1 cup all-purpose flour

1 cup old-fashioned rolled oats

¾ cup ground flaxseed meal

½ cup oat flour

½ cup raisins

1 TB. baking powder

1 tsp. salt

¾ tsp. ground cinnamon

1 cup fat-free milk

1 large egg, at room temperature, or the equivalent amount of egg substitute

3 TB. honey

1. Preheat the oven to 400°F. Coat 2³/₄-inch (regular-size) muffin cups with nonstick cooking spray.

2. Stir together all-purpose flour, rolled oats, flaxseed meal, oat flour, raisins, baking powder, salt, and cinnamon in a large bowl.

3. Combine milk, egg, and honey in a medium bowl, and blend well. Stir into flour mixture until moistened.

4. Spoon batter into the prepared muffin cups, filling ³/₄ full. Bake for 15 to 18 minutes or until a cake tester or toothpick inserted into the middle of muffins comes out clean. Cool in the pan for 5 minutes before removing to a wire rack to cool.

Variation: If you can't find oat flour, substitute ¹/₄ cup all-purpose flour for the ¹/₂ cup oat flour in this recipe.

Heroic Hints

When shopping for ground flaxseed meal in your supermarket's organic section or the baking aisle, be certain it's in opaque packaging, which helps protect the ground flaxseeds' nutrients. Just 2 tablespoons ground flaxseed provides 4 grams fiber plus those important lignans and alphalinolenic acid.

Homemade Granola

Sprinkle this crisp mix over yogurt, stir it into your morning cereal, or simply enjoy it out of hand.

2 cups old-fashioned rolled oats

1 cup shelled, unsalted sunflower seeds

½ cup untoasted wheat germ

½ cup unsalted chopped walnuts

½ cup unsalted sliced almonds

½ cup dried cranberries

⅓ cup peanut oil

⅓ cup honey

1 tsp. vanilla extract

Yield: 6 cups
Prep time: 12 minutes
Cook time: 30 minutes
Cool time: 15 to 30 minutes
Serving size: ¼ cup
Each serving has:
153 calories
10 g total fat
1 g saturated fat
4 g protein
13 g carbohydrate
2 g fiber
0 mg cholesterol
6 mg sodium

1. Preheat the oven to 325°F.

2. Stir together oats, sunflower seeds, wheat germ, walnuts, almonds, and dried cranberries in a large (about 17×11×1-inch) nonstick baking sheet. Spread out evenly.

3. Combine peanut oil, honey, and vanilla extract in a measuring cup and stir until blended. Drizzle over oat mixture, and stir until evenly coated, spreading out evenly again. Bake for 30 minutes or until golden and toasted, stirring to redistribute and spreading out evenly every 10 minutes during baking.

4. Cool granola and transfer to an airtight container. Store refrigerated for up to 4 weeks.

Super Knowledge

This snack isn't a low-fat treat, but keep in mind that the fat comes from nuts and seeds so it's mostly the heart-healthy, unsaturated type.

Homey Three-Meat Meatloaf

If meatloaf isn't a favorite at your house, give this mix a try; it's more healthful than traditional meatloaf, and your family might enjoy the taste enough to request it again!

Yield: 8 servings
Prep time: 12 minutes
Cook time: 70 to 75 minutes
Stand time: 10 to 15 minutes
Serving size: 1 slice
Each serving has:
226 calories
8 g total fat
2 g saturated fat
26 g protein
16 g carbohydrate
1 g fiber
113 mg cholesterol
551 mg sodium

1 tsp. extra-virgin or light olive oil

1 medium yellow onion, diced

2 medium cloves garlic, minced

2 TB. dried parsley flakes

1 tsp. salt

½ tsp. freshly ground black pepper

½ tsp. dried thyme

¼ tsp. cayenne

¼ tsp. dry mustard

½ cup fat-free plain yogurt

2 large eggs, at room temperature, or the equivalent amount of egg substitute

⅔ cup uncooked quick oats

1 lb. ground sirloin

½ lb. 99 percent fat-free ground turkey breast

½ lb. ground chicken breast

½ cup ketchup

2 TB. honey

4 tsp. cider vinegar

1. Preheat the oven to 350°F.

2. Heat olive oil in a small nonstick skillet over medium heat. Add onion and garlic, and sauté for 5 minutes or until softened and just beginning to color. Set aside.

3. Combine parsley flakes, salt, black pepper, thyme, cayenne, dry mustard, yogurt, and eggs in a large bowl, and stir until well blended. Add onion mixture, oats, ground sirloin, turkey breast, and chicken breast. Mix until thoroughly blended and turn into a nonstick 9¼×5¼×2¾-inch loaf pan. Bake for 45 minutes.

4. Meanwhile, combine ketchup, honey, and cider vinegar in a small bowl, and stir until blended. Remove the loaf pan from the oven and drain. Spoon ketchup mixture over the top of meatloaf, and bake for another 20 to 25 minutes or until done (165°F on a food thermometer). Drain again carefully (or remove meatloaf from the pan) and let stand for 10 to 15 minutes before slicing to serve.

★ **Heroic Hints**

If you're reducing sodium in your diet, replace the salt in this recipe with a salt substitute seasoning blend and use no-salt-added ketchup.

Part 5

From the Rivers and Ranges

Although most of us get plenty of protein from beef, chicken, and pork, as well as milk, cheese, and other dairy, some other protein sources are less frequently seen on our dinner tables. Fish, especially salmon, and turkey provide amazing health benefits above and beyond being fantastic protein sources.

If you're not quite sure how to prepare them, never fear. Keep reading to find a multitude of ways to start enjoying these super ingredients.

Chapter 13

Excel with Salmon

In This Chapter

- ◆ Salmon's super health benefits
- ◆ What salmon should you buy?
- ◆ Delicious, healthful salmon recipes

Does it feel like everywhere you go someone is telling you to eat more fish? If so, listen up—they're trying to help you out! Fish, no matter what kind, is a great addition to a healthy diet. It contains very little sodium, most contains very little fat and cholesterol, and it gives you a great dose of protein.

Sensational Salmon

Although all fish are good-for-you foods, salmon ranks particularly high in that category. Granted, it does contain more fat than most other fish, but it's the good kind of fat—*omega-3 fatty acids*.

Omega-3s help battle heart disease in more than one way. First, they help maintain healthy blood pressure; high blood pressure is one of the risk factors for cardiovascular disease. Omega-3s also help prevent blood clots from forming, and less blood clotting in the arteries means fewer chances for a clot to block blood flow in the heart or brain and cause a heart attack or stroke. And they can help lower all the bad cholesterol levels—total, LDL, and triglycerides.

def•i•ni•tion

Omega-3 fatty acids are a group of fats found in fish oils essential to the body and lower blood cholesterol levels. Three main ones are EPA (eicosapentaenoic acid), DHA (docosahexaenoic acid), and ALA (alphalinolenic acid).

And for any of you who are pregnant, planning to become pregnant, or breast-feeding, omega-3s can help your precious little one, too. The DHA-type of omega-3 fatty acids is especially beneficial for brain development, which is most crucial in the 3 months before and 3 months after birth.

Wild Versus Farmed Salmon

You may notice two types of salmon when you go to buy it—wild and farmed. Nutritionally, the two are pretty much identical. However, because of how and where it's raised, the farmed salmon usually contains contaminates that could increase your risk of cancer (but not nearly as much as salmon in general reduces your risk of heart disease).

Heroic Hints

Include fish in your diet, especially fatty fish like salmon, twice a week to reap the health benefits.

Your best bet is to purchase fish raised in Chile and Washington State and avoid it from Scotland and the Faroe Islands. When cooking, make small cuts in the flesh and grill or broil the fish so the juices drip off. And don't eat the skin. These steps go a long way in reducing the amount of contaminants in the fish and allow you to safely eat up to 12 ounces a month.

Marinated Salmon Salad Pitas

A touch of lemon and your favorite Italian dressing bring out the rich, meaty flavor of wild-caught salmon for a delicious, easy sandwich.

1 (3-oz.) pouch skinless, boneless pink salmon	1 TB. low-fat Italian salad dressing
1 green onion, finely chopped	1 (6-in.) whole-wheat pita bread pocket, halved
1 TB. lemon juice	

1. Stir together salmon, green onion, lemon juice, and salad dressing in a small bowl. Cover and chill for at least 1 hour.

2. Spoon ¼ cup salmon mixture into each pita pocket half to serve.

Variation: To amp up these pitas, stuff them with your favorite salad or other fixings such as lettuce leaves, tomato slices, alfalfa sprouts, shredded carrots, pickles, cheese, and more.

 Heroic Hints _____

When you need a last-minute lunch, omit the chilling step and serve these sandwiches immediately.

Yield: 2 servings
Prep time: 2 minutes
Chill time: 1 hour
Serving size: 1 pocket half
Each serving has:
131 calories
3 g total fat
<1 g saturated fat
13 g protein
14 g carbohydrate
2 g fiber
30 mg cholesterol
346 mg sodium

Maple Dijon Salmon Fillets

A few kitchen staples come together to create a sweet, spicy marinade that coats the salmon for a real taste treat.

Yield: 4 servings
Prep time: 3 minutes
Chill time: 20 minutes
Cook time: 10 minutes
Serving size: 1 fillet
Each serving has:
266 calories
13 g total fat
3 g saturated fat
25 g protein
11 g carbohydrate
0 g fiber
82 mg cholesterol
206 mg sodium

3 TB. Dijon mustard

3 TB. maple syrup

1 TB. balsamic vinegar

$\frac{1}{8}$ tsp. freshly ground black pepper

4 (4-oz.) boneless, skinless salmon fillets

1. Combine Dijon mustard, maple syrup, balsamic vinegar, and black pepper in a gallon-size resealable plastic bag. Add salmon, press the air out of the bag, seal the bag, and marinate in the refrigerator for 20 minutes.

2. Preheat the broiler. Coat the rack of a broiler pan with nonstick cooking spray.

3. Remove salmon from marinade, reserve marinade, and place salmon bottom side up on the broiler pan's rack. Broil 4 to 6 inches from the heat source for 5 minutes per inch of thickness. Turn salmon and baste with remaining marinade. Broil for 5 minutes per inch of thickness or until fish flakes easily with a fork or reads 145°F on a food thermometer. (Be certain to broil for at least 3 minutes after basting with marinade to prevent possible food poisoning.)

Super Knowledge

Many consumers are wary of seafood for fear of their mercury content. Fortunately, salmon typically contains only very low levels of mercury. As of this writing, the Food and Drug Administration (FDA) recommends limiting your intake of swordfish, king mackerel, shark, and tilefish because of mercury, too. For the most up-to-date advisories, visit www.cfsan.fda.gov/seafood1.html.

Creole Salmon

The piquancy of the sauce lends a complementary flavor to the charbroiled fish in this dish.

1 small yellow onion, diced

½ large red bell pepper, ribs and seeds removed, and diced

1 small jalapeño pepper, seeded and minced

½ cup no-salt-added tomato sauce

¼ cup tarragon white wine vinegar or white wine vinegar

2 TB. extra-virgin olive oil

½ tsp. dried basil

½ tsp. dried oregano

¼ tsp. salt

¼ tsp. freshly ground black pepper

4 (4-oz.) boneless salmon fillets

Yield: 4 servings
Prep time: 5 minutes
Cook time: 10 minutes per inch of thickness
Serving size: 1 salmon fillet with ¹/₃ cup sauce
Each serving has:
308 calories
20 g total fat
4 g saturated fat
26 g protein
6 g carbohydrate
1 g fiber
82 mg cholesterol
208 mg sodium

1. Combine onion, red bell pepper, and jalapeño pepper in a medium bowl. Add tomato sauce, vinegar, olive oil, basil, oregano, salt, and black pepper. Stir well and set aside.

2. Preheat the broiler. Coat the rack of a broiler pan with nonstick cooking spray.

3. Place salmon fillets skin side down on the broiler rack and broil 4 to 6 inches from the heat source for 10 minutes per inch of thickness at the thickest part of the salmon or until fish flakes easily with a fork or reads 145°F on a food thermometer.

4. Slide a spatula between the flesh and the skin to remove the skin. Serve fillets topped with sauce.

Super Knowledge

At first glance, it may seem this entrée is a bit high in fat, but keep in mind most of it is the heart-healthy unsaturated kind and almost 2 grams are the powerful omega-3 fatty acids.

Greek Isle Salmon Cakes

Pairing cool cucumber sauce with crisp, olive-studded salmon patties gives this meal Mediterranean flair.

Yield: 4 servings
Prep time: 12 minutes
Cook time: 4 minutes per batch
Serving size: 2 salmon cakes with ¼ cup sauce
Each serving has:
304 calories
6 g total fat
<1 g saturated fat
36 g protein
30 g carbohydrate
5 g fiber
73 mg cholesterol
774 mg sodium

⅔ cup seeded, finely diced cucumber

⅔ cup fat-free plain yogurt

¼ tsp. dried dill weed

2 medium cloves garlic, crushed

1 (15-oz.) can garbanzo beans, rinsed and drained

2 (7.1-oz.) pouches skinless, boneless pink salmon

¼ cup plain dry breadcrumbs

¼ cup drained sliced black olives

½ cup chopped fresh parsley

2 TB. lime juice

1 tsp. hot pepper sauce

½ tsp. ground cumin

¼ tsp. salt

2 large egg whites, slightly beaten

1. Stir together cucumber, yogurt, dill weed, and garlic in a small bowl. Cover and chill while preparing salmon cakes.

2. Turn garbanzo beans into a medium bowl and mash with the back of a fork. Add salmon, breadcrumbs, and olives, and mix well, breaking up salmon.

3. Combine parsley, lime juice, hot pepper sauce, cumin, salt, and egg whites in a small bowl, and stir until blended. Pour over salmon mixture, and stir until combined.

4. Heat a large nonstick skillet over medium-high heat and coat liberally with nonstick cooking spray.

5. Press ½ cup salmon mixture firmly into ¾-inch-thick patties, add to the skillet, and cook for 2 minutes on each side or until crisp and browned, cooking in batches as needed. Serve salmon cakes hot with cucumber sauce on the side.

Heroic Hints

To seed a cucumber, cut it in half lengthwise and run a small metal spoon between the flesh and the pulp to scoop out the seeds.

Creamy Salmon Macaroni Bake

Perk up your taste buds with this cottage cheese–based salmon-and-macaroni bake that's a change of pace from the usual tuna noodle casserole.

1 cup uncooked whole-wheat elbow macaroni

2 (7.1-oz.) pouches skinless, boneless pink salmon

1 cup low-fat small-curd cottage cheese

1 cup fat-free sour cream

1 small yellow onion, very finely diced

2 TB. fat-free milk

¼ tsp. salt

¼ tsp. freshly ground black pepper

½ tsp. paprika

Yield: 7 servings
Prep time: 3 minutes
Cook time: 40 minutes
Serving size: ³/₄ cup
Each serving has:
186 calories
3 g total fat
1 g saturated fat
22 g protein
20 g carbohydrate
1 g fiber
47 mg cholesterol
458 mg sodium

1. Preheat the oven to 350°F. Coat a 1½-quart glass casserole dish with nonstick cooking spray.

2. Cook macaroni according to the package directions until al dente and then drain.

3. Combine macaroni, salmon, cottage cheese, sour cream, onion, milk, salt, and black pepper in a large bowl. Stir until blended and pour into the casserole dish. Sprinkle paprika across the top and bake, uncovered, for 30 minutes or until bubbly and heated through.

Heroic Hints

Pouched and canned salmon are easy and inexpensive ways to include this super fish in your diet. Plus, it's typically wild-caught salmon, so no worries about its contaminants.

Chapter 14

Terrific Turkey

In This Chapter

- ◆ To sleep or not to sleep?
- ◆ Boost your energy with turkey
- ◆ Turkey recipes for any time of the year (not just with Thanksgiving leftovers!)

Is it really the turkey's fault you fall asleep after Thanksgiving dinner? Chances are, if you gorge yourself on a big meal and then zone out on the couch for a while, you'd go into a food coma no matter what you ate. But it's true that turkey contains a substance involved in sleep regulation.

Tom Turkey

Tryptophan is the amino acid found in turkey that helps create neurotransmitters and hormones in the body that promote relaxation and sleep. In addition, tryptophan can change to *serotonin* in the body.

def•i•ni•tion

Tryptophan is an essential amino acid the body uses for protein-building. Serotonin is a nervous system transmitter that helps regulate sleep as well as appetite and mood.

Not all tryptophan gets converted to serotonin, however. Some transforms into the B-vitamin niacin. Interestingly, turkey meat is also a fantastic source of niacin. So a meal including turkey gets you a bonus amount of this vitamin. Niacin works to change the food you eat—protein, fat, and carbohydrate—into the energy your body needs to function. It creates two types of energy—one to be used right away and another to be stored in your muscles and liver for later use.

Keep in mind it's skinless turkey breast meat that's the superfood. In addition to the beneficial nutrients, it's also high in protein but low in sodium and very low in fat and saturated fat. For those reasons, it's a well-received addition to a heart-healthy diet.

Other cuts of turkey that come from the breast include tenderloins, cutlets, and medallions. Just remove the skin if they have it to get rid of the excess saturated fat.

Fruited Turkey Rice Salad

The combination of ingredients in this salad might seem unusual, but the flavors meld nicely and make a delicious lunchtime offering.

2 cups cooked long-grain brown rice

1½ cups finely chopped cooked 99 percent fat-free turkey breast

2 green onions, finely chopped

1 small Granny Smith apple, cored and finely chopped

1 small Red Delicious apple, cored and finely chopped

½ cup halved seedless green grapes

¼ cup extra-virgin olive oil

¼ cup tarragon white wine vinegar

1 tsp. honey

¼ tsp. salt

¼ tsp. ground cinnamon

Yield: 6 servings
Prep time: 5 minutes
Chill time: 2 hours
Serving size: 1 cup
Each serving has:
234 calories
10 g total fat
1 g saturated fat
13 g protein
24 g carbohydrate
2 g fiber
29 mg cholesterol
121 mg sodium

1. Stir together rice, turkey breast, green onions, apples, and grapes in a medium bowl.

2. Whisk together olive oil, vinegar, honey, salt, and cinnamon in a small bowl until well blended. Pour olive oil mixture over rice mixture, and stir until evenly coated.

3. Cover and chill for at least 2 hours or until cold. Stir again before serving.

Heroic Hints

Never shy away from adding a new vinegar variety to your pantry. Vinegar keeps indefinitely when stored in a cool, dark place and is always on hand when called for in a recipe.

Southwestern Turkey Soft Tacos

These soft tacos are easy to personalize by adding sour cream, guacamole, diced tomatoes, shredded lettuce, sliced black olives, and all your Mexican favorites.

Yield: 10 servings
Prep time: 5 minutes
Cook time: 11 minutes
Serving size: 1 taco
Each serving has:
187 calories
4 g total fat
2 g saturated fat
19 g protein
26 g carbohydrate
3 g fiber
28 mg cholesterol
391 mg sodium

Heroic Hints

Frozen corn and peas are easy last-minute additions to recipes because they can be quickly rinsed under cool, running water to thaw.

1 lb. 99 percent fat-free extra-lean ground turkey breast

2 TB. chili powder

1 small yellow onion, chopped

½ large red bell pepper, ribs and seeds removed, and coarsely chopped

½ medium green bell pepper, ribs and seeds removed, and coarsely chopped

1 cup salsa

1 cup frozen whole-kernel corn, rinsed and drained to thaw

2 TB. chopped fresh cilantro or 2 tsp. dried

10 (soft-taco-size) whole-wheat tortillas, warmed

1¼ cups 2 percent milk shredded Mexican blend cheese

1. Place ground turkey in a large nonstick skillet over medium heat and cook, stirring to break up meat, for 3 minutes or until beginning to brown. Stir in chili powder, and add onion and bell peppers. Cook and stir for 5 minutes or until meat is browned and vegetables are crisp-tender.

2. Stir in salsa and corn, and cook for 2 minutes or until heated through. Stir in cilantro, and cook for 1 minute more.

3. Spoon ½ cup mixture down the center of each tortilla. Sprinkle 2 tablespoons cheese over top, and fold tortilla to enclose filling.

Busy-Day Turkey Burgers

Quick and easy to make, you can top these turkey burgers with individual favorites for fewer calories and less fat than traditional hamburgers.

1 lb. 99 percent fat-free extra-lean ground turkey breast

¼ cup plain dry breadcrumbs

2 TB. fat-free milk

½ TB. Worcestershire sauce

1 egg, at room temperature, or egg substitute

¼ tsp. dried crushed rosemary

¼ tsp. garlic powder

¼ tsp. onion powder

¼ tsp. freshly ground black pepper

Yield: 4 servings
Prep time: 6 minutes
Cook time: 8 to 10 minutes
Serving size: 1 burger
Each serving has:
171 calories
3 g total fat
<1 g saturated fat
31 g protein
6 g carbohydrate
0 g fiber
98 mg cholesterol
158 mg sodium

1. Preheat the broiler. Coat the rack of a broiler pan with nonstick cooking spray.

2. Combine ground turkey, breadcrumbs, milk, Worcestershire sauce, egg, rosemary, garlic powder, onion powder, and black pepper in a medium bowl. Using your hands, mix until blended and divide into 4 equal portions. Shape each portion into a ¹/₂-inch-thick patty, and place on the rack of the broiler pan.

3. Broil 4 to 6 inches from the heat source for 8 to 10 minutes, turning halfway through cooking time, or until done (165°F on a food thermometer). Serve on whole-grain buns topped with cheese, tomato slices, pickles, onions, lettuce, ketchup, and mustard, if desired.

Kryptonite

Be sure to look for either "99 percent fat-free" or "turkey breast" on the label when buying ground turkey. Otherwise, you may end up with a product that includes not only the lean meat, but also the fatty skin.

Tasty Turkey Tetrazzini

This creamy casserole is a welcome meal to warm the stomach on a wintry day and can be completed with a green salad and crusty bread.

Yield: 4 servings
Prep time: 3 minutes
Cook time: 28 minutes
Serving size: 1¹⁄₂ cups
Each serving has:
282 calories
5 g total fat
2 g saturated fat
22 g protein
37 g carbohydrate
2 g fiber
68 mg cholesterol
159 mg sodium

4½ cups uncooked extra-wide yolk-free whole-wheat egg noodles

1 TB. light butter with canola oil

1 TB. all-purpose flour

¾ cup fat-free milk

½ cup fat-free, less-sodium chicken broth

***Pinch* freshly ground black pepper**

Pinch cayenne

¾ cup frozen green peas

¼ cup fat-free plain yogurt

2 TB. grated Parmesan cheese

8 oz. sliced button mushrooms

1 cup diced cooked 99 percent fat-free turkey breast

1. Preheat the oven to 425°F. Coat an 8×8×2-inch glass baking dish with nonstick cooking spray.

2. Cook egg noodles according to the package directions. Drain and return to the pan.

3. Meanwhile, melt light butter in a small saucepan over medium heat. Whisk in flour until smooth. Whisking, add milk, broth, black pepper, and cayenne. Cook and whisk over medium heat for 10 minutes or until boiling and thickened. Turn off heat and whisk in peas, yogurt, and 1 tablespoon cheese. Pour over noodles, and stir in mushrooms and turkey breast.

4. Turn mixture into the prepared baking dish. Sprinkle remaining 1 tablespoon cheese over top, and bake for 15 minutes or until bubbly and top is golden brown.

def•i•ni•tion

Pinch is a nonspecific measurement indicating the amount of a dry ingredient you can hold between your thumb and finger.

Tropical Turkey with Honeyed Pineapple Sauce

A few common ingredients blend to create a sauce that deliciously coats turkey cutlets with a sweet Dijon flavor.

½ cup honey

¼ cup Dijon mustard

2 TB. unsweetened pineapple juice

1 tsp. sesame seeds

½ tsp. lemon juice

1½ lb. 99 percent fat-free turkey breast cutlets

Yield: 6 servings
Prep time: 5 minutes
Cook time: 15 minutes
Serving size: 4 ounces turkey with 2 tablespoons sauce
Each serving has:
212 calories
1 g total fat
<1 g saturated fat
27 g protein
23 g carbohydrate
0 g fiber
74 mg cholesterol
179 mg sodium

1. Preheat the oven to 350°F. Coat a medium nonstick baking sheet with nonstick cooking spray.

2. Combine honey, Dijon mustard, pineapple juice, sesame seeds, and lemon juice in a small saucepan. Whisk until well blended.

3. Pour ¼ cup honey mixture into a pie plate or other shallow dish. Cut turkey breast cutlets into serving-size pieces, if needed, and coat each piece with honey mixture. Place turkey on the prepared baking sheet, and bake for 15 minutes or until done (170°F on a food thermometer).

4. Meanwhile, cook remaining honey mixture in the saucepan over medium heat for 5 minutes or until simmering, whisking occasionally. (Do not boil.) Spoon warm honey mixture over turkey cutlets to serve.

Kryptonite _____

You can't always tell if poultry and meats are done by visually inspecting them. Juices that run clear are a good indicator, but a food thermometer is the only sure test. Instant-read thermometers are quick and easy to use. Use one every time.

Part 6

Tongue-Tingling Tastes

You might know that yogurt is good for you, but who would have thought ingredients like spices and herbs and even chocolate can improve your health? It's true, as you'll see in the upcoming chapters. And if you like your tea sweetened with a little honey, you're getting two super health foods in one.

The following chapters contain a generous helping of unique and tasty ways for you to incorporate these flavor-filled foods into your diet.

Heroic Yogurt

In This Chapter

- Building strong bones (and more)
- Bacteria that's good?
- Creative ways to cook with yogurt

Yogurt seems to be one of those foods people either love or hate. (Our editor's mother eats it as a snack, but our editor can barely choke it down unless it's packed with fruit or chocolate or other "disguising" flavors!) If you're a hater (We're talking to you, editor), hopefully after reading about it, you'll convert to a lover.

Yo-Yo-Yogurt

Whether you choose the creamy white plain or vanilla yogurt or opt for one of the dozens of fancy flavors, you're getting a healthful food. Yogurt is a great source of both protein and calcium, each of which offer tremendous benefits, including building and maintaining healthy bones, keeping blood pressure in check, building healthy skin and teeth, and more. Both nutrients are found in other foods as well, such as low-fat milk and cheese and lean meats.

Super Knowledge _____

The only yogurts you really should watch out for are those that come with some sort of mix-in. These products are usually a smaller 4- to 6-ounce cup and come with sprinkles or cookie bits or some other "extra." The result is less of the good stuff and more unnecessary sugar and calories.

def•i•ni•tion _____

Probiotics are microscopic living organisms that provide an array of health benefits, particularly for the digestive system.

But what makes yogurt unique is the bacteria it contains. That's right, bacteria. Before you say "Yuck!" and turn to the next chapter (agreeing with our editor that yogurt isn't worth your time), stay with us a second, because this is *good* bacteria called *probiotics*. Believe it or not, your body—specifically your intestines—is filled with good bacteria. And the probiotics in yogurt help that bacteria work better.

Think about some of the ailments affecting your digestive tract: ulcers, lactose intolerance, and diarrhea are just a few. Yogurt, with its probiotics, can help all of them.

Ulcers are usually caused by a bacterium residing in the stomach. Probiotics can help prevent it from growing and thus causing a painful ulcer.

Lactose intolerance is a condition where your body can't digest the sugar found in dairy products. The symptoms can range from mild to severe stomach pain, bloating, gas, and diarrhea. Probiotics help in two ways. First, they can actually help break down the milk sugar your body can't digest itself, and, therefore, prevent the uncomfortable symptoms. And second, by the simple fact that probiotics help your digestive tract work well, they may help lessen your body's sensitivity to the sugar in milk.

Super Knowledge _____

For the benefits mentioned, you must eat yogurt containing live cultures. Many in your grocer's refrigerated case do, and the package should say so. In addition, yogurt needs to be part of your daily diet to obtain these results.

If you're experiencing diarrhea, eating yogurt daily may help lessen the severity of it. This has been shown to work when diarrhea is the result of taking antibiotics, if you're suffering traveler's diarrhea, and in kids with rotavirus. In addition, those who enjoy yogurt on a regular basis may be able to ward off this problem in the first place.

This good bacteria in yogurt with live active cultures provide another benefit our female readers may appreciate. It may help prevent decrease the frequency of yeast infections. A yeast infection is basically an overgrowth if yeast in a particular part of the body. Good bacteria can help prevent this overgrowth from happening and, therefore, may help to prevent infection. And if you've ever suffered through the itch of a yeast infection we think you'll be more than happy to try adding a cup of yogurt to your daily diet. When you're at the market just be sure to buy the kind that lists live active cultures somewhere on the label.

Spiced Banana Smoothies

Adding a creamy smoothness, yogurt is a great base for the heady spices and sweet bananas in this smoothie.

Yield: 3 servings
Prep time: 2 minutes
Serving size: 1 cup
Each serving has:
146 calories
0 g total fat
0 g saturated fat
4 g protein
35 g carbohydrate
2 g fiber
2 mg cholesterol
42 mg sodium

2 medium ripe bananas, peeled

½ cup fat-free plain yogurt

½ cup fat-free milk

2 TB. honey

½ tsp. vanilla extract

¼ tsp. ground cinnamon

Dash ground nutmeg

6 large ice cubes

1. Break bananas into large chunks and place into a blender. Add yogurt, milk, honey, vanilla extract, cinnamon, and nutmeg. Cover and blend on high speed for 30 seconds or until smooth.

2. Remove the cap from the blender's lid and, with the blender running, add ice cubes one at a time until well blended. Serve cold.

Kryptonite

Wonder why you should take the time to whip up this smoothie when you can just go to the store and buy one? Here's why: those store-bought smoothies can be loaded with sugar and calories—some as many as 800 calories per serving! Plus, after you drink the caloric equivalent to a fast-food deluxe burger, there's a good chance you'll go on and eat the same amount of food you'd have eaten if you'd had a calorie-free water or diet cola because drinks don't provide the same lasting full sensation foods do. So you may possibly end up with almost a day's worth of calories in one sitting.

Tropical Island Smoothies

Treat yourself to a breezy island break by sipping the sultry taste of this cool smoothie you'll want to indulge in again and again.

1 medium ripe banana, peeled, broken into chunks

¼ cup fresh or unsweetened orange juice

1¼ cups fat-free vanilla or plain yogurt

¼ tsp. coconut extract

1½ cups unsweetened frozen pineapple chunks

Yield: 2 servings	
Prep time: 5 minutes	
Serving size: 1¾ cups	
Each serving has:	
185 calories	
<1 g total fat	
0 g saturated fat	
8 g protein	
43 g carbohydrate	
3 g fiber	
3 mg cholesterol	
89 mg sodium	

1. Combine banana, orange juice, yogurt, and coconut extract in a blender. Cover and blend on high speed for 10 seconds or until blended.

2. Add pineapple chunks to the blender. Cover and blend on high speed for 1 or 2 minutes or until well blended and pineapple is no longer in large chunks. Serve cold.

Super Knowledge

Just one glass of this smoothie gives you more than 200 milligrams of bone-building calcium.

Cold Cucumber Soup with Lemon and Dill

This low-calorie appetizer not only tastes fresh and tangy, but a bowl of this cold soup at the beginning of the meal may just allow you to enjoy a tremendous treat at the finish.

Yield: 12 servings	
Prep time: 5 minutes	
Chill time: 2 hours	
Serving size: ¹/₂ cup	
Each serving has:	
29 calories	
<1 g total fat	
0 g saturated fat	
3 g protein	
5 g carbohydrate	
<1 g fiber	
2 mg cholesterol	
93 mg sodium	

2 cups fat-free plain yogurt

1 (14-oz.) can fat-free, less-sodium chicken broth

2 TB. lemon juice

2 TB. chopped fresh dill or 2 tsp. dried dill weed

1 tsp. grated lemon zest

¹/₂ tsp. ground cumin

¼ tsp. salt

¼ tsp. freshly ground black pepper

2 large cucumbers, peeled, seeded, and finely chopped

1 medium yellow onion, diced

1. Combine yogurt, broth, lemon juice, dill, lemon zest, cumin, salt, and black pepper in a large bowl, and stir until blended.

2. Add cucumbers and onion, and stir. Cover and chill for at least 2 hours or until cold. Stir again before serving.

Heroic Hints

When you substitute dried herbs for fresh, use a 1:3 ratio. Dried herbs are more concentrated than their fresh counterparts so you can use 1 teaspoon dried or 1 tablespoon fresh. Always adjust to taste.

Veggie Lover's Curried-Yogurt Macaroni Salad

Packed with garden vegetables, this macaroni salad gets its creamy yellow coloring from the spicy curry powder and dry mustard that flavor the yogurt dressing.

1 (16-oz.) pkg. multi-grain elbow macaroni	½ cup diced green bell peppers
2 cups fat-free plain yogurt	½ cup diced tomatoes
½ cup reduced-fat mayonnaise	½ cup peeled, seeded, and diced cucumbers
½ cup red wine vinegar	½ cup shredded carrots
1 TB. curry powder	½ cup diced sweet pickles
¼ tsp. honey	¼ cup finely chopped green onions
¼ tsp. dry mustard	¼ cup finely chopped celery
½ cup thinly sliced radishes	

Yield: 16 servings
Prep time: 25 minutes
Chill time: 4 hours
Serving size: ¼ cup
Each serving has:
146 calories
3 g total fat
<1 g saturated fat
6 g protein
26 g carbohydrate
3 g fiber
3 mg cholesterol
108 mg sodium

1. Cook macaroni according to the package directions. Drain and rinse in cold water.

2. Meanwhile, combine yogurt, mayonnaise, red wine vinegar, curry powder, honey, and dry mustard in a medium bowl. Stir until blended.

3. Stir together macaroni, radishes, green bell peppers, tomatoes, cucumbers, carrots, sweet pickles, green onions, and celery in a large bowl. Stir in yogurt mixture until evenly coated. Cover and chill for at least 4 hours or overnight. Stir again before serving.

Super Knowledge

Although we call for peeled cukes in this recipe, feel free to leave them on if you like to retain the vitamin A. Many supermarket cucumbers are waxed, however, and you should clean it with a commercial fruit-and-vegetable wash before preparation.

Dijon Chicken Salad

Spread this tangy chicken salad over rye bread for a flavorful sandwich, stuff a ripe tomato, or scoop onto assorted crackers.

Yield: 2 servings
Prep time: 3 minutes
Serving size: ½ cup plus 2 tablespoons
Each serving has:
202 calories
8 g total fat
1 g saturated fat
29 g protein
4 g carbohydrate
1 g fiber
88 mg cholesterol
348 mg sodium

1 (7-oz.) pkg. ready-to-use chicken breast

¼ cup fat-free plain yogurt

1 TB. Dijon mustard

2 TB. diced celery

2 TB. unsalted diced walnuts

¼ tsp. freshly ground black pepper

1. Combine chicken breast, yogurt, and Dijon mustard in a small bowl, and stir until blended. Add celery, walnuts, and black pepper, and stir until evenly distributed.

2. Refrigerate any leftovers.

Variation: You can toast the walnuts in a small, dry, nonstick skillet over medium heat for 3 minutes or until golden.

Super Knowledge

Dijon mustard originated in Dijon, France. A creamy, smooth blend using white wine, its darker color comes from brown or black mustard seeds.

Easy Spinach Dip

The tangy yogurt base and tasty seasonings keep your family and guests scooping up good-for-your-health spinach.

1 cup packed fresh spinach

¾ cup fat-free plain yogurt

¼ cup reduced-fat mayonnaise

½ tsp. salt

¼ tsp. dried basil

¼ tsp. dry mustard

¼ tsp. garlic powder

¼ tsp. onion powder

¼ tsp. dried oregano

¼ tsp. dried parsley flakes

⅛ tsp. cayenne

⅛ tsp. dried thyme

Yield: 1¼ cups		
Prep time: 5 minutes		
Chill time: 30 minutes		
Serving size: 2 tablespoons		
Each serving has:		
18 calories		
1 g total fat		
0 g saturated fat		
1 g protein		
2 g carbohydrate		
0 g fiber		
0 mg cholesterol		
181 mg sodium		

1. Wash spinach, drain, and roll in paper towels to dry completely. Chop spinach into small pieces.

2. In a small bowl, stir together yogurt and mayonnaise until blended. Stir in salt, basil, dry mustard, garlic powder, onion powder, oregano, parsley flakes, cayenne, and thyme. Stir in spinach to mix.

3. Cover and chill for at least 30 minutes before serving. Serve with baked tortilla chips, baby carrots, celery sticks, mushroom caps, and more of your favorite dippers.

Super Knowledge

The active cultures in yogurt that aid in digestion are heat sensitive. Frozen yogurt has inactive bacteria. Conversely, heating yogurt over 120°F also kills the beneficial bacteria.

Getting Spicy

In This Chapter

◆ Heating things up with cayenne

◆ A spoonful of cinnamon helps the blood sugar go down

◆ Peppermint to calm your stomach

◆ Recipes for your spice rack (or mint garden)

Spices and herbs do more than just add flavor. They can offer tremendous health boosts. This chapter offers something for everyone. We've got sweet, and we've got hot. With cayenne, you can crank the heat up a bit as well as your metabolism. And if you think cinnamon is just for apple pie, think again. Sure, it's great in sweet treats, but it can also be for savory dishes. And while peppermint makes a great breath freshener, it also does so much more. Give it a whirl for a refreshing twist to a variety of foods.

Kickin' Cayenne

We probably don't have to tell you that most chile peppers are *h-o-t*. That's especially true for cayenne peppers. *Capsaicin* is the chemical in peppers that produces the heat. And while the heat from cayenne peppers may burn up your throat, it actually does some good, too.

Think of the last time you ate spicy food. Did your nose run? If you happened to have had a cold at the time, that probably provided some relief. The capsaicin—and, therefore the heat—in the peppers stimulates mucus production in your nose and respiratory tract and helps clear them out when you're congested.

def•i•ni•tion

Capsaicin is an odorless, flavorless chemical that's responsible for the burn you feel when you eat peppers or foods that contain them.

You might also notice when you eat those fiery foods that you get warmer. Foods and sauces made with cayenne and other peppers raise your body temperature. And to do that, your body needs energy and burns more calories to push up the thermometer. In fact, for up to 20 minutes after eating spicy, spicy food, your body burns calories at a faster speed. How's that for a super bonus?

Exceptional Cinnamon

When you think of cinnamon, you probably think of a dessert or other sweet you love it in. Grandma's cinnamon rolls? Mom's apple-cinnamon pie? While cinnamon does speak your sweet-tooth's language, its biggest contributions to health involve heart disease and diabetes, thanks to the *cinnamaldehyde* it contains.

def•i•ni•tion

Cinnamaldehyde is an essential oil that gives cinnamon its spicy flavor. It's found in the bark of cinnamon trees.

Cinnamaldehyde helps make blood platelets more resistant to clotting. Excessive clotting can limit the flow in blood vessels and lead to strokes and heart attacks. By helping to lessen some of this clotting, cinnamaldehyde may help lower your risk of having one of these events.

Taking cinnamon regularly has also been shown to help lower blood sugar levels in people with diabetes. As little as $^1/_4$ to $^1/_2$ teaspoon a day dropped blood sugar levels significantly. In addition, this amount of cinnamon lowered heart disease risk factors such as cholesterol and triglycerides levels. This is important because having diabetes increases your risk of developing heart disease.

Kryptonite _____

If you decide to supplement with cinnamon, be aware that large doses on a regular basis can be dangerous because of cinnamaldehyde's affect on blood clotting. So while cooking with cinnamon is completely safe, if you supplement, be sure to use a water-soluble extract and not a fat-soluble one or whole cinnamon. An online search can turn up several brands to look for.

Protective Peppermint

The oil found in peppermint leaves can help soothe an irritated stomach. When you're suffering from indigestion, whether by itself or as a result of having a condition such as irritable bowel syndrome, give peppermint a try. It helps relax the smooth muscle surrounding the digestive tract, and in doing so, it lowers the chances of spasms that can cause indigestion.

Peppermint also contains _rosmarinic acid_, which affects various chemicals that are involved in asthma. By slowing the production of the inflammation-causing chemicals and increasing the production of those that help keep the airways open, rosmarinic acid may help asthma sufferers breathe easier.

def•i•ni•tion _____

Rosmarinic acid is a phytochemical that works as an anti-inflammatory and antioxidant.

Cayenne-Spiced Roasted Garbanzo Beans

Enjoy these spicy bites out of hand or use them to top a green salad for a crunchy, spicy delight.

Yield: 5 servings	
Prep time: 3 minutes	
Cook time: 25 to 35 minutes	
Serving size: ¼ cup	
Each serving has:	
115 calories	
6 g total fat	
1 g saturated fat	
4 g protein	
11 g carbohydrate	
3 g fiber	
0 mg cholesterol	
455 mg sodium	

1 (15-oz.) can garbanzo beans, rinsed and drained

2 TB. extra-virgin or light olive oil

½ tsp. cayenne

½ tsp. garlic powder

⅛ tsp. salt

1. Preheat the oven to 450°F.

2. Dry garbanzo beans with a paper towel and pour into a medium bowl. Add olive oil, stirring to coat. Sprinkle on cayenne, garlic powder, and salt, and stir to coat evenly.

3. Spread beans in a single layer on a medium nonstick baking sheet, and bake for 25 to 35 minutes or until golden brown and crunchy, stirring to redistribute halfway through cooking time. (Watch carefully near the end of cooking time to prevent burning.) Store in an airtight container in the refrigerator.

Heroic Hints

Check the bottom of your oven after it cools, because you might have had a couple beans pop off the baking sheet as they cooked.

Sassy Salsa

This fresh tomato salsa provides a little heat for your taste buds. If you like it h-o-t, stir in more cayenne until it makes you sweat.

1½ cups diced tomatoes

¼ cup finely diced sweet onions

1 medium jalapeño pepper, seeded and minced

2 TB. chopped fresh cilantro

2 tsp. fresh lime juice

⅛ tsp. cayenne or to taste

Yield: 2 cups
Prep time: 3 minutes
Serving size: ¼ cup
Each serving has:
12 calories
0 g total fat
0 g saturated fat
<1 g protein
2 g carbohydrate
1 g fiber
0 mg cholesterol
109 mg sodium

1. Combine tomatoes, sweet onions, jalapeño pepper, cilantro, lime juice, and cayenne in a small bowl. Stir until blended.

2. Serve immediately with tortilla chips or your favorite dippers, or cover and chill until serving time.

Kryptonite

Take care when seeding and cutting a hot pepper, and wash your hands immediately afterward—especially before rubbing your eyes! The heat will transfer to your fingers and onto anything else you touch. If your skin is especially sensitive and your pepper especially hot, you may want to wear gloves.

White Hot Chili

Slow cooking infuses this ready-when-you-are meal with its peppery bite, but if you're tender-tongued, you can add a dollop of sour cream to help quell the fiery flavor.

Yield: 8 servings
Prep time: 8 minutes
Soak time: 6 to 8 hours
Cook time: 10 hours, 25 minutes
Serving size: 1 cup
Each serving has:
310 calories
4 g total fat
1 g saturated fat
36 g protein
33 g carbohydrate
11 g fiber
64 mg cholesterol
362 mg sodium

1 (16-oz.) pkg. dry great northern beans

2 lb. boneless, skinless chicken breast halves, trimmed of fat and cut into bite-size pieces

1 medium yellow onion, chopped

3 medium cloves garlic, minced

2 (4.5-oz.) cans chopped green chilies, undrained

1½ tsp. cayenne

1½ tsp. ground cumin

1 tsp. dried oregano

½ tsp. salt

1 (14-oz.) can fat-free, less-sodium chicken broth

1 cup water

1. Sort beans in a large saucepan, and cover with water by 3 inches. Cover saucepan and soak beans 6 to 8 hours or overnight. Drain beans and cover with fresh water by 1 inch. Bring to a boil over high heat. Reduce heat, cover with a slightly vented lid, and simmer for 20 minutes. Drain.

2. Meanwhile, brown chicken in a large nonstick skillet for 6 minutes or until browned on all sides, stirring often. Drain well.

3. Combine beans, chicken, onion, garlic, green chilies, cayenne, cumin, oregano, salt, broth, and 1 cup water in a 3½- to 4-quart slow cooker. Stir until well mixed, cover, and cook on low for 10 hours or until done. Serve hot.

Variation: When you're short on time, cook on high heat for 5 hours.

★☆ Heroic Hints

When a recipe calls for you to sort or "pick over" dried beans, you simply need to run them through your fingers, looking for any shriveled or otherwise irregular beans. Occasionally, you'll even find pebbles. Remove these unwanted pieces before soaking the beans.

Quick Cinnamon Crisps

Enjoy these sweet, spicy crisps alone or in a sundae dish with a scoop of ice cream or frozen yogurt.

3 (10-in.) whole-wheat tortillas

2 TB. honey

1 scant tsp. ground cinnamon

Yield: 6 servings	
Prep time: 5 minutes	
Cook time: 6 to 8 minutes	
Serving size: 3 crisps	
Each serving has:	
67 calories	
<1 g total fat	
0 g saturated fat	
2 g protein	
18 g carbohydrate	
1 g fiber	
0 mg cholesterol	
105 mg sodium	

1. Preheat the oven to 350°F.

2. Cut each tortilla into 6 wedges and arrange in a single layer on a large nonstick baking sheet. Spread honey evenly over tortilla wedges. Sprinkle cinnamon evenly over top.

3. Bake for 6 to 8 minutes or until bubbly and crisp. Remove from the baking sheet immediately. Store in an airtight container when cool.

Kryptonite

Don't get distracted after removing the baking sheet from the oven. If the crisps aren't removed immediately, the honey will "glue" them to the baking sheet. To save your baking sheet, return it to the oven until the honey is heated again. You'll be able to remove the crisps, but they'll likely be overcooked.

Cinnamon-Spiced Fried Apples

This sweet side dish rounds out pork and poultry meals nicely—
and quickly.

Yield: 4 servings
Prep time: 2 minutes
Cook time: 7 minutes
Serving size: ¹/₂ cup
Each serving has:
70 calories
5 g total fat
<1 g saturated fat
<1 g protein
15 g carbohydrate
2 g fiber
0 mg cholesterol
3 mg sodium

½ TB. extra-virgin olive oil

1 medium Golden Delicious apple, cored and thinly sliced

1 medium Braeburn apple, cored and thinly sliced

¼ cup apple juice

2 TB. dried cranberries

½ tsp. ground cinnamon

¼ tsp. ground nutmeg

1. Heat olive oil in an 11-inch nonstick skillet over medium heat. Add Golden Delicious and Braeburn apple slices, and sauté for 2 minutes.

2. Add apple juice, dried cranberries, cinnamon, and nutmeg, and cook, stirring often, for 5 minutes or until apples are tender. Serve warm.

Variation: Substitute any cooking apples you have on hand.

 Heroic Hints

Mark the date you open a ground spice. Stored in a cool, dark place, it will keep for up to six months.

Greek Marinated Chicken Breasts

Serve these chicken breasts, marinated with a mingling of Mediterranean flavors, freshly baked or sliced over salad greens with a drizzling of Sweet-to-Your-Heart Salad Dressing (recipe in Chapter 17).

¼ cup lemon juice

2 TB. extra-virgin olive oil

1 tsp. dried oregano

½ tsp. ground cinnamon

¼ tsp. freshly ground black pepper

4 (3-oz.) boneless, skinless chicken breast halves, trimmed of fat

Yield: 4 servings	
Prep time: 5 minutes	
Chill time: 1 hour	
Cook time: 20 minutes	
Serving size: 1 chicken breast half	
Each serving has:	
157 calories	
9 g total fat	
2 g saturated fat	
17 g protein	
2 g carbohydrate	
<1 g fiber	
47 mg cholesterol	
41 mg sodium	

1. Combine lemon juice, olive oil, oregano, cinnamon, and black pepper in a gallon-size resealable plastic bag. Add chicken breast halves, press out the air from the bag, and seal the bag. Marinate in the refrigerator for at least 1 hour.

2. Preheat the oven to 425°F. Coat a medium nonstick baking sheet with nonstick cooking spray.

3. Remove chicken from marinade and discard marinade. Place chicken on the baking sheet, and bake for 20 minutes or until done (170°F on a food thermometer).

Heroic Hints

For freshly ground black pepper, purchase black peppercorns and grind them in a peppermill as needed. Freshly ground pepper can be ground as coarsely or finely as desired and is more aromatic than preground pepper.

Balsamic Mint Vinaigrette

This sweetly refreshing dressing is delicious drizzled over a bowl of your favorite fruit salad.

Yield: ¹/₄ *cup*
Prep time: 3 minutes
Serving size: 1 tablespoon
Each serving has:
42 calories
1 g total fat
0 g saturated fat
<1 g protein
10 g carbohydrate
0 g fiber
0 mg cholesterol
2 mg sodium

2 TB. balsamic vinegar   1 TB. chopped fresh mint

2 TB. honey   ½ tsp. extra-virgin olive oil

1. Combine balsamic vinegar and honey in a small bowl and whisk until blended. Whisk in mint and olive oil.

2. Serve with halved strawberries, blueberries, seedless grapes, pitted cherries, pineapple chunks, melon balls, or your favorites. Refrigerate any leftovers and stir again before serving.

 Heroic Hints _____

Use a sharp knife or kitchen shears to chop fresh mint. If you tend to tear fresh herbs, you'll stain your fingers with the easily bruised mint leaves.

Bountiful Garden Zucchini Salad

When your garden (or your neighbor's) begins to burgeon, reap the rewards of the bumper crop with this easy zucchini recipe.

1 TB. extra-virgin olive oil

4 medium (about 8-in.) zucchini, *julienne* cut

3 medium cloves garlic, minced

1 TB. chopped fresh basil

1 TB. chopped fresh mint

¼ tsp. salt

¼ cup unsalted finely chopped pecans

Yield: 9 servings
Prep time: 3 minutes
Cook time: 3 minutes
Stand time: 10 minutes
Serving size: ¹/₂ cup
Each serving has:
52 calories
4 g total fat
<1 g saturated fat
1 g protein
4 g carbohydrate
1 g fiber
0 mg cholesterol
74 mg sodium

1. Heat olive oil in a large nonstick skillet over medium heat. Add zucchini and garlic, and sauté for 3 minutes or until zucchini is just slightly softened. Remove from heat to cool.

2. Turn zucchini mixture into a medium bowl. Stir in basil, mint, and salt. Stir in pecans until evenly distributed. Serve at room temperature or cover and chill to serve cold.

def•i•ni•tion

Julienne describes foods cut into long, thin strips sometimes referred to as matchsticks. For this recipe, the zucchini can be cut in half crosswise and then cut into thin, 4-inch-long strips.

Chilled Minty Green Beans

This delicious make-ahead green bean salad is a welcome taste at summertime meals.

Yield: 6 servings
Prep time: 3 minutes
Cook time: 5 minutes
Stand time: 10 to 15 minutes
Chill time: 2 hours
Serving size: ¹/₂ cup
Each serving has:
38 calories
2 g total fat
<1 g saturated fat
1 g protein
4 g carbohydrate
1 g fiber
0 mg cholesterol
114 mg sodium

1 (12-oz.) pkg. ready-to-microwave fresh green beans

1 large clove garlic, minced

1 TB. extra-virgin olive oil

½ TB. red wine vinegar

1 TB. chopped fresh mint

¹/₈ tsp. salt

¹/₈ tsp. freshly ground black pepper

1. Prepare green beans in their packaging according to the package directions. Transfer to a medium bowl and let cool.

2. Stir in garlic, olive oil, and vinegar until green beans are coated. Stir in mint, salt, and black pepper. Cover and chill for at least 2 hours or until cold. Stir again before serving.

Variation: If you can't find microwave-ready fresh green beans in your grocer's produce section, you can substitute 3 cups cooked fresh or frozen cut green beans.

 Super Knowledge

Frozen vegetables can be just as nutritious as fresh ones. Plus, they're available year-round and are often less expensive.

Baked Snapper with Minty Cucumber Salsa

Pair this firm-fleshed, mild-flavored fish with a citrus-y, biting salsa to delight your taste buds.

1 (1-lb.) boneless red snapper fillet	**¾ cup finely chopped seedless cucumber**
¼ cup lemon juice	**¼ cup chopped fresh mint**
½ tsp. dried oregano	**2 TB. drained capers**
¼ tsp. paprika	**1 TB. extra-virgin olive oil**
⅛ tsp. salt	**½ tsp. grated lemon zest**

Yield: *4 servings*
Prep time: 5 minutes
Cook time: 10 minutes per inch of thickness
Serving size: 3 ounces fish with ¼ cup salsa

Each serving has:
185 calories
5 g total fat
1 g saturated fat
30 g protein
3 g carbohydrate
1 g fiber
53 mg cholesterol
266 mg sodium

1. Preheat the oven to 400°F. Coat a medium nonstick baking sheet with nonstick cooking spray.

2. Place red snapper on the baking sheet, cutting into pieces to facilitate more even cooking if necessary. Drizzle 2 tablespoons lemon juice over top, and sprinkle on oregano, paprika, and salt. Bake for 10 minutes per inch of thickness or until fish flakes easily with a fork or reads 145°F on a food thermometer.

3. Meanwhile, combine cucumber, mint, capers, remaining 2 tablespoons lemon juice, olive oil, and lemon zest in a small bowl, and stir to mix well. Let stand while fish bakes.

4. Remove skin from fish by sliding a spatula between the flesh and the skin. Cut fish into serving-size pieces and spoon cucumber salsa over top to serve.

Heroic Hints

The salsa looks pretty and has a nice mouthfeel when you leave the peel on the cucumber. Wash the seedless cucumber's peel with a commercial fruit-and-vegetable wash before cutting to ensure cleanliness.

Chapter 17

Sweet Tooth Tamers

In This Chapter

◆ Chocoholics, rejoice!

◆ Help yourself to honey

◆ Tea: good for the queen, good for you

◆ Sweet treats for any time

To us, a big part of healthy eating is not feeling deprived. In other words, not avoiding your favorite foods because they fall a bit low on the nutritional totem pole. Thanks to some recent research, allowing yourself some guilt-free sweet treats is a bit easier, at least when it comes to a couple formerly forbidden foods. And if you can't get through the day without your cup of hot tea, there's good news for you, too.

Whether you enjoy them for comfort, relaxation, or just as a little pleasure, this sweet trio offers much more.

Chocolate Triumph

So many people say if something tastes good it's not good for you. That might be true many times, but it's not the case when it comes to chocolate. It's delicious *and* good for you. Like the other foods in this book, chocolate contains phytochemicals. Those found in chocolate are *epicatechin* and *catechin*.

The flavonoids found in chocolate help reduce the clotting action of blood platelets, enabling blood to flow throughout the body better, lowering the risk of having a heart attack or stroke. In addition, these flavonoids may help make arteries healthier.

Even with all its super powers, chocolate still contains fats, but even that isn't all bad news. The first kind, *palmitic acid*, is your run-of-the-mill unhealthful saturated kind. However, the other two, *stearic acid* and *oleic acid*, are a different story. Stearic acid is also saturated, but it's unlike other saturated fats that raise cholesterol and clog arteries; it has no effect on cholesterol at all, good or bad. Oleic acid, on the other hand, may help lower both total cholesterol and LDL (bad) cholesterol levels.

def•i•ni•tion

Epicatechin is a flavonoid found in cocoa, red wine, and green tea. It helps maintain heart health by improving blood flow. **Catechin** is a flavonoid and antioxidant found in cocoa as well as white and green teas

Super Knowledge

The flavonoid content and, therefore, health benefits of chocolate are greater the more cocoa the chocolate has. Dark and baking chocolates have the most cocoa. And when it comes to cocoa powder, the natural kind contains more flavonoids than Dutched or alkalinized cocoa.

Herculean Honey

Athletes, listen up! Honey is all carbohydrate, no fat or protein. Your body absorbs this type of carbohydrate slowly and can immediately and easily use it. This is an important benefit for those participating or competing in sports, especially long-lasting events such as distance runs or bike rides or long games. When your body is working strenuously and for a long time, it burns the sugar or carbohydrate in your blood quickly. By offering a slow, steady, and easy absorption, honey enables you to continue that activity instead of running out of steam as quickly.

> **Super Knowledge**
>
> Depending on the type of flower visited, bees create a variety of different honeys that vary in color, texture, and taste. The darker the honey, the greater the antioxidant content.

And believe it or not this syrupy sweet stuff may also help wounds heal. Now don't go heading to the pantry the next time you end up on the wrong side of your chef's knife just yet. There's been promising results with honey healing wounds faster but more research is needed. Just keep your eyes and ears open for more information on this one in the future.

Mighty Tea

It might surprise you that such a simple and common drink as tea offers so many benefits to your health, but it's true. Tea contains a variety of flavonoids that may help protect you against cancer as well as heart disease.

In terms of cancer protection, tea may help prevent the development and growth of cancer cells by boosting your immune power. It also helps promote the death of cancer cells.

Studies show those who drink 1¹/₂ to 2¹/₂ cups per day have a lower chance of developing colon, rectal, and urinary tract cancer compared to nontea drinkers. Other studies show that 3 to 4¹/₂ cups a day can help lower the risk of colon, rectal, and pancreatic cancer. And even more studies show that at least 2 cups a day can lower a woman's chances for ovarian cancer.

> **Super Knowledge**
>
> Studies about tea's benefits have been done using the type of plant that's used to make black, green, oolong, and white tea. Herbal teas come from different plants and, therefore, their effect or lack thereof on these diseases has not yet been studied. To obtain the benefits described, choose black, green, oolong, or white teas.

When it comes to heart health, tea has a lot to offer as well, including a lower risk of high blood pressure. By decreasing that risk, tea may also help lower the chances of having a stroke or heart attack, high blood pressure being a risk factor for both. Regularly drinking tea also appears to promote healthier blood vessels, which can help allow better blood flow through the body. Most of the research in this area is based on 3 or more cups of tea per day.

Mint Chocolate Smoothies

Indulge in this tempting treat knowing you're enjoying the benefits of dark chocolate as well.

2 oz. bittersweet chocolate

2 cups fat-free plain yogurt

¼ cup honey

1 TB. loosely packed small fresh mint leaves

⅛ tsp. ground cinnamon

12 large ice cubes

Yield: 4 servings
Prep time: 12 minutes
Serving size: 1 cup
Each serving has:
185 calories
6 g total fat
3 g saturated fat
6 g protein
34 g carbohydrate
1 g fiber
3 mg cholesterol
70 mg sodium

1. Break chocolate into small pieces and place in a small, heavy-bottomed, nonstick saucepan. Heat over very low heat for 5 minutes, stirring frequently and removing from heat before completely melted. Stir to melt completely and let cool.

2. Combine yogurt, chocolate, honey, mint, and cinnamon in a blender. Cover and blend on high speed for 1 minute or until well blended, stopping to scrape down the sides as necessary.

3. Remove the cap from the blender's lid and, with the blender running, add ice cubes one at a time until well blended. Serve immediately.

Kryptonite

Honey makes a great sweetener in drinks and other foods, but it's not recommended for young children under the age of 1 because it may contain botulinum spores that once ingested could produce a toxin their digestive systems can't yet handle. However, it's perfectly safe for older kids and adults.

Mayan-Spiced Hot Chocolate

You'll welcome wintry days when you know you have this thick, chocolaty, cinnamon-laced hot mug to look forward to.

Yield: 2 servings
Prep time: 2 minutes
Cook time: 10 minutes
Serving size: 1 heaping cup
Each serving has:
199 calories
1 g total fat
1 g saturated fat
10 g protein
42 g carbohydrate
3 g fiber
5 mg cholesterol
142 mg sodium

3 TB. unsweetened cocoa powder

¼ cup granulated sugar

Pinch salt

¼ tsp. ground cinnamon

¼ cup water

2 cups fat-free milk

½ tsp. vanilla extract

1. In a medium saucepan, whisk together cocoa powder, sugar, salt, and cinnamon. Add water and whisk until smooth. Heat over medium-high heat just until mixture starts to boil and then reduce heat to medium and simmer, whisking constantly, for 1 minute.

2. Whisk in 1 cup milk and cook, whisking constantly, for 5 minutes or until hot. Remove from heat and whisk in remaining 1 cup milk and vanilla extract. Serve hot.

Super Knowledge

Spiced with a bit of cinnamon to give it a Central American flair, this cocoa gives a double shot of super power.

Mexican Turkey Molé with Chocolate-Chili Sauce

The legendary habanero pepper lends a fiery bite to the almond-thickened sauce that envelops the thinly sliced turkey breast.

1 lb. 99 percent fat-free thin scaloppini-cut turkey breast

1 (14-oz.) can fat-free, less-sodium chicken broth

1 tsp. olive oil

2 small yellow onions, chopped

2 medium cloves garlic, minced

2 TB. chili powder

1 dried habanero or other small red chili pepper, seeded and finely chopped

1 cup unsalted ground almonds

½ oz. bittersweet chocolate, chopped

Yield: 4 servings	
Prep time: 7 minutes	
Cook time: 25 minutes	
Serving size: 2 slices turkey with 3 tablespoons sauce	

Each serving has:

325 calories

16 g total fat

2 g saturated fat

35 g protein

13 g carbohydrate

5 g fiber

77 mg cholesterol

112 mg sodium

1. Coat a large nonstick skillet with nonstick cooking spray and heat over medium heat. Add turkey and cook for 2 minutes on each side or until browned. Drain. Pour in broth and bring to a boil over high heat. Reduce heat and simmer for 15 minutes or until turkey is tender.

2. Meanwhile, heat olive oil in a small nonstick skillet over medium heat. Add onions and sauté for 6 minutes or until golden brown.

3. Add onions, garlic, chili powder, habanero pepper, ground almonds, and chocolate to turkey mixture, and stir to blend. Simmer for 10 minutes, stirring occasionally, until heated through and well blended to a deep, rich color. Serve over rice or noodles, if desired.

Heroic Hints

To make ground almonds, grind unsalted sliced almonds on high speed in your blender to measure 1 cup.

Asian Sesame Dip

Serve this creamy, robust dip dotted with sesame seeds to awaken your appetite for deeply flavored Asian dishes.

Yield: 1 cup
Prep time: 5 minutes
Serving size: 2 table-spoons
Each serving has:
76 calories
4 g total fat
1 g saturated fat
<1 g protein
10 g carbohydrate
0 g fiber
0 mg cholesterol
174 mg sodium

⅔ **cup reduced-fat mayonnaise**

3 TB. sodium-free rice vinegar

3 TB. honey

2 TB. toasted sesame seeds

2 tsp. finely grated gingerroot

1 small clove garlic, minced

½ tsp. dark sesame seed oil

Pinch crushed red pepper flakes

1. Combine mayonnaise, vinegar, and honey in a small bowl and stir until blended. Stir in sesame seeds, gingerroot, garlic, sesame seed oil, and crushed red pepper flakes until blended.

2. Serve with broccoli florets, carrot sticks, bell pepper spears, cucumber slices, celery sticks, or your other favorite veggies. Refrigerate any leftovers.

Kryptonite

If you're cutting sodium from your diet, take care when purchasing rice vinegar. Regular or seasoned rice vinegar is loaded with sodium. Be sure to choose the no-salt version that lists 0 milligrams sodium on the label.

Sweet-to-Your-Heart Salad Dressing

Dress your favorite salad greens with this sweet and tangy—and guilt-free!—blend.

⅓ cup tarragon white wine vinegar

⅓ cup water

⅓ cup honey

Yield: 1 cup
Prep time: 3 minutes
Serving size: 2 table-spoons
Each serving has:
43 calories
0 g total fat
0 g saturated fat
<1 g protein
11 g carbohydrate
0 g fiber
0 mg cholesterol
15 mg sodium

1. Combine vinegar, water, and honey in a measuring cup. Whisk for 1 minute or until smooth and well blended.

2. Store any leftovers in the refrigerator and stir again before serving.

Heroic Hints

Store honey at room temperature out of direct sunlight. Don't store honey in the refrigerator, as it will crystallize. To restore honey that has crystallized, fill a saucepan with water and bring it to a boil; then remove the saucepan from the heat and place the container of honey in the hot water until the honey is liquefied again. Crystallization can be reversed in the microwave if your honey is in a microwave-safe container. Cook on high power for 2 or 3 minutes, stirring every 30 seconds until crystals liquefy.

Barbecue-Glazed Chicken Breasts

The sweet honey-barbecue sauce makes this chicken a dinnertime hit.

Yield: 4 servings
Prep time: 5 minutes
Cook time: 25 to 30 minutes
Serving size: 1 chicken breast half
Each serving has:
220 calories
3 g total fat
1 g saturated fat
24 g protein
24 g carbohydrate
1 g fiber
63 mg cholesterol
366 mg sodium

1 lb. boneless, skinless chicken breast halves, trimmed of fat and cut into serving-size pieces

1 medium yellow onion, thinly sliced into rings

¾ cup tomato sauce

¼ cup cider vinegar

¼ cup honey

2 TB. Worcestershire sauce

1 tsp. paprika

¼ tsp. hot pepper sauce

1. Preheat the oven to 375°F.

2. Arrange chicken breast halves in a 13×9×2-inch nonstick baking pan. Scatter onion rings over chicken.

3. Combine tomato sauce, vinegar, honey, Worcestershire sauce, paprika, and hot pepper sauce in a small bowl. Stir until well blended and pour over chicken and onions.

4. Bake, uncovered, for 25 to 30 minutes or until chicken is done (170°F on a food thermometer). Serve hot with onions and barbecue sauce.

Variation: When substituting 1 cup honey in your baked goods, reduce the recipe's liquid by ¼ cup, add ½ teaspoon baking soda, and reduce the oven temperature by 25°F.

 Super Knowledge

Honey is a great substitute for other sweeteners in your recipes. Because honey has a higher sweetening power than sugar, reduce the amount by half, adjusting to taste.

Honey-Basted Salmon

Sweeten salmon's superb health benefits with a super, honey-based marinade.

½ **cup honey**	**2 TB. white vinegar**
3 TB. reduced-sodium soy sauce	**1 lb. salmon fillet**

1. Whisk together honey, soy sauce, and vinegar in a small bowl until well blended. Pour into a gallon-size resealable plastic bag and add salmon. Press out the air from the bag, seal the bag, and turn to coat salmon. Marinate in the refrigerator for 1 hour.

2. Preheat the oven to 350°F.

3. Remove salmon from the bag, reserving marinade, and arrange salmon on a large sheet of aluminum foil. Pull up the long sides of the foil, fold over 2 times, and roll the ends in to form a well-sealed pouch. Place the pouch on a baking sheet and bake for 15 minutes.

4. Meanwhile, pour reserved marinade into a small saucepan. Whisk over medium-high heat until boiling, watching closely to prevent boil-overs. Boil for 2 minutes and remove from heat.

5. Remove salmon pouch from the oven and carefully open. Pour marinade over salmon and tightly reseal the pouch. Bake for 15 minutes or until fish flakes easily with a fork. Serve hot.

Yield: 4 servings
Prep time: 5 minutes
Chill time: 1 hour
Cook time: 30 minutes
Serving size: 3 ounces salmon
Each serving has:
396 calories
15 g total fat
4 g saturated fat
30 g protein
35 g carbohydrate
<1 g fiber
96 mg cholesterol
469 mg sodium

Kryptonite

A foil pouch is a great way to lock in moisture and flavor. Take caution when opening a hot pouch, though. Always open it away from you to prevent burns from the hot steam.

Orange Spiced Tea

With tea, honey, cinnamon, and oranges this pleasant sipper is a super choice.

Yield: 4 servings
Prep time: 3 minutes
Cook time: 10 minutes
Serving size: 1 cup
Each serving has:
68 calories
0 g total fat
0 g saturated fat
<1 g protein
18 g carbohydrate
<1 g fiber
0 mg cholesterol
1 mg sodium

4 cups freshly brewed green tea

¼ cup honey

4 cinnamon sticks

4 whole cloves

4 thin slices navel orange

1. Combine tea, honey, cinnamon sticks, and cloves in a medium saucepan and stir to blend. Bring to a simmer over medium heat. Continue to simmer gently, reducing heat as needed, for 5 minutes.

2. Discard cinnamon sticks and cloves. Pour hot tea into individual tea cups, and float 1 orange slice in each to serve.

Heroic Hints

To make removing the cinnamon sticks and whole cloves easier, place them in a cheesecloth bag. The flavor will still infuse the tea, and you only then have to fish out one thing instead of several.

Green Tea Smoothies

This simple and refreshing way to sip the clean flavor of green tea is sure to become a family favorite.

1 cup fat-free plain yogurt

1 cup prepared green tea, cold

2 TB. honey

¼ tsp. ground cinnamon

12 large ice cubes

Yield: 4 servings
Prep time: 3 minutes
Serving size: 1 cup
Each serving has:
57 calories
0 g total fat
0 g saturated fat
3 g protein
13 g carbohydrate
0 g fiber
1 mg cholesterol
36 mg sodium

1. Combine yogurt, green tea, honey, and cinnamon in a blender. Cover and blend on high speed for 30 seconds or until well blended.

2. Remove the cap from the blender's lid and, with the blender running, add ice cubes one at a time until well blended. Serve immediately.

Variation: Substitute your favorite tea—black, oolong, or white tea.

Heroic Hints

Tea keeps for up to 1 year if stored in its original packaging and/or an airtight container in a cool, dark place.

Tea-Time Quick Bread

Complement your afternoon cup of tea with a slice of this simple, mildly flavored quick bread.

Yield: 16 servings
Prep time: 12 minutes
Cook time: 60 to 70 minutes
Serving size: 1 slice
Each serving has:
124 calories
4 g total fat
<1 g saturated fat
4 g protein
21 g carbohydrate
3 g fiber
26 mg cholesterol
159 mg sodium

1⅔ cups whole-wheat flour

¾ cup ground flaxseed meal

⅓ cup oat flour

1 TB. baking powder

½ tsp. salt

1 cup prepared green tea, at room temperature

½ cup honey

2 large eggs, at room temperature, or the equivalent amount of egg substitute

2 TB. grated orange zest

1 tsp. vanilla extract

1. Preheat the oven to 350°F. Coat a 9×5×3-inch loaf pan with nonstick cooking spray.

2. Stir together whole-wheat flour, flaxseed meal, oat flour, baking powder, and salt in a large bowl. Combine green tea, honey, eggs, orange zest, and vanilla extract in a medium bowl and stir until well blended. Pour into flour mixture and stir until moistened.

3. Pour batter into the loaf pan and bake for 60 to 70 minutes or until a cake tester or toothpick inserted into the middle of loaf comes out clean. Let cool in the pan for 10 minutes before removing to a wire rack to cool completely. Cut into ½-inch slices to serve.

Variation: Substitute your favorite tea—black, oolong, or white tea.

 Heroic Hints

Healthy quick breads like this freeze well. When you want a healthful snack or quick breakfast, cut a slice or two, thaw or heat, and eat.

Honey Wheat Corn Bread

Complete your soup or salad meal with this hearty, slightly sweet, lightly corn-flavored bread.

1 cup fat-free milk

1 TB. cider vinegar

2 cups whole-wheat flour

1 cup yellow cornmeal

1 tsp. baking soda

¾ tsp. salt

¾ cup unsweetened apple-sauce

¾ cup honey

Yield: 16 servings
Prep time: 30 minutes
Cook time: 45 minutes
Serving size: 2×2-inch square
Each serving has:
137 calories
<1 g total fat
0 g saturated fat
3 g protein
32 g carbohydrate
2 g fiber
0 mg cholesterol
302 mg sodium

1. In a liquid measuring cup, measure milk. Stir in cider vinegar. Let stand for 20 minutes or until curdled.

2. Meanwhile, preheat the oven to 375°F. Spray an 8×8×2-inch baking pan with nonstick cooking spray.

3. In a medium bowl, stir together whole-wheat flour, cornmeal, baking soda, and salt. In a large bowl, combine applesauce, honey, and milk mixture. Stir until blended. Add whole-wheat flour mixture and stir until moistened.

4. Pour batter into the prepared pan. Bake for 45 minutes or until golden brown around edges that are pulled away from the sides and a cake tester inserted in the center comes out clean. Let stand for at least 5 minutes on a wire rack before cutting to serve.

Super Knowledge

When baking soda comes in contact with liquid and acid, it produces the carbon dioxide that causes leavening in baked goods. Batters prepared with baking soda must be baked immediately upon combining the dry ingredients with the wet ingredients.

Part 7

Superfood Combinations

Throughout the preceding six parts, we've described the countless health benefits superfoods offer. But to get the most bang for your buck, why not eat more than one at a time? Including more than one of the superfoods or flavors in a single meal or recipe doubles your nutritional benefits. But more than that, some of the beneficial compounds found in these foods actually become more powerful when combined with others. Double- or even triple-duty breakfast, lunch, dinner, and treat recipes can be found on the following pages.

Chapter 18

Breaking for Breakfast

In This Chapter

- Breaking the fast
- Preventing weight gain and disease
- Loading up on nutrition
- Tasty ways to start the day

It never ceases to amaze us how many people skip this ever-so important first meal of the day. Many claim a lack of time in the morning, but setting that alarm clock 10 to 15 minutes earlier is all you need to make a world of difference in your day. Others state they aren't hungry when they awaken. There's a good chance that skipping breakfast regularly has conditioned these folks to not *notice* that hunger that likely is there. In fact, often when a person begins to eat in the morning again they find that hunger creeping back into their mornings. While many folks seem to think of morning hunger as bad thing because it makes dieting and cutting out foods more difficult, its actually a good thing. It's a sign that your metabolism is up and running. Your body has worked hard digesting your last meal and its ready for more food to keep it going. So listen to your body—give it a nutritious breakfast to rev up its engine and get your day started.

If your mornings are a hectic race to get out the door on time, this chapter, has some quick breakfast ideas for you. If you've got a bit more time in the mornings or for lazy weekends, we've got recipes for you, too, as well as some that may take a bit longer to prepare and are perfect for a lazy weekend morning.

Breakfast Bonanza

Why is breakfast so important? By eating in the morning, you are breaking the fast of not eating for several hours throughout the night. Breakfast gives you energy and gets your metabolism and all of your body's systems up and running. This jump-start helps keep your body using and burning food more efficiently throughout the day, which might be why studies have shown those who eat breakfast regularly weigh less than nonbreakfast eaters. Plus, those who've lost a significant amount of weight are more likely to keep it off if they start the day with a healthful meal versus leaving the house on an empty stomach.

Plus, eating breakfast in the morning leads to less overeating/bingeing in the afternoon and evening. Starting the day on an empty stomach leaves your body looking to make up those calories, which leads to afternoon slumps and nighttime cravings—when we tend to choose the least nutritious foods to fill the void. Even eating larger portions at dinner can be a result of skipping the important morning meal. All this late-day overeating can lead to weight gain.

> **Super Knowledge**
>
> A great healthful breakfast includes one serving from at least three, if not four, of the five food groups. For example, one serving of fruit (ideally whole, not juice), a serving of high-quality protein (such as an egg or peanut butter), a dairy serving (low-fat milk or yogurt), and a whole-grain (such as whole-grain bread/toast or cereal).

Additionally, those who pass up their morning nosh have a greater risk of developing diabetes. Isn't it worth taking a few extra minutes in the morning to eat a yummy meal to help keep yourself trimmer and healthier?

Starting the day off with a balanced meal also gives you a better chance of meeting your body's nutrient needs. Common breakfast foods include cereal, milk, yogurt, and fruit. These foods are all filled with not only super nutrients, but also the standard vitamins, minerals, and fiber we all need. Skipping breakfast cuts out one of your daily opportunities to eat these foods. And while they should be eaten throughout the day, for many folks they're less likely to be included in lunch or dinner.

Another bonus about breakfast—if you've got a family this may be the only time of day when everyone is home at the same time. Our days get pretty full between work, school, sports practices, various lessons, working out, need I go on? Carving out a few extra minutes in the morning to enjoy a meal together may actually be easier than trying to do so in the evening. And family breakfasts provide more than just nourishment. Sure people who eat breakfast have been shown to have more fruits, vegetables, fiber, and calcium in their diets as well as less fat and saturated fat, but there's more. Kids and teens who eat family meals regularly are more successful in school and are less likely to smoke or try drugs.

So what have you got to lose? Less risk of disease, a healthier family life, a more nutritious diet. All of this and it will only cost you a few extra morning minutes for enjoying a tasty meal.

Morning Sunshine French Toast with Oranges

A warm, refreshing way to enjoy your morning orange, this sweet, citrus-y dish doesn't have to be reserved for special occasions.

Yield: 2 servings
Prep time: 8 minutes
Cook time: 12 minutes
Serving size: 2 slices French toast with 1 orange and ½ cup syrup
Each serving has:
409 calories
4 g total fat
1 g saturated fat
9 g protein
95 g carbohydrate
17 g fiber
106 mg cholesterol
489 mg sodium

1 large egg or the equivalent amount of egg substitute

1¼ cups fresh or unsweetened orange juice

1 tsp. fresh lemon juice

¼ tsp. vanilla extract

1 TB. finely grated orange zest

3 TB. honey

1 TB. cornstarch

¼ tsp. salt

4 (1-oz.) slices whole-grain bread

2 medium navel oranges, peeled and divided into segments

1. In an 8- or 9-inch pie plate or other shallow dish, beat egg with a whisk. Add ¼ cup orange juice, lemon juice, vanilla extract, 1 teaspoon orange zest, and 1 tablespoon honey, and whisk until thoroughly blended. Set aside.

2. Add cornstarch, salt, and remaining 2 teaspoons orange zest to a small saucepan. Pour in remaining 1 cup orange juice and remaining 2 tablespoons honey, and whisk until well blended. Bring to a boil over high heat, stirring continuously until beginning to thicken. Reduce heat to low and continue stirring to desired consistency. Remove from heat and set aside. (Syrup will thicken slightly upon standing.)

3. Meanwhile, coat a large nonstick skillet with nonstick cooking spray and heat over medium heat. Coat both sides of each bread slice with egg mixture, allowing all excess mixture to drip back into the pie plate. Add to the skillet and cook for 3 minutes or until golden brown on the undersides. Turn and cook for 3 minutes or until the other sides are golden.

4. Cut French toast slices on the diagonal and arrange 2 slices on each serving plate. Scatter orange segments on top and drizzle orange syrup over all.

Kryptonite

When buying whole-wheat or whole-grain breads, look for the words *100 percent whole-wheat* or *whole-grain* on the label or ingredients list. Without them, chances are the bread is no better for you, nutritionally speaking, than white bread.

Spiced Pumpkin Pancakes

Pleasantly spice-speckled with a pleasing pumpkin taste, these pancakes make a special morning treat.

2 cups reduced-fat baking mix (such as Bisquick Heart Smart all-purpose baking mix)

2 TB. ground flaxseed meal

2 tsp. ground cinnamon

1 tsp. ground allspice

1 (12-oz.) can fat-free evaporated milk

½ cup canned pure pumpkin

2 large eggs, at room temperature, or the equivalent amount of egg substitute

1 TB. peanut oil

1 TB. honey

1 tsp. vanilla extract

Yield: 5 servings
Prep time: 5 minutes
Cook time: 6 minutes per batch
Serving size: 3 pancakes
Each serving has:
339 calories
9 g total fat
2 g saturated fat
12 g protein
51 g carbohydrate
3 g fiber
85 mg cholesterol
684 mg sodium

1. Stir together baking mix, flaxseed meal, cinnamon, and allspice. Add evaporated milk, pumpkin, eggs, oil, honey, and vanilla extract, and whisk until dry ingredients are moistened.

2. Heat a large nonstick skillet or griddle over medium heat and coat with nonstick cooking spray. Pour ¼ cup batter into the hot skillet for each pancake, cooking in batches. Cook for 3 minutes or until the top is bubbly and the edge is dry. Turn and cook the other side for 3 minutes or until golden brown. Serve warm with maple syrup, honey, or your favorite toppings.

 Kryptonite _____

If someone in your house has a peanut allergy, substitute your favorite cooking oil for the peanut oil in this recipe.

Speedy Spinach and Feta Frittata

A quick and easy hot breakfast special enough for overnight guests, this Greek-inspired frittata with the briny bite of feta cheese also makes a good busy-weeknight dinner dish.

Yield: 4 servings
Prep time: 2 minutes
Cook time: 9 minutes
Serving size: 1 wedge
Each serving has:
189 calories
14 g total fat
5 g saturated fat
15 g protein
3 g carbohydrate
1 g fiber
326 mg cholesterol
437 mg sodium

Heroic Hints

If your skillet isn't ovenproof, you can cover the handle completely with aluminum foil to use it under the broiler.

1 TB. extra-virgin or light olive oil

¼ tsp. crushed red pepper flakes or to taste

1 cup firmly packed fresh spinach

6 large eggs or the equivalent amount of egg substitute

2 TB. cold water

¾ cup reduced-fat crumbled feta cheese

6 thin tomato slices

2 TB. chopped fresh chives

1. Preheat the broiler.

2. Heat olive oil in a 10-inch ovenproof skillet over medium heat. Stir in crushed red pepper flakes and cook for 30 seconds. Add spinach and sauté for 2 minutes or until wilted.

3. Meanwhile, beat eggs with water in a medium bowl using a wire whisk. Reduce heat to medium-low, pour in egg mixture, and stir, scraping up bottom, for 1 minute. Add feta cheese and stir, scraping up bottom, for 3 minutes or until eggs are beginning to set. Using a spatula, even and smooth out top of frittata. Arrange tomato slices on top and sprinkle on chives.

4. Place frittata on uppermost oven shelf nearest the heat source and broil for 3 minutes or until top is set and lightly browned. Cut into wedges to serve.

Salmon and Cheese Omelet with Broccoli and Red Peppers

Whether a weekend-morning indulgence or a breakfast dish for overnight guests, this hearty, veggie-packed omelet is stuffed with superfoods and their health benefits to start your day off right.

4 large eggs or the equivalent amount of egg substitute

2 TB. cold water

1 (3-oz.) pouch boneless, skinless pink salmon

1 cup broccoli florets

½ small red bell pepper, ribs and seeds removed, and cut into thin strips

¼ cup 2 percent milk shredded Colby and Monterey Jack cheese

Yield: 2 servings
Prep time: 6 minutes
Cook time: 6 to 8 minutes
Serving size: ½ omelet
Each serving has:
251 calories
15 g total fat
5 g saturated fat
28 g protein
4 g carbohydrate
1 g fiber
463 mg cholesterol
432 mg sodium

1. Heat a 10-inch nonstick skillet coated with nonstick cooking spray over medium heat.

2. In a medium bowl, whisk eggs with cold water until lightly beaten. Whisk in salmon, breaking up as needed. Pour into the skillet and cook for 5 or 6 minutes or until top is nearly set, lifting around the edge and tilting the skillet to allow eggs to run to the bottom of the skillet.

3. When eggs are nearly set and the underside is golden brown, slide onto a large plate. Invert the skillet over the plate and then flip the skillet and the plate together. Cook for 1 to 2 minutes or until the underside of omelet is golden brown. Slide out onto a different plate.

4. Meanwhile, fill a steamer pot or a medium pot or saucepan with enough water to fall below the steamer basket when added, and bring to a boil over high heat. Add broccoli florets and red bell pepper strips to the steamer basket or a collapsible steamer basket, place the basket in the pot, and cover. Steam over boiling water, reducing heat as necessary to just maintain a boil, for 5 minutes or until crisp-tender.

5. Scatter broccoli and red bell pepper over ½ of omelet and top with ½ of cheese. Fold omelet over filling and sprinkle remaining cheese on top. Cut in half crosswise to serve.

Super Knowledge

Steaming is the preferred cooking method for vegetables. Steaming adds no fat to your healthful vegetables; more nutrients are retained when vegetables are steamed instead of boiled or simmered; and your foods don't end up water-logged.

Spicy Scrambled Eggs

Wake up your tired taste buds by stirring a little zing into your morning eggs.

Yield: 2 servings	
Prep time: 2 minutes	
Cook time: 5 minutes	
Serving size: ³/₄ cup	
Each serving has:	
162 calories	
10 g total fat	
3 g saturated fat	
14 g protein	
4 g carbohydrate	
1 g fiber	
423 mg cholesterol	
258 mg sodium	

4 large eggs or the equivalent amount of egg substitute

2 TB. cold water

½ cup Sassy Salsa (recipe in Chapter 16) or your favorite

2 TB. fat-free plain yogurt

1. Coat a 10-inch nonstick skillet with nonstick cooking spray and heat over medium heat.

2. In a medium bowl, whisk together eggs and cold water until lightly beaten. Pour into the skillet and cook, stirring, for 3 minutes or until eggs are nearly set. Stir in ¹/₄ cup Sassy Salsa. Cook and stir for 2 minutes or until eggs are set and a food thermometer reads 160°F.

3. Spoon scrambled eggs onto serving plates while hot. Over each serving, spoon remaining 2 tablespoons Sassy Salsa and 1 tablespoon yogurt. Serve immediately.

def•i•ni•tion

To **whisk** is to beat or whip ingredients rapidly using a cooking utensil of the same name with interlooped wires. If you don't have a whisk, you can use a fork instead.

Blueberry-Topped Sweet Rice

Reinvent rice left over from last night's dinner for a delicious, sweet, and creamy breakfast bowl.

1 cup cooked long-grain brown rice	**½ TB. honey**
½ cup fat-free milk	**¼ tsp. ground cinnamon**
	½ cup fresh blueberries

Yield: 1 serving
Prep time: 3 minutes
Cook time: 5 minutes
Each serving has:
334 calories
2 g total fat
<1 g saturated fat
10 g protein
71 g carbohydrate
6 g fiber
2 mg cholesterol
62 mg sodium

1. Combine rice, milk, honey, and cinnamon in a small saucepan. Stir and bring to a boil over high heat. Reduce heat to medium and cook for 3 minutes or until thickened, stirring frequently.

2. Turn rice mixture into a serving bowl and set aside to cool while you clean blueberries. Stir blueberries into rice mixture and serve hot.

Variation: If you don't have cooked leftover brown rice and you need a fast, hot breakfast, use instant brown rice instead.

Super Knowledge

Using brown rice instead of white rice gives each serving of this morning meal almost 2 extra grams of health-boosting fiber.

Make-Your-Day Morning Parfait

Garnish this sweet and satisfying breakfast parfait with a fanned whole strawberry for a pretty dish that's ready to eat as soon as you are.

Yield: 1 serving
Prep time: 5 minutes
Chill time: 6 to 8 hours
Each serving has:
450 calories
3 g total fat
0 g saturated fat
17 g protein
96 g carbohydrate
7 g fiber
5 mg cholesterol
137 mg sodium

1 cup fat-free plain yogurt

2 TB. honey

½ cup uncooked quick oats

½ cup fresh blueberries

¼ cup sliced fresh strawberries

1. Combine yogurt and honey in a small bowl and stir until blended. Stir in oats until evenly coated.

2. In a parfait glass or a tall 2-cup container, layer ¹/₂ cup oat mixture, ¹/₄ cup blueberries, ¹/₂ cup oat mixture, strawberries, remaining oat mixture, and remaining ¹/₄ cup blueberries. Cover and chill overnight. Serve cold for breakfast.

Super Knowledge

You may be able to trick your eyes into thinking you're delighting in a luscious dessert while your stomach's waking up to three of the five food groups—dairy, whole-grain, and whole fruits.

Peach Crisp Breakfast Bowl

This hot, delectable breakfast treat can be on the table in just 10 minutes … so of course you have time!

1 cup fat-free soy milk or milk

½ cup old-fashioned rolled oats

1 TB. fat-free plain yogurt

1 TB. honey

¼ tsp. almond extract

1 medium peach

Yield: 1 serving
Prep time: 2 minutes
Cook time: 8 minutes
Each serving has:
343 calories
3 g total fat
0 g saturated fat
15 g protein
65 g carbohydrate
7 g fiber
<1 mg cholesterol
114 mg sodium

1. Pour soy milk into a medium nonstick saucepan and bring to a boil over high heat. Stir in oats, reduce heat to medium, and cook for 5 minutes, stirring occasionally.

2. Meanwhile, combine yogurt, honey, and almond extract in a small bowl, and stir until blended.

3. Wash peach, remove pit, and cut peach into thin slices.

4. When oatmeal is thickened, remove from heat. Stir in yogurt mixture until blended. Pour into a serving bowl and stir in peach slices. Serve hot.

Heroic Hints

To slice a peach, cut it in half lengthwise around the pit with a small knife. Hold the peach with both hands on either of the cut sides and twist the halves in opposite directions until they separate. Remove the pit with your fingers or the tip of the knife and discard it. Then, slice each half as needed.

Honey Nut Oatmeal

Sweet and crunchy, the honey-nut addition makes a hearty breakfast tasty and satisfying.

Yield: 1 serving
Prep time: 2 minutes
Cook time: 9 minutes
Each serving has:
505 calories
22 g total fat
2 g saturated fat
14 g protein
69 g carbohydrate
9 g fiber
0 mg cholesterol
12 mg sodium

2 TB. unsalted sliced almonds

2 TB. unsalted diced walnuts

1 cup water

½ cup old-fashioned rolled oats

2 TB. honey

1 TB. flaxseeds

1. Place almonds and walnuts in a small, dry, nonstick skillet over medium heat. Cook for 5 minutes or until lightly toasted, shaking the skillet occasionally to prevent burning.

2. Pour water in a medium nonstick saucepan and bring to a boil over high heat. Stir in oats and reduce heat to medium. Cook for 5 or 6 minutes or until done, stirring occasionally.

3. When nuts are toasted, pour into a serving bowl. Drizzle 1 tablespoon honey over nuts, and toss to coat. When oats are done, remove from heat and stir in flaxseeds and remaining 1 tablespoon honey. Add to the serving bowl and stir to combine with nuts. Serve hot.

Variation: Substitute fat-free soy milk for water for yet another superfood ingredient.

 Kryptonite

This belly-warming cereal might be a tad high in calories for breakfast, but keep in mind that it contains very little saturated fat or sodium and it's packed with super nutrition.

Speedy Sweet-Topped English Muffins

Honey adds its sweet touch to bring creamy peanut butter and sassy strawberries together atop a whole-grain breakfast favorite.

2 whole-wheat English muffins

2 TB. natural peanut butter

1½ TB. honey

4 large frozen strawberries, thawed and drained

1. Split English muffins into halves. Toast to desired doneness.

2. In a small bowl, stir together peanut butter and honey until blended. In another small bowl, mash strawberries with the back of a fork until broken up. Stir into peanut butter mixture to blend.

3. Spread 1 heaping tablespoon peanut butter mixture on top of each English muffin half.

Yield: 2 servings
Prep time: 3 minutes
Serving size: 1 English muffin
Each serving has:
290 calories
9 g total fat
1 g saturated fat
10 g protein
45 g carbohydrate
6 g fiber
0 mg cholesterol
483 mg sodium

Heroic Hints

Even if you wake to find you've forgotten to thaw the strawberries, you can still make this breakfast in a flash. Place the frozen strawberries in a small microwave-safe bowl and defrost (30-percent power) for 1 minute or until thawed. Drain well and mash in the bowl as directed.

Chapter 19

Loving Lunch

In This Chapter

◆ Midday energizers

◆ Fast and healthful lunches

◆ Flavorful lunchbox fillers

Sixty years ago it wasn't uncommon for men to come home at lunch time for a hot meal. Of course, 60 years ago it also wasn't uncommon for his wife to be home all day and able to cook that meal! Times certainly have changed. Today, lunch has all but dwindled to a quick meal on the run or worse, its skipped altogether.

For the energy you need to make it through the afternoon, lunch is a must. And there's certainly nothing wrong with a simple sandwich, but that noon-time meal can be so much more, even if you don't have all morning to prepare it like in days of old.

Let's Do Lunch

If you're like most people, when 12 noon hits, your breakfast has worn off and you're in need of an energy reviver. That's exactly what lunch does. Once breakfast is out of your belly, its lunch's job to get in there, get things going again, and help you make it through the rest of the afternoon.

But there's no need to rely solely on the office vending machine or local fast-food joint. With a little bit of advance planning, you can enjoy a different delicious and healthful lunch every day of the week. And most likely, you'll save yourself a few bucks while you're at it.

Kryptonite

Many fast-food combo meals provide more than a day's worth of heart-clogging saturated fat and almost an entire day's worth of calories—in just one meal!

Blueberry and Walnut Spinach Salad

With an intriguing combination of flavors, this novel salad is guaranteed to tantalize your taste buds.

2 TB. unsalted chopped walnuts

1 cup packed fresh spinach

¼ cup fresh blueberries

2 TB. reduced-fat crumbled feta cheese

Pinch freshly ground black pepper

1 TB. Sweet-to-Your-Heart Salad Dressing (recipe in Chapter 17)

Yield: 1 serving
Prep time: 5 minutes
Cook time: 5 minutes
Each serving has:
178 calories
12 g total fat
2 g saturated fat
7 g protein
15 g carbohydrate
3 g fiber
7 mg cholesterol
269 mg sodium

1. Place walnuts in a small, dry, nonstick skillet over medium heat. Cook for 5 minutes or until lightly toasted, shaking the skillet occasionally to prevent burning. Remove walnuts from the skillet to cool.

2. Combine spinach, blueberries, walnuts, feta cheese, and black pepper in a serving bowl. Drizzle salad dressing over top and toss to coat evenly. Serve immediately.

Heroic Hints

Toasting nuts enables them to develop a golden crispness and deeper flavor. You can pretoast nuts to save time and have them on hand when needed. Let them cool completely before storing in an airtight container at room temperature, and use them within one week.

Zippy Four-Bean Salad

Great for a carry-in dish, this palate-pleasing bean salad is chock-full of superfoods and great taste.

Yield: 14 servings
Prep time: 10 minutes
Chill time: 2 hours
Serving size: ¹/₂ cup
Each serving has:
107 calories
5 g total fat
1 g saturated fat
4 g protein
12 g carbohydrate
4 g fiber
0 mg cholesterol
243 mg sodium

½ cup cider vinegar

¼ cup *extra-virgin olive oil*

1 TB. honey

½ tsp. dry mustard

¼ tsp. garlic powder

¼ tsp. onion powder

¼ tsp. freshly ground black pepper

¼ tsp. cayenne

1 (14.5-oz.) can no-salt-added cut green beans, rinsed and drained

1 (14.5-oz.) can cut wax beans, rinsed and drained

1 (15-oz.) can dark red kidney beans, rinsed and drained

1 (15-oz.) can garbanzo beans, rinsed and drained

4 green onions, trimmed and finely chopped

½ small red bell pepper, ribs and seeds removed, and finely diced

1. Combine vinegar, olive oil, honey, dry mustard, garlic powder, onion powder, black pepper, and cayenne in a large, shallow bowl. Stir until well blended.

2. Stir in green beans, wax beans, kidney beans, garbanzo beans, green onions, and red bell pepper until evenly coated. Cover and chill for at least 2 hours before serving. Stir again before serving.

def•i•ni•tion

Extra-virgin olive oil is the product of the first pressing of olives without the use of heat or chemicals. Fragrant and low-acid (and a bit more costly than other olive oils), extra-virgin olive oil is best used in dressings and marinades and as a condiment. Extra-virgin olive oil is notably high in healthful monounsaturated fat.

Simple Pasta Salad with Veggies and Kidney Beans

Toss together this collection of superfoods when you need an easy and tasty make-ahead dish for a picnic or potluck.

1 (12-oz.) pkg. whole-wheat rotini pasta

1 (15-oz.) can dark red kidney beans, rinsed and drained

¾ cup diced tomatoes

½ cup small broccoli florets

½ cup diced red bell pepper

¼ cup thinly sliced carrots

1 (16-oz.) bottle low-fat Italian salad dressing

Yield: 24 servings
Prep time: 5 minutes
Cook time: 15 minutes
Chill time: 6 to 8 hours
Serving size: ¹/₂ cup
Each serving has:
103 calories
3 g total fat
<1 g saturated fat
4 g protein
15 g carbohydrate
3 g fiber
<1 mg cholesterol
192 mg sodium

1. Cook pasta according to the package directions. Drain and rinse under cold water, and transfer to a 3-quart container.

2. Stir in beans, tomatoes, broccoli florets, red bell pepper, and carrots. Pour salad dressing over top, and stir until evenly coated. Cover and chill for 6 to 8 hours or overnight. Stir again before serving.

Super Knowledge

When shopping for red bell peppers, select ones that are firm, unblemished, and heavy. Store them in the refrigerator in the plastic produce bag and use them within a week.

Classic Middle Eastern Tabbouleh

Set your taste buds tingling with this nutty-flavored whole-grain salad that relies heavily on the refreshing, faintly peppery taste of parsley.

Yield: 8 servings
Prep time: 3 minutes
Soak time: 30 minutes
Chill time: 2 hours
Serving size: ½ cup
Each serving has:
125 calories
9 g total fat
1 g saturated fat
2 g protein
10 g carbohydrate
2 g fiber
0 mg cholesterol
47 mg sodium

½ cup *bulgur*

½ cup water

2 medium tomatoes, seeded and finely diced

1½ cups very finely chopped fresh parsley

4 green onions, very finely chopped

2 TB. very finely chopped fresh mint

⅓ cup extra-virgin olive oil

3 TB. lemon juice

⅛ tsp. salt

⅛ tsp. cayenne

1. Place bulgur in a small bowl and pour in water. Soak for 30 minutes or until softened and water is absorbed.

2. Meanwhile, combine tomatoes, parsley, green onions, and mint in a medium bowl.

3. In another small bowl, whisk together olive oil, lemon juice, salt, and cayenne until blended.

4. When bulgur is softened, stir into tomato mixture. Pour olive oil mixture over top, and stir to coat evenly. Cover and chill for at least 2 hours or until cold. Stir again before serving with romaine lettuce leaves to scoop it up or on a sample platter of Middle Eastern delights.

def•i•ni•tion

Bulgur is wheat that's been steamed or parboiled, dried, and ground into different textures: fine, medium, and coarse. Use fine bulgur for this salad, if available.

Chilly Cherry Soup

Get your taste buds tingling from the start of your meal with this cold, tart, spiced soup.

½ **cup fresh or unsweetened orange juice**

¼ **cup honey**

2 TB. lime juice

1 tsp. grated lime zest

Scant ½ **tsp. ground cinnamon**

2 (14.5-oz.) cans pitted red tart cherries in water, drained

Yield: 6 servings
Prep time: 4 minutes
Cook time: 15 minutes
Chill time: 4 hours
Serving size: ½ cup
Each serving has:
107 calories
0 g total fat
0 g saturated fat
2 g protein
27 g carbohydrate
2 g fiber
0 mg cholesterol
4 mg sodium

1. Stir together orange juice, honey, lime juice, lime zest, and cinnamon in a medium saucepan.

2. Turn cherries into a blender and chop on low speed for 15 seconds or until finely chopped. Stir into orange juice mixture and bring to a boil over high heat. Stir, reduce heat, cover, and simmer for 10 minutes.

3. Pour soup into a storage container, and plunge it into ice water to cool quickly. Cover and chill for at least 4 hours or until cold. Stir again before serving.

 Super Knowledge

Thanks almost entirely to the cherries, a serving of this cool soup supplies hefty doses of vitamin A and beta-carotene.

Very Berry Strawberry Soup

Solely superfood ingredients blend to make this creamy, cold soup every berry lover will delight in.

Yield: 4 servings
Prep time: 2 minutes
Chill time: 1 hour
Serving size: ¾ cup
Each serving has:
94 calories
<1 g total fat
0 g saturated fat
4 g protein
22 g carbohydrate
3 g fiber
1 mg cholesterol
35 mg sodium

4 cups hulled fresh whole strawberries

1 cup fat-free plain yogurt

¼ cup fresh or unsweetened orange juice

1 TB. honey

1. Combine strawberries, yogurt, orange juice, and honey in a blender. Cover and purée on low speed for 45 seconds or until blended.

2. Cover and chill soup for at least 1 hour. Stir again before serving.

 Kryptonite _____

Flavored yogurts often have a good deal of added sugar. Using plain yogurt in this sweet soup saves you almost 1½ teaspoons extra sugar per serving.

Golden Pumpkin Soup

Start your meal off right with this broth-based soup of spiced pumpkin with an undertone of fresh tomatoes.

1 tsp. extra-virgin or light olive oil	**1 small tomato, peeled and diced**
½ cup chopped green onions	**¼ tsp. ground nutmeg**
1 (14-oz.) can fat-free, less-sodium chicken broth	**¼ tsp. freshly ground black pepper**
1 (15-oz.) can pure pumpkin	**1 cup fat-free evaporated milk**

Yield: 9 servings
Prep time: 7 minutes
Cook time: 25 minutes
Serving size: ¹/₂ cup
Each serving has:
52 calories
1 g total fat
<1 g saturated fat
3 g protein
8 g carbohydrate
2 g fiber
1 mg cholesterol
68 mg sodium

1. Heat olive oil in a medium nonstick saucepan over medium heat. Add green onions and sauté for 2 minutes. Add 1 cup broth, pumpkin, tomato, nutmeg, and black pepper, stirring to blend. Bring just to a boil over medium heat. Reduce heat and gently simmer for 15 minutes.

2. Transfer mixture to a blender and purée for 30 to 45 seconds or until smooth. Return to the saucepan and stir in remaining broth and evaporated milk. Heat over very low heat for 5 minutes or until heated through. (Do not boil.) Serve hot or cold with a dollop of sour cream and a sprinkling of chopped green onions, if desired.

Heroic Hints

To peel a tomato, score an X in the blossom end and then submerge the tomato in boiling water for 20 to 60 seconds. Immediately immerse the tomato in very cold water. Use the tip of a small knife to remove the skin, which should slide right off.

Secret-Ingredient Chili con Carne

Sprinkle in a little cocoa powder for a rich, brown sauce on this meaty chili.

Yield: 5 servings
Prep time: 5 minutes
Cook time: 1 hour, 25 minutes
Serving size: 1 cup
Each serving has:
253 calories
8 g total fat
3 g saturated fat
23 g protein
20 g carbohydrate
5 g fiber
56 mg cholesterol
930 mg sodium

1 lb. ground sirloin

1 medium yellow onion, chopped

2 medium cloves garlic, minced

1 TB. chili powder

1 tsp. salt

1 tsp. dried oregano

1 tsp. unsweetened cocoa powder

1 tsp. hot pepper sauce

¼ tsp. ground ginger

1 (14.5-oz.) can diced tomatoes, undrained

1 (15-oz.) can dark red kidney beans, rinsed and drained

1. Cook ground sirloin, onion, and garlic in a large nonstick saucepan over medium heat for 8 minutes or until meat is browned, stirring to break up meat. Drain well.

2. Return the saucepan to the heat, and stir in chili powder, salt, oregano, cocoa powder, hot pepper sauce, ginger, and tomatoes. Bring to a boil over medium heat. Reduce heat, cover, and simmer for 1 hour, stirring occasionally.

3. Stir in beans, cover, and simmer for 15 minutes or until heated through. Serve hot.

Heroic Hints

When you want to cook a recipe that calls for hot pepper sauce but find you don't have any on hand, substitute a mixture with a superfood ingredient. Blend ¾ teaspoon cayenne with 1 teaspoon white vinegar for each teaspoon of hot pepper sauce called for.

Raw Veggie Wraps

When you need a quick, nutrient-packed pick-me-up for lunch, build this wonderful wrap stuffed with superfoods.

1 TB. fat-free plain yogurt

1 TB. yellow mustard or to taste

2 (7-in.) whole-wheat tortillas

½ small red bell pepper, ribs and seeds removed, and cut into thin strips

⅓ cup small broccoli florets

⅓ cup diced tomatoes

¼ cup shredded carrots

¼ cup broccoli sprouts or alfalfa sprouts

Yield: 2 servings
Prep time: 5 minutes
Serving size: 1 tortilla
Each serving has:
100 calories
1 g total fat
<1 g saturated fat
5 g protein
25 g carbohydrate
4 g fiber
<1 mg cholesterol
285 mg sodium

1. In a small bowl, stir together yogurt and mustard until blended. Spread evenly over tortillas, leaving 1-inch margins around edges.

2. Top tortillas with red bell pepper, broccoli florets, tomatoes, carrots, and sprouts. Fold over left sides of tortillas, fold up bottoms, and fold over right sides to enclose filling. Serve immediately.

Super Knowledge

An alternative to alfalfa sprouts, broccoli sprouts contain many times more of the cancer-fighting phytochemical sulforaphane than full-grown broccoli does.

Walnut Hummus Pitas

Scoop up the delicious flavor of this nutty hummus with torn pieces of warm pita bread for a Middle East–inspired lunch.

Yield: 6 servings
Prep time: 5 minutes
Cook time: 5 minutes
Serving size: 1 pita pocket with ¼ cup hummus
Each serving has:
210 calories
5 g total fat
<1 g saturated fat
9 g protein
35 g carbohydrate
6 g fiber
0 mg cholesterol
426 mg sodium

¼ **cup unsalted chopped walnuts**

1 (15-oz.) can garbanzo beans, undrained

3 medium cloves garlic

2 TB. lemon juice

½ **tsp. ground cumin**

6 (6-in.) whole-wheat pita pockets, warmed

1. Place walnuts in a small, dry, nonstick skillet over medium heat. Cook for 5 minutes or until lightly toasted, shaking the skillet occasionally to prevent burning.

2. Drain garbanzo beans, reserving ¼ cup liquid. Combine garbanzo beans, reserved liquid, walnuts, garlic, lemon juice, and cumin in a blender. Cover and grind on high speed for 2 minutes or until well blended, stopping the blender to scrape down the sides as needed. Serve hummus alongside warmed pita pockets.

Heroic Hints

For an extra-super boost, dip raw veggies, such as red bell peppers, carrots, and broccoli, in the hummus.

Thanksgiving Memories Open-Faced Turkey Sandwiches

Whenever you get a hankering for the taste of the traditional holiday feast, you can savor the flavors in this simple sandwich.

½ cup Whole Orange Cranberry Relish (recipe in Chapter 3) or store-bought cranberry-orange relish

¼ cup reduced-fat mayonnaise

2 TB. chopped green onions

½ TB. prepared horseradish

4 slices rye bread from a round loaf

¾ lb. thinly sliced cooked turkey breast

4 (1-oz.) slices provolone cheese

Yield: 4 servings
Prep time: 5 minutes
Chill time: 1 hour
Cook time: 10 minutes
Serving size: 1 sandwich
Each serving has:
354 calories
11 g total fat
6 g saturated fat
36 g protein
27 g carbohydrate
5 g fiber
90 mg cholesterol
500 mg sodium

1. Combine 2 tablespoons relish, mayonnaise, green onions, and horseradish in a small bowl until well blended. Cover and chill for at least 1 hour to allow flavors to meld.

2. Preheat the oven to 400°F.

3. Place bread slices on a large nonstick baking sheet. Evenly spread relish mixture over bread slices, place turkey on top, and cover with cheese. Bake for 10 minutes or until heated through and cheese is melted. Serve hot with remaining relish.

Kryptonite

This recipe calls for fresh cooked turkey breast. If you use deli meat instead, be aware that the sodium content is much higher. For convenience and sodium sensibility, look for low-sodium deli selections.

Grown-Up Grilled Soy Cheese Sandwiches

Growing up doesn't mean foregoing an ooey, gooey lunchtime favorite, but your palate may crave a bit more sophisticated sandwich these days ….

Yield: 2 servings
Prep time: 2 minutes
Cook time: 9 to 11 minutes
Serving size: 1 sandwich
Each serving has:
228 calories
7 g total fat
1 g saturated fat
13 g protein
31 g carbohydrate
7 g fiber
0 mg cholesterol
587 mg sodium

1 tsp. olive oil

1 small yellow onion, thinly sliced and halved

½ small red bell pepper, ribs and seeds removed, and thinly sliced

½ cup packed fresh spinach

4 (1-oz.) slices whole-wheat or multi-grain bread

Fat-free, calorie-free buttery spray

2 slices cheddar-flavor soy cheese alternative

1. Heat olive oil in a large nonstick skillet over medium heat. Add onion and red bell pepper, and sauté for 5 minutes or until onion is softened. Stir in spinach and sauté for 2 minutes or until spinach is wilted.

2. Meanwhile, spray one side of each bread slice with buttery spray. Top unbuttered sides of 2 bread slices with 1 piece of cheese each. Evenly divide onion mixture over cheese. Close sandwiches with remaining bread slices, butter side up.

3. Transfer sandwiches to the skillet over medium heat and cook for 1 or 2 minutes on each side or until golden brown. Cut in half diagonally to serve.

Variation: Substitute your favorite flavor soy cheese. Try smoked provolone or pepper jack slices.

 Kryptonite

Foods added to oils for sautéing should be dry. Moisture can cause splattering and/or steaming instead of sautéing.

Tasty Two-Bean Soup with Carrots

Ready in 15 minutes, this soup can add its warm, earthy flavor to any short-on-time lunch.

1½ cups drained cooked or canned garbanzo beans

1½ cups drained cooked or canned pinto beans

½ cup shredded carrots

1 (14-oz.) can fat-free, less-sodium chicken broth

⅛ tsp. cayenne or more to taste

Yield: 3 servings	
Prep time: 5 minutes	
Cook time: 10 minutes	
Serving size: 1 cup	
Each serving has:	
242 calories	
3 g total fat	
<1 g saturated fat	
16 g protein	
38 g carbohydrate	
13 g fiber	
3 mg cholesterol	
724 mg sodium	

1. Combine garbanzo beans, pinto beans, carrots, and chicken broth in a medium pan. Stir in cayenne. Bring to a boil over high heat.

2. Reduce heat to medium-high. Cook, stirring occasionally, for 5 minutes or until carrots are tender.

3. Transfer soup to a serving bowl. Using the back of a fork, mash the beans to break up. Serve hot.

Super Knowledge

A staple of salad bars, garbanzo beans are cream-colored, peach-shaped beans. When shopping, you'll want to watch for the garbanzo beans' aliases: chickpeas and ceci beans.

Chapter 20

Dinnertime Delights

In This Chapter

- ◆ Add some variety to the dinner table
- ◆ Two for dinner?
- ◆ Enjoyable evening eating

Dinner is more than just the last time in the day to eat. If you're single, this is the time to relax and unwind from the day. If you have a family, it's the time to catch up and reconnect. Whatever your situation, try to remember that the goal is to enjoy it and nourish yourself.

But you're in a dinner rut, you say? No need to be. The following pages offer lots of great ways to add excitement and health to your end-of-the-day meal.

Dinner Date

By preparing your meals with a variety of superfoods, you get many benefits at one time. In some cases, the benefits are even stronger when superfoods are combined than when the foods are eaten by themselves.

One example of this is the Fiesta Salsa Pork Chops. This flavorful entrée includes both broccoli and canned tomatoes. You've already read about the cancer-fighting properties these two foods possess. However, research has shown that when these two foods are eaten together their prostate cancer–fighting power is even stronger—possibly stronger than some medications used to treat the disease. More research is being done to find other extra-potent superfood combinations.

Super Knowledge

You might think that ordering take-out is a faster way to get dinner on the table than cooking yourself. But that can often take a half hour or more, while several of the recipes in this chapter take 20 minutes or less to prepare. In addition, when you cook your own dinner, you're in control. That means the food is most likely healthier, fresher, and less expensive. Plus, you can jazz it up to your tastes with extra spices, less salt, or a different kind of pasta—whatever *you* desire.

Fiesta Salsa Pork Chops

A mingling of Tex-Mex flavors spice up your everyday pork chops for a family-pleasing favorite.

1½ lb. boneless pork chops, trimmed of fat and cut into serving-size pieces

1 (14.5-oz.) can diced tomatoes with garlic and onion

½ cup salsa

1 tsp. chili powder

2 cups broccoli florets

½ small red bell pepper, ribs and seeds removed, and cut into small strips

½ cup frozen whole-kernel corn

1 (15-oz.) can black beans, rinsed and drained

Yield: 6 servings
Prep time: 5 minutes
Cook time: 18 minutes
Serving size: 4 ounces pork with ¾ cup sauce
Each serving has:
288 calories
12 g total fat
5 g saturated fat
28 g protein
17 g carbohydrate
5 g fiber
73 mg cholesterol
439 mg sodium

1. Coat a large, deep skillet with nonstick cooking spray and heat over medium heat. Add pork chops and cook for 4 minutes on each side or until browned.

2. Stir in tomatoes with garlic and onion, salsa, and chili powder. Cover and cook over medium heat for 5 minutes.

3. Add broccoli, red bell pepper, and corn. Turn pork chops over on top of vegetables and add black beans. Cover and cook over medium heat for 5 minutes or until pork chops read 160°F on a food thermometer and vegetables are tender. Serve vegetable mixture over pork chops.

Kryptonite

Take care when using canned black beans. The packing liquid takes on the beans' purplish-black color, and it can stain easily. Be sure to rinse all equipment well, and watch for any countertop rings from the can.

Italian-Style Turkey Loaf

This spinach-stuffed loaf is so attractive and delicious, your family will forget they're eating humble meatloaf and instead compliment your culinary skills.

Yield: 8 servings
Prep time: 12 minutes
Cook time: 50 to 55 minutes
Stand time: 10 minutes
Serving size: 1 slice
Each serving has:
176 calories
4 g total fat
1 g saturated fat
26 g protein
12 g carbohydrate
2 g fiber
83 mg cholesterol
441 mg sodium

1 (1.2-lb.) pkg. 99 percent fat-free extra-lean ground turkey breast

1¼ cups plain spaghetti sauce or marinara sauce

½ cup diced yellow onions

½ cup plain dry breadcrumbs

2 TB. shredded Parmesan cheese

½ TB. Italian seasoning

2 large eggs, at room temperature, or the equivalent amount of egg substitute

1 (10-oz.) pkg. frozen chopped spinach, thawed and well drained

¾ cup fat-free shredded mozzarella cheese

1. Preheat the oven to 350°F.

2. Combine ground turkey, ¼ cup spaghetti sauce, onions, breadcrumbs, Parmesan cheese, Italian seasoning, and eggs in a large bowl, and mix with your hands or stir to blend well. Place ⅔ of mixture in a 9¼×5¼×2¾-inch nonstick loaf pan and pat down evenly. Make a 1-inch-deep indentation in the center of mixture, leaving 1-inch margins around the edges.

3. Stir together spinach and mozzarella cheese in a medium bowl. Fill the indentation with spinach mixture, pressing in evenly.

4. Top with remaining turkey mixture, pressing down evenly to seal edges. Bake for 40 to 45 minutes or until edges are slightly pulled away from the pan and the internal temperature reads 165°F on a food thermometer. Spoon remaining 1 cup spaghetti sauce over top of loaf. Bake for 10 minutes or until sauce is bubbling. Let stand for 10 minutes before slicing to serve.

Heroic Hints

To prepare well-drained spinach for recipes, press initially drained spinach between layers of paper towels until dry.

Spinach-Bedded Salmon Bake

Simple and appealing, this seasoned-spinach fish dish is the dinner you're looking for on those rushed evenings.

3 cups packed fresh spinach

3 (4-oz.) boneless salmon fillets

⅛ tsp. cayenne

⅛ tsp. onion powder

⅛ tsp. salt

1. Preheat the oven to 400°F. Coat an 8×8×2-inch glass baking dish with nonstick cooking spray.

2. Wash spinach, loosely drain, and place it in the baking dish with any water that clings to the leaves. Arrange salmon fillets on top. Sprinkle cayenne, onion powder, and salt evenly over salmon.

3. Bake for 15 minutes or until fish flakes easily with a fork. Remove skin from fillets and discard skin. Serve salmon atop spinach.

Heroic Hints

To remove the skin from the salmon fillets easily, slide a spatula between the flesh and the skin. The skin should slip off easily after cooking.

Yield: 3 servings
Prep time: 5 minutes
Cook time: 15 minutes
Serving size: 3 ounces salmon atop ¼ cup spinach
Each serving has:
230 calories
13 g total fat
3 g saturated fat
26 g protein
1 g carbohydrate
1 g fiber
82 mg cholesterol
179 mg sodium

Greek Spinach, Feta, and Cannellini Orzo

A medley of Mediterranean tastes meld for a simple, mouthwatering meal.

Yield: 8 servings
Prep time: 5 minutes
Cook time: 12 minutes
Serving size: 1 cup
Each serving has:
213 calories
4 g total fat
2 g saturated fat
12 g protein
35 g carbohydrate
4 g fiber
7 mg cholesterol
642 mg sodium

1 tsp. extra-virgin or light olive oil

2 medium cloves garlic, minced

1 (28-oz.) can diced tomatoes, undrained

1 (15.5-oz.) can cannellini beans, rinsed and drained

½ cup chopped fresh basil or 3 TB. dried

1 TB. chopped fresh oregano or 1 tsp. dried

4 cups packed fresh spinach

4 cups cooked orzo pasta

1 cup reduced-fat crumbled feta cheese

1. Heat olive oil in a large, deep skillet over medium heat. Add garlic and sauté for 1 minute. Add tomatoes, cannellini beans, basil, and oregano. Stir and bring to a boil. Reduce heat to low or medium-low and simmer for 5 minutes. Add spinach and stir for 2 minutes or until wilted.

2. Stir in orzo pasta until evenly coated. Turn off heat. Stir in feta cheese until evenly distributed. Serve hot.

 Heroic Hints

When preparing pasta, omit the salt and oil sometimes called for in the package directions. You'll save on unnecessary sodium and fat in your dishes.

After-Work Mac and Bean Stew

When you need a quick, filling supper, let this veggie-studded stew simmer on the stove while you toss a green salad and warm the bread.

1 (16-oz.) can navy beans, rinsed and drained

1 (15-oz.) can black beans, rinsed and drained

1 (14-oz.) can fat-free, less-sodium chicken broth

1 cup coarsely chopped tomatoes

¾ cup uncooked whole-wheat elbow macaroni

¼ cup chopped yellow onions

¼ cup chopped green bell pepper

1 medium clove garlic, minced

1 TB. chopped fresh basil

1 tsp. Worcestershire sauce

Yield: 5 *servings*
Prep time: 3 minutes
Cook time: 20 minutes
Serving size: 1 cup
Each serving has:
196 calories
1 g total fat
<1 g saturated fat
13 g protein
38 g carbohydrate
10 g fiber
2 mg cholesterol
656 mg sodium

1. Stir together navy beans, black beans, broth, tomatoes, macaroni, onions, green bell pepper, garlic, basil, and Worcestershire sauce in a large saucepan. Bring to a boil over high heat, stirring occasionally.

2. Reduce heat, cover, and simmer for 15 minutes or until macaroni is done, stirring occasionally. Serve hot.

Variation: Substitute red bell pepper for green to add another superfood to this stew.

 Heroic Hints _____

To reduce the sodium content of this quick dish, look for no-salt-added canned beans and reduced-sodium Worcestershire sauce.

Veggie Lentil Bake over Rice

Try this protein-packed vegetarian meal on meatless Mondays … or any other day of the week you want a delicious, Asian-flavored dinner.

Yield: 4 servings

Prep time: 5 minutes

Cook time: 70 to 80 minutes

Serving size: 1 cup lentils over 1 cup rice

Each serving has:

498 calories

4 g total fat

1 g saturated fat

19 g protein

100 g carbohydrate

15 g fiber

0 mg cholesterol

571 mg sodium

1 cup dried lentils

4 cups water

1 tsp. olive oil

½ cup thinly sliced carrots

¼ cup diced yellow onions

¼ cup diced celery

⅓ cup honey

¼ cup reduced-sodium soy sauce

1 tsp. dry mustard

½ tsp. freshly ground black pepper

¼ tsp. ground ginger

4 cups cooked long-grain brown rice

1. Place lentils in a large saucepan, add water, and bring to a boil over high heat. Reduce heat, cover with a slightly vented lid, and simmer for 15 to 20 minutes or until tender. Drain.

2. Meanwhile, heat olive oil in a small nonstick skillet over medium heat. Add carrots, onions, and celery, and sauté for 3 to 5 minutes or until onions are softened.

3. Preheat the oven to 350°F.

4. Whisk together honey, soy sauce, dry mustard, black pepper, and ginger in a small bowl until blended. When lentils are done, pour into an 8×8×2-inch glass baking dish. Pour honey mixture over lentils. Add carrot mixture, stir until mixed, and cover. Bake for 40 minutes and then uncover and bake for 5 to 10 minutes or until bubbly but not dry. Spoon lentil mixture over rice to serve.

Kryptonite

While beans are generally packaged carefully with today's modern cleaning equipment, you should still sort them before cooking. Sift though the beans to remove any shriveled beans or—ouch!—small pebbles.

Super Pizza Sauce

Enjoy this rich, deeply flavored pizza sauce in all your favorite ways—ladle over your pizza crust, dunk your breadsticks, scoop onto your cheese sticks—while reaping its health benefits.

1 tsp. olive oil

1 medium yellow onion, diced

3 medium cloves garlic, minced

2 (6-oz.) cans tomato paste

1 (28-oz.) can crushed tomatoes

½ cup cabernet sauvignon or other red wine

1 TB. honey

1 tsp. chopped fresh basil or ¼ tsp. dried

½ tsp. dried oregano

¼ tsp. ground savory

¼ tsp. dried thyme

⅛ tsp. cayenne

⅛ tsp. salt

⅛ tsp. freshly ground black pepper

Yield: 5 cups
Prep time: 5 minutes
Cook time: 30 minutes
Serving size: ¹/₂ cup
Each serving has:
80 calories
1 g total fat
<1 g saturated fat
3 g protein
16 g carbohydrate
3 g fiber
0 mg cholesterol
404 mg sodium

1. Heat olive oil in a large saucepan over medium heat. Add onion and garlic, and sauté for 5 minutes or until onion is golden.

2. Reduce heat to medium-low. Add tomato paste, crushed tomatoes, wine, honey, basil, oregano, savory, thyme, cayenne, salt, and black pepper, and stir to blend. Bring to a simmer over medium-low or medium heat. Reduce heat and gently simmer for 20 minutes, stirring occasionally. Serve hot.

Super Knowledge

Cabernet sauvignon is the wine with the greatest amount of flavonoids. Other top choices are petit syrah and pinot noir. Pass on merlots and red zinfandels if you're looking for flavonoids, as these contain the least.

Greek Stuffed Red Bell Peppers

Favorite Mediterranean flavors—feta, olives, spinach, orzo, and mint—pack sweet bell peppers for an enticing taste treat.

Yield: 6 servings

Prep time: 5 minutes

Cook time: 30 minutes

Serving size: ¹/₂ bell pepper

Each serving has:

140 calories

4 g total fat

2 g saturated fat

10 g protein

19 g carbohydrate

4 g fiber

9 mg cholesterol

402 mg sodium

2 cups cooked orzo pasta

1 (10-oz.) pkg. chopped frozen spinach, thawed and drained

1 cup reduced-fat crumbled feta cheese

1 TB. chopped fresh mint

3 medium red bell peppers, ribs and seeds removed, and halved

6 large pitted black olives, halved

1. Preheat the oven to 350°F. Coat a 13×9×2-inch or other large glass baking dish with nonstick cooking spray.

2. Stir together pasta, spinach, feta, and mint in a medium bowl. Spoon into red bell pepper halves and place in the baking dish. Garnish with olives. Bake for 30 minutes or until heated through and red bell peppers are crisp-tender.

 Heroic Hints

> If you want to keep these stuffed peppers authentically Greek, choose kalamata olives. As long as they're not too large, you can use a cherry pitter to remove the pits.

Cranberry and Walnut Rice Medley

The flavors might put you in mind of the Thanksgiving feast, but you'll want to enjoy this simple-to-prepare side dish year-round.

½ cup long-grain brown rice

¼ cup wild rice

1 (14-oz.) can fat-free, less-sodium chicken broth

¾ cup water

¼ cup dried cranberries

¼ cup unsalted diced walnuts

¼ tsp. onion powder

Yield: 7 servings	
Prep time: 3 minutes	
Cook time: 1 hour	
Serving size: ¹/₂ cup	
Each serving has:	
119 calories	
3 g total fat	
<1 g saturated fat	
4 g protein	
19 g carbohydrate	
2 g fiber	
1 mg cholesterol	
39 mg sodium	

1. Combine brown rice and wild rice in a medium nonstick saucepan, and add broth and water. Bring to a boil over high heat. Reduce heat to low or medium-low, cover, and simmer for 45 minutes.

2. Stir dried cranberries, walnuts, and onion powder into rice mixture. Cover and continue to simmer for 15 minutes or until rice is tender and liquid is absorbed. Fluff with a fork before serving.

Super Knowledge

Wild rice is technically not a rice at all, but the seed of an aquatic grass. Once harvested by Native Americans of the northern Great Lakes region, wild rice is now cultivated. The dark brown grains have a nutty flavor and chewy texture.

Hint-of-Dijon Broccoli with Toasted Almonds

Dress up your broccoli with the tangy flavor of Dijon mustard and an almond crunch that's ready in minutes.

Yield: 6 servings
Prep time: 2 minutes
Cook time: 6 minutes
Serving size: ¹/₂ cup
Each serving has:
165 calories
16 g total fat
2 g saturated fat
3 g protein
4 g carbohydrate
2 g fiber
0 mg cholesterol
24 mg sodium

4 cups broccoli florets

½ cup unsalted sliced almonds

⅓ cup extra-virgin olive oil

¼ cup tarragon white wine vinegar

1 tsp. Dijon mustard

1. Fill a steamer pot or a medium pot or saucepan with enough water to fall below the steamer basket when added, and bring to a boil over high heat. Add broccoli to the steamer basket or a collapsible steamer basket, place the basket in the pot, and cover. Steam broccoli florets over boiling water, reducing heat as necessary to just maintain a boil, for 6 minutes or until crisp-tender.

2. Place almonds in a small, dry, nonstick skillet over medium heat. Cook for 6 minutes or until almonds are golden brown, shaking skillet occasionally to prevent burning.

3. Meanwhile, combine olive oil, vinegar, and Dijon mustard in a serving bowl. Stir until blended. Add cooked broccoli and toss to coat. Stir in almonds until evenly distributed and serve.

 Heroic Hints

Savor every last bit of Dijon mustard by pouring the vinegar over the teaspoon to wash it out into the serving bowl.

Thai-Sauced Mixed Vegetables

Prepare this quick and easy veggie side dish awash in a peanut butter and soy sauce flavor combination when you're expecting a crowd, or cut the recipe in half when you don't need as much.

4 cups sliced carrots

4 cups broccoli florets

1 (6-oz.) pkg. snow peas (about 3 cups)

½ cup honey

¼ cup no-salt natural peanut butter

2 TB. reduced-sodium soy sauce

1 TB. chopped fresh cilantro

⅛ tsp. crushed red pepper flakes

8 cups cooked long-grain brown rice

Yield: 16 servings
Prep time: 2 minutes
Cook time: 5 to 7 minutes
Serving size: ¹/₂ cup vegetables with ¹/₂ cup rice
Each serving has:
189 calories
3 g total fat
<1 g saturated fat
5 g protein
36 g carbohydrate
4 g fiber
0 mg cholesterol
99 mg sodium

1. Fill a steamer pot or a large pot or saucepan with enough water to fall below the steamer basket when added, and bring to a boil over high heat. Add carrots, broccoli florets, and snow peas to the steamer basket or a collapsible steamer basket, place the basket in the pot, and cover. Steam carrots, broccoli florets, and snow peas over boiling water, reducing heat as necessary to just maintain a boil, for 5 to 7 minutes or until crisp-tender.

2. Meanwhile, combine honey, peanut butter, soy sauce, cilantro, and crushed red pepper flakes in a small bowl, and stir until well blended.

3. Transfer steamed vegetables to a large serving bowl, pour honey mixture over top, and stir to coat. Line individual serving plates with rice and spoon vegetables with sauce over top to serve.

def•i•ni•tion

Steam indicates the method of suspending a food over boiling water to allow the heat of the water vapor to cook the food. Steaming can also be accomplished by microwaving. Specially designed plastic bags are commercially available for great convenience. Or you might wrap foods tightly in foil or parchment paper and bake them until steamed. Foil packages can steam on the grill, too.

Tremendous Treats

In This Chapter

- ◆ Guilt-free treats
- ◆ Everything in moderation
- ◆ Sweet temptations

Most of us have our guilty pleasures. Maybe you don't feel like a meal is finished until you have a little sweet? Or is it that sugary bite that gets you through a rough day? Whatever the case is for you, go ahead and enjoy. But there's no need for the guilt. The pages to follow are filled with sweet-tooth satisfiers that are healthful to boot.

Treat Yourself

So many people view sweets and treats as "forbidden foods" and feel there's no place for such foods in a healthy diet. For many, however, that all-or-nothing mentality can lead to problems. Banning these foods from your diet can lead to feelings of deprivation, which in turn trigger cravings, which are usually followed by binges. Binges cause guilty feelings, which can go one of two ways—more bingeing or a reinstatement of the ban,

Heroic Hints _____

For some, having a little sweet taste after dinner actually helps maintain a healthy diet because the sweet flavor signifies the end of the meal and helps prevent evening snacking. Not having it may lead to munching all night in hopes of finding some satisfaction.

which follows the same cycle. In the end, you overeat your forbidden foods over and over again.

Instead, let yourself have a small treat occasionally. Depending on your situation and the treat, it could be once a day, once a week, or once or twice a month. You enjoy it, feel satisfied, and have no guilt because the treat fits into your healthy plan.

On top of allowing once-in-a-while treats, what if they were actually good for you? Even less guilt and more reason to allow the indulgence. It's hard to beat a sweet treat that tastes great and also may improve your health!

Super-Moist Orange Honey Cake

Even the most insatiable of sweet tooths will delight in this super-sweet honey-of-a-treat.

2¼ cups uncooked farina or 1 (14-oz.) pkg. Cream of Wheat

¾ cup whole-wheat flour

½ cup all-purpose flour

2 tsp. baking powder

1 tsp. baking soda

½ cup unsalted blanched slivered almonds

3 cups honey

2 cups fat-free plain yogurt

¼ cup partially thawed frozen orange juice concentrate

1 TB. grated orange zest

1½ cups fresh or unsweetened orange juice

Yield: 16 servings
Prep time: 12 minutes
Cook time: 45 minutes
Serving size: 3¹/₄×2¹/₄-inch piece
Each serving has:
369 calories
2 g total fat
<1 g saturated fat
6 g protein
84 g carbohydrate
2 g fiber
1 mg cholesterol
212 mg sodium

1. Preheat the oven to 350°F. Coat a 13×9×2-inch baking pan with nonstick cooking spray.

2. Stir together farina, whole-wheat flour, all-purpose flour, baking powder, baking soda, and almonds in a large bowl.

3. Combine 1¹/₂ cups honey, yogurt, orange juice concentrate, and orange zest in a medium bowl, and stir until blended. Add to farina mixture, stirring until well blended. Pour batter into the baking pan. Bake for 45 minutes or until golden and a cake tester or toothpick inserted into the middle of cake comes out clean.

4. Meanwhile, combine remaining 1¹/₂ cups honey and orange juice in a small nonstick saucepan and stir to blend. Bring to a boil over high heat, reduce heat to low or medium-low, and simmer for 5 minutes. Skim foam from the surface and pour syrup over cake, poking holes in cake with a toothpick to allow more syrup to be absorbed. Cool completely on a wire rack. Cut into pieces to serve. Store any leftovers in the refrigerator.

Heroic Hints

When testing baked goods for doneness, insert a cake tester, a needlelike metal or plastic baking tool, into the center. If crumbs cling to it, the baked good isn't done. When the cake tester comes out clean, the food is finished. A wooden toothpick or even a strand of spaghetti makes a good substitute.

Angelic Pumpkin Trifle

Healthful superfood ingredients, just over 100 calories, and less than 1 gram fat make this dessert indulgent and guilt-free!

Yield: 20 servings	
Prep time: 20 minutes	
Chill time: 2 hours	
Serving size: 1/2 cup	
Each serving has:	
109 calories	
<1 g total fat	
<1 g saturated fat	
3 g protein	
24 g carbohydrate	
2 g fiber	
0 mg cholesterol	
244 mg sodium	

1 (15-oz.) can pure pumpkin

4 (4-serving-size) pkg. sugar-free butterscotch instant pudding mix

1 tsp. ground cinnamon

1/4 tsp. ground allspice

1/4 tsp. ground nutmeg

2 1/2 cups cold fat-free soy milk or milk

1 (16-oz.) prepared angel food cake

1 (8-oz.) pkg. fat-free frozen whipped topping, thawed

1. Combine pumpkin, pudding mix, cinnamon, allspice, nutmeg, and soy milk in a large bowl. Stir until thoroughly blended.

2. Gently tear 1/4 of angel food cake into bite-size pieces and layer on the bottom of a trifle bowl or a 3-quart container. Spoon 1/2 of pumpkin mixture over top. Tear another 1/4 of angel food cake into bite-size pieces and layer over pumpkin mixture. Spoon 1/2 of whipped topping over top. Repeat layering to use all ingredients.

3. Cover and chill for at least 2 hours or until cold. Garnish with a light sprinkling of ground cinnamon, if you like.

Super Knowledge

Angel food cake is butterless and is leavened with egg whites. Baked in a tube pan to be light and airy, angel food cake (without additions) is a fat-free dessert—perfect for weight-watching cake lovers.

Creamy Gelled Fruit Cups

Frothy-topped offerings, these gelatin cups are a great creamy and fruity ending to any meal.

1 cup fat-free soy milk or milk

1 (.25-oz.) pkg. unflavored gelatin

1 cup fresh or unsweetened orange juice

2 TB. honey

1 (10.5-oz.) can mandarin orange segments in mandarin orange juice, drained and coarsely chopped

1 medium banana, peeled and thinly sliced

¼ cup thinly sliced fresh strawberries

Yield: 4 servings
Prep time: 10 minutes
Chill time: 2 hours
Serving size: 1 cup
Each serving has:
142 calories
<1 g total fat
0 g saturated fat
4 g protein
32 g carbohydrate
2 g fiber
0 mg cholesterol
41 mg sodium

1. Pour soy milk into a blender, sprinkle gelatin on top, and let stand for 3 minutes to soften.

2. Meanwhile, heat orange juice in a small saucepan over high heat until boiling. Pour into the blender. Add honey, cover, and blend on low speed for 2 minutes. Pour into a medium bowl and chill for 1 hour, stirring occasionally, until thickened to egg-white consistency. (Mixture will be frothy.)

3. Gently stir in mandarin oranges, banana, and strawberries. Spoon into 4 dessert dishes and chill for 1 hour or until firm.

Variation: Use mandarin orange juice drained from the can as part of your orange juice measure. You should have about ⅔ of the called for cup.

Super Knowledge

Softening gelatin in cold liquid allows it to dissolve evenly upon mixing. You shouldn't stir the gelatin into the cold liquid, but mix it well with warm liquid to activate the protein that causes gelling when cooled.

Berry-Dotted Rice Pudding

Homey and comforting rice pudding can be filled with superfood ingredients, too.

Yield: 7 servings
Prep time: 5 minutes
Cook time: 10 minutes
Stand time: 5 minutes
Serving size: ¹/₂ cup
Each serving has:
152 calories
3 g total fat
2 g saturated fat
4 g protein
27 g carbohydrate
2 g fiber
8 mg cholesterol
122 mg sodium

3 cups cooked long-grain brown rice, cold

2 cups fat-free soy milk or milk

1 TB. honey

½ tsp. vanilla extract

¼ tsp. salt

¼ tsp. ground cinnamon

¼ tsp. ground nutmeg

½ cup fresh blueberries

⅓ cup light cream

1. Stir together rice and soy milk in a medium nonstick saucepan. Bring to a boil over high heat, stirring constantly to prevent scorching and boil-overs. Reduce heat to medium, and cook, stirring, for 5 minutes or until mixture begins to thicken. Remove from heat.

2. Stir in honey, vanilla extract, salt, cinnamon, nutmeg, and blueberries. Let stand for 5 minutes to cool slightly. Stir in light cream. Serve warm or cover and chill to serve cold.

Variation: You can substitute raisins for half or all of the blueberries.

Super Knowledge

Soy milk is not a dairy product, but a milk-replacement option made by puréeing soybeans with water. You'll find plain and flavored soy milks, as well as fat-free, low-fat, and regular selections.

Cherry-Walnut Bread

This fruit-and-nut-studded bread makes for a sweet treat filled with the benefits of a half-dozen superfoods.

3 cups whole-wheat flour

6 TB. ground flaxseed meal

1 TB. baking powder

½ tsp. salt

1 tsp. ground cinnamon

¼ tsp. ground nutmeg

1 cup dried sour cherries

½ cup raisins

½ cup unsalted diced walnuts

1¼ cups fat-free soy milk or milk

1 cup honey

1 large egg, at room temperature, or the equivalent amount of egg substitute

Yield: 16 servings
Prep time: 12 minutes
Cook time: 60 to 65 minutes
Serving size: 1 slice
Each serving has:
233 calories
4 g total fat
1 g saturated fat
6 g protein
46 g carbohydrate
6 g fiber
13 mg cholesterol
164 mg sodium

1. Preheat the oven to 350°F. Coat a 9×5×3-inch loaf pan with nonstick cooking spray.

2. Stir together whole-wheat flour, flaxseed meal, baking powder, salt, cinnamon, and nutmeg in a large bowl. Stir in cherries, raisins, and walnuts to coat.

3. Combine soy milk, honey, and egg in a medium bowl, and stir until well blended. Add to flour mixture and stir until moistened.

4. Pour batter into the loaf pan and bake for 60 to 65 minutes or until a cake tester or toothpick inserted into the middle of loaf comes out clean. Let stand for 10 minutes before removing from the pan to cool completely on a wire rack. Cut into ¹/₂-inch slices to serve.

Heroic Hints

One 12-ounce container of honey equals 1 cup. The honey's flavor and color are testaments to the flowers visited by the honey bees. Generally, deeper colored honey boasts a bolder flavor than more mild light-colored honey.

Cinnamon-Swirled Applesauce Bread

A loaf of this pretty quick bread makes a nice hostess gift—and tastes great, too!

Yield: 16
Prep time: 12 minutes
Cook time: 50 to 60 minutes
Serving size: 1 slice
Each serving has:
96 calories
<1 g total fat
<1 g saturated fat
3 g protein
21 g carbohydrate
2 g fiber
13 mg cholesterol
135 mg sodium

1½ cups all-purpose flour

1 cup whole-wheat flour

2 tsp. baking powder

½ tsp. salt

1 cup unsweetened apple-sauce

1 cup fat-free soy milk or milk

¼ cup honey

1 large egg, at room temperature, or the equivalent amount of egg substitute

1½ TB. ground cinnamon

1. Preheat the oven to 350°F. Coat a 9×5×3-inch nonstick loaf pan with nonstick cooking spray.

2. Stir together all-purpose flour, whole-wheat flour, baking powder, and salt in a large bowl. Combine applesauce, soy milk, honey, and egg in a medium bowl, and stir until blended. Pour into flour mixture, and stir until moistened.

3. Transfer 1¹/₂ cups batter to the medium bowl. Add cinnamon and stir until thoroughly blended. Turn plain batter into the loaf pan. Pour cinnamon batter over top. Using a knife, cut cinnamon batter into plain batter, swirling together without blending.

4. Bake for 50 to 60 minutes or until loaf tests done with a cake tester. Cool in the pan for 5 minutes before removing to a wire rack to cool completely. Cut into ¹/₂-inch slices to serve.

 Super Knowledge _____

Wire racks are called for to cool baked goods because they allow air to circulate all around, resulting in even cooling.

Honey Pot Cocoa Fruit Dip

Delight in this rich, creamy, chocolately blend.

½ cup fat-free sour cream

¼ cup unsweetened cocoa powder

¼ cup honey

½ tsp. vanilla extract

Yield: 7 servings
Prep time: 5 minutes
Serving size: 2 table-spoons
Each serving has:
61 calories
1 g total fat
<1 g saturated fat
2 g protein
14 g carbohydrate
1 g fiber
2 mg cholesterol
14 mg sodium

1. Combine sour cream, cocoa powder, honey, and vanilla extract in a small bowl and stir until well blended.

2. Serve swirled around fresh strawberries, banana chunks, apple slices, pitted cherries, or your favorite chocolate-friendly fruits. Store any leftovers in the refrigerator.

Heroic Hints

Measure the cocoa powder in a ¼-cup measure before measuring the honey in the same cup. The dusting of cocoa powder that remains in the measuring cup helps the honey to release easily.

Cran-Orange Yogurt Freeze

Sip this cool, creamy, fruity dessert drink on hot summer days.

Yield: 2 servings
Prep time: 4 minutes
Serving size: 1 cup
Each serving has:
301 calories
5 g total fat
3 g saturated fat
10 g protein
57 g carbohydrate
4 g fiber
65 mg cholesterol
63 mg sodium

1 medium navel orange, peeled, seeded, and chopped

1 cup cranberry juice

1 tsp. honey

1 cup low-fat vanilla frozen yogurt

1. Combine orange, cranberry juice, and honey in a blender. Cover and blend on high speed for 30 to 60 seconds or until well blended.

2. Add frozen yogurt to the blender. Cover and blend on high speed for 10 seconds or just until mixed. Serve immediately.

Kryptonite _____

Be sure to buy 100 percent cranberry juice for this drink. You'll find lots of cranberry juice "drinks" and "cocktails" on the market, but they have added sugar and, therefore, extra calories.

Melonana Berry Smoothies

This delicious beverage proves the adage: the whole is greater than the sum of its parts. So give it a taste, even if you're not partial to the individual ingredients.

1 cup cubed cantaloupe

1 cup hulled fresh straw-berries

1 very ripe banana, peeled and broken into chunks

⅔ cup fat-free plain yogurt

⅓ cup white grape juice

2 TB. honey

⅛ tsp. dried mint

12 large ice cubes

Yield: 4 servings
Prep time: 3 minutes
Serving size: 1 cup
Each serving has:
112 calories
<1 g total fat
0 g saturated fat
3 g protein
27 g carbohydrate
2 g fiber
<1 mg cholesterol
33 mg sodium

1. Combine cantaloupe, strawberries, banana, yogurt, grape juice, honey, and mint in a blender. Cover and blend on high speed for 30 seconds or until well blended.

2. Remove the cap from the blender's lid and, with the blender running, add ice cubes one at a time. Serve cold.

Heroic Hints

Cantaloupes are best in the summer months. Choose a ripe cantaloupe by smelling for a sweet fragrance and pressing on the ends; both the stem end and the blossom end should give slightly. Its peel should be evenly netted and free of blemishes and green areas

Chocolate Chip Cookie Balls

Watch these nutty, chocolaty bites disappear without your family ever suspecting your secret ingredient—pinto beans.

Yield: 6 dozen
Prep time: 12 minutes
Cook time: 8 minutes per batch
Serving size: 2 cookies
Each serving has:
124 calories
6 g total fat
1 g saturated fat
4 g protein
16 g carbohydrate
3 g fiber
12 mg cholesterol
103 mg sodium

1 cup puréed drained cooked or canned pinto beans

2 large eggs, at room temperature

½ cup fat-free milk

½ cup honey

1 tsp. vanilla extract

1½ cups ground flaxseed meal

1 cup all-purpose flour

1 cup whole-wheat flour

1¼ tsp. baking soda

½ tsp. salt

1 cup unsalted diced walnuts

1 cup semi-sweet chocolate chips

1. Preheat the oven to 350°F. Line cookie sheets with parchment paper.

2. Combine puréed pinto beans, eggs, milk, and honey in a large mixing bowl. Stir until well blended. Stir in vanilla extract.

3. Stir together flaxseed meal, all-purpose flour, whole-wheat flour, baking soda, and salt in a medium mixing bowl. Gradually stir into bean mixture until moistened. (Batter will be stiff.) Fold in walnuts and chocolate chips until evenly distributed.

4. Using a 1-tablespoon cookie scoop, drop dough onto the prepared cookie sheets 1-inch apart. Bake for 8 minutes or until golden brown around edges. Remove to a wire rack to cool. Store in an airtight container in the refrigerator.

Heroic Hints

To make the pinto bean purée, place drained cooked or canned pinto beans in a blender. You'll need about 1½ cups beans to make 1 cup purée. Cover and purée on low speed for 3 minutes or until all beans are broken and a paste forms, scraping down the sides of the blender and stirring as needed to redistribute beans.

Glossary

al dente Italian for "against the teeth." Refers to pasta or rice that's neither soft nor hard, but just slightly firm against the teeth.

all-purpose flour Flour that contains only the inner part of the wheat grain. Usable for all purposes from cakes to gravies.

allspice Named for its flavor echoes of several spices (cinnamon, cloves, nutmeg), allspice is used in many desserts and in rich marinades and stews.

almonds Mild, sweet, and crunchy nuts that combine nicely with creamy and sweet food items.

alpha-carotene A carotenoid that the body converts to vitamin A.

alpha-linolenic acid An essential fatty acid (EFA), meaning it's needed for the body to work properly and the body cannot make its own. This EFA is found mostly in flaxseeds, canola oil, and walnuts.

anthocyanidin Phytochemicals that work to maintain healthy blood vessels. They're also responsible for the dark reds, blues, and purples in some fruits and vegetables.

antioxidants Substances that provide protection to the cells in the body from damage caused by free radicals. In doing so, they may reduce the risks of certain cancers and age-related diseases. *See also* free radicals.

bake To cook in a dry oven. Dry-heat cooking often results in a crisping of the exterior of the food being cooked. Moist-heat cooking, through methods such as steaming, poaching, etc., brings a much different, moist quality to the food.

balsamic vinegar Vinegar produced primarily in Italy from a specific type of grape and aged in wood barrels. It's heavier, darker, and sweeter than most vinegars.

barbecue To quick-cook over high heat, or to cook something long and slow in a rich liquid (barbecue sauce).

basil A flavorful, almost sweet, resinous herb delicious with tomatoes and used in all kinds of Italian or Mediterranean-style dishes.

baste To keep foods moist during cooking by spooning, brushing, or drizzling with a liquid.

beat To quickly mix substances.

beta-carotene An antioxidant that the body converts to vitamin A. Several antioxidants do this, but beta-carotene is the easiest for the body to transform.

beta-cryptoxanthin A carotenoid family that the body turns into vitamin A.

beta-glucan A soluble fiber that, when combined with water, creates viscous, jelly-like liquid.

black pepper A biting and pungent seasoning, freshly ground pepper is a must for many dishes and adds an extra level of flavor and taste.

blanch To place a food in boiling water for about 1 minute (or less) to partially cook the exterior and then submerge in or rinse with cool water to halt the cooking.

blend To completely mix something, usually with a blender or food processor, more slowly than beating.

blue cheese A blue-veined cheese that crumbles easily and has a somewhat soft texture, usually sold in a block. The color is from a flavorful, edible mold that's often added or injected into the cheese.

boil To heat a liquid to a point where water is forced to turn into steam, causing the liquid to bubble. To boil something is to insert it into boiling water. A rapid boil is when a lot of bubbles form on the surface of the liquid.

breadcrumbs Tiny pieces of crumbled dry bread, often used for topping or coating.

brine A highly salted, often seasoned, liquid used to flavor and preserve foods. To brine a food is to soak, or preserve, it by submerging it in brine. The salt in the brine penetrates the fibers of the meat and makes it moist and tender.

broil To cook in a dry oven under the overhead high-heat element.

broth *See* stock.

brown rice Whole-grain rice including the germ with a characteristic pale brown or tan color. Brown rice is more nutritious and flavorful than white rice.

brown To cook in a skillet, turning, until the food's surface is seared and brown in color, to lock in the juices.

bulgur A wheat kernel that's been steamed, dried, and crushed and is sold in fine and coarse textures.

capers Flavorful buds of a Mediterranean plant, ranging in size from *nonpareil* (about the size of a small pea) to larger, grape-size caper berries produced in Spain.

capsaicin The odorless, flavorless chemical that causes the burn when you eat peppers or foods that contain them.

carbohydrate A nutritional component found in starches, sugars, fruits, and vegetables that can cause a rise in blood glucose levels. Carbohydrates are a primary energy source for the body.

carotenoids Strong antioxidants that may lower the risk of heart disease, some types of cancer, age-related eye diseases, and lung diseases. Carotenoids are responsible for the vibrant orange and red colors of many vegetables.

catechin A flavonoid and antioxidant found in cocoa as well as white and green tea.

cayenne A fiery spice made from (hot) chili peppers, especially the cayenne chili, a slender, red, and very hot pepper.

cheddar The ubiquitous hard cow's milk cheese with a rich, buttery flavor that ranges from mellow to sharp. Originally produced in England, cheddar is now produced worldwide.

chili powder A seasoning blend that includes chili pepper, cumin, garlic, and oregano. Proportions vary among different versions, but they all offer a warm, rich flavor.

chilies (or **chilis** or **chiles**) Any one of many different "hot" peppers, ranging in intensity from the relatively mild ancho pepper to the blisteringly hot habanero.

chives A member of the onion family, chives grow in bunches of long leaves that resemble tall grass or the green tops of onions. They lend a light onion flavor to dishes.

chop To cut into pieces, usually qualified by an adverb such as "*coarsely* chopped," or by a size measurement such as "chopped into $1/2$-inch pieces." "Finely chopped" is much closer to mince.

cider vinegar Vinegar produced from apple cider, popular in North America.

cilantro A member of the parsley family and used in Mexican cooking (especially salsa) and some Asian dishes. Use in moderation, as the flavor can overwhelm. The seed of cilantro is the spice coriander.

cinnamaldehyde An oil that gives cinnamon its spicy flavor. It's found in the bark of cinnamon trees.

cinnamon A sweet, rich, aromatic spice commonly used in baking or desserts. Cinnamon can also be used for delicious and interesting entrées.

clove A sweet, strong, almost wintergreen-flavor spice used in baking and with meats such as ham.

collagen A protein that plays a role in building the body's connective tissues like tendons, ligaments, skin, and bones.

couscous Granular semolina (durum wheat) that's cooked and used in many Mediterranean and North African dishes.

c-reactive protein A protein found in the blood that rises with inflammation. It is often used as a marker of heart disease and other inflammatory-related diseases.

cumin A fiery, smoky-tasting spice popular in Middle Eastern and Indian dishes. Cumin is a seed; ground cumin seed is the most common form used in cooking.

curd A gelatinous substance resulting from coagulated milk used to make cheese. Curd also refers to dishes of similar texture, such as dishes made with egg (lemon curd).

curry powder A ground blend of rich and flavorful spices used as a basis for curry and many other Indian-influenced dishes. Common ingredients include hot pepper, nutmeg, cumin, cinnamon, pepper, and turmeric. Some curry can also be found in paste form.

dash A few drops, usually of a liquid, released by a quick shake of, for example, a bottle of hot sauce.

dice To cut into small cubes about ¼-inch square.

Dijon mustard A hearty, spicy mustard made in the style of the Dijon region of France.

dill An herb perfect for eggs, salmon, cheese dishes, and, of course, vegetables (pickles!).

dollop A spoonful of something creamy and thick, like sour cream or whipped cream.

dredge To cover a piece of food with a dry substance such as flour or cornmeal.

drizzle To lightly sprinkle drops of a liquid over food, often as the finishing touch to a dish.

dry In the context of wine, one that contains little or no residual sugar, so it's not very sweet.

ellagic acid This polyphenol has antioxidant properties and may help reduce the risk of certain cancers.

entrée The main dish in a meal. In France, the entrée is considered the first course.

epicatechin A flavonoid found in cocoa, red wine, and green tea that helps maintain heart health by improving blood flow.

extra-virgin olive oil *See* olive oil.

fat-soluble vitamins Vitamins that are dissolvable in fat and stored in the body's fat.

feta A white, crumbly, sharp, and salty cheese popular in Greek cooking and on salads. Traditional feta is usually made with sheep milk, but feta-style cheese can be made from sheep, cow, or goat milk.

fillet A piece of meat or seafood with the bones removed.

flake To break into thin sections, as with fish.

flavonoids The most powerful and abundant phytochemical group in the diet.

floret The flower or bud end of broccoli or cauliflower.

flour   Grains ground into a meal. Wheat is perhaps the most common flour. Flour is also made from oats, rye, buckwheat, soybeans, etc. *See also* all-purpose flour; whole-wheat flour.

folate (or **folic acid**)   A B-vitamin that plays a big role in preventing birth defects and producing red blood cells.

fold   To combine a dense and light mixture with a circular action from the middle of the bowl.

free radicals   The natural result of the process of food being turned into energy. They also come from exposure to UV radiation, smoke, and pollution. They damage the body's cells. *See also* antioxidants.

frittata   A skillet-cooked mixture of eggs and other ingredients that's not stirred but is cooked slowly and then either flipped or finished under the broiler.

fry   *See* sauté.

garbanzo beans (or **chickpeas**)   A yellow-gold, roundish bean used as the base ingredient in hummus. Chickpeas are high in fiber and low in fat.

garlic   A member of the onion family, a pungent and flavorful element in many savory dishes. A garlic bulb contains multiple cloves. Each clove, when chopped, provides about 1 teaspoon garlic. Most recipes call for cloves or chopped garlic by the teaspoon.

garnish   An embellishment not vital to the dish but added to enhance visual appeal.

ginger   Available in fresh root or dried, ground form, ginger adds a pungent, sweet, and spicy quality to a dish.

grate   To shave into tiny pieces using a sharp rasp or grater.

grind   To reduce a large, hard substance, often a seasoning such as peppercorns, to the consistency of sand.

HDL cholesterol   The cholesterol in the blood that helps carry LDL ("bad") cholesterol out of the body. Often referred to as "good" cholesterol.

hesperetin   A flavonoid shown in animal studies to possess many health-promoting properties involving blood pressure, inflammation, and heart disease.

hors d'oeuvre   French for "outside of work" (the "work" being the main meal), an hors d'oeuvre can be any dish served as a starter before the meal.

horseradish   A sharp, spicy root that forms the flavor base in many condiments from cocktail sauce to sharp mustards. Prepared horseradish contains vinegar and oil, among other ingredients. Use pure horseradish much more sparingly than the prepared version, or try cutting it with sour cream.

hummus   A thick, Middle Eastern spread made of puréed garbanzo beans, lemon juice, olive oil, garlic, and often tahini (sesame seed paste).

hypoglycemia   The condition of having episodes of low sugar levels in the blood. It's the opposite of hyperglycemia, a classic sign of diabetes.

insoluble fiber   The part of plant-based foods that the body cannot digest. It's found in wheat bran, whole grains, fruits, and vegetables, and it increases the rate of food going through the intestines.

isoflavones   Plant compounds that somewhat copy what the hormone estrogen does, which plays a role in the development of sexual characteristics and menstruation as well as reproduction.

Italian seasoning   A blend of dried herbs, including basil, oregano, rosemary, and thyme.

julienne   A French word meaning "to slice into very thin pieces."

kaempferol   A flavonoid that acts as a strong antioxidant.

kalamata olives   Traditionally from Greece, these medium-small long black olives have a smoky rich flavor.

Key limes   Very small limes grown primarily in Florida and known for their tart taste.

LDL cholesterol   Low density lipoprotein cholesterol that more easily deposits triglycerides and cholesterol in the arteries, potentially leading to the formation of atherosclerotic plaques and increasing the risk of heart attack and stroke. Often referred to as "bad" cholesterol.

lentils   Tiny lens-shape pulses used in European, Middle Eastern, and Indian cuisines.

lignans   Substances from plants that work both as antioxidants and phytoestrogens.

lutein   An antioxidant that does a great deal to improve and maintain eye health. It also plays a role in helping the heart and preventing cancer.

lycopene   A compound in the carotenoid group of phytochemicals. It works primarily as an antioxidant.

magnesium   A mineral that's essential for the body to function properly.

marinate   To soak meat, seafood, or other food in a seasoned sauce, called a marinade, which is high in acid content. The acids break down the muscle of the meat, making it tender and adding flavor.

marjoram   A sweet herb, a cousin of and similar to oregano, popular in Greek, Spanish, and Italian dishes.

melatonin   A hormone involved in regulating sleeping and waking cycles.

meld   To allow flavors to blend and spread over time. Melding is often why recipes call for overnight refrigeration and is also why some dishes taste better as leftovers.

mince   To cut into very small pieces smaller than diced pieces, about $1/8$ inch or smaller.

mold   A decorative, shaped metal pan in which contents, such as mousse or gelatin, set up and take the shape of the pan.

mull (or **mulled**)   To heat a liquid with the addition of spices and sometimes sweeteners.

myricetin   A flavonoid shown to have anti-inflammatory and anti-cancer properties in studies. It's found in fruits and vegetables, primarily berries, grapes, parsley, and spinach.

naringenin   A flavonoid shown in animal studies to possess many health-promoting properties involving blood pressure, inflammation, and heart disease.

niacin   One of the B-vitamins, also known as vitamin B_3, niacin is a water-soluble vitamin, which means the body does not store it so it must be consumed regularly.

nitric oxide   A substance within the blood stream and vessel walls that contributes to a healthy cardiovascular system.

nutmeg   A sweet, fragrant, musky spice used primarily in baking.

olive oil   A fragrant liquid produced by crushing or pressing olives. Extra-virgin olive oil—the most flavorful and highest quality—is produced from the first pressing of a batch of olives; oil is also produced from later pressings.

olives   The fruit of the olive tree commonly grown on all sides of the Mediterranean.

Black olives are also called ripe olives. Green olives are immature, although they are also widely eaten. *See also* kalamata olives.

omega-3 fatty acids   A group of fats that is essential to the body and lower blood cholesterol levels. They are found in fish oils; salmon in particular contains a high amount. The three main ones are EPA (eicosapentaenoic acid), DHA (docosahexaenoic acid), and ALA (alphalinolenic acid).

oregano   A fragrant, slightly astringent herb used in Greek, Spanish, and Italian dishes.

orzo   A rice-shape pasta used in Greek cooking.

paprika   A rich, red, warm, earthy spice that lends a rich red color to many dishes.

Parmesan   A hard, dry, flavorful cheese primarily used grated or shredded as a seasoning for Italian-style dishes.

parsley   A fresh-tasting green leafy herb, often used as a garnish.

pecans   Rich, buttery nuts, native to North America, that have a high unsaturated fat content.

peppercorns   Large, round, dried berries ground to produce pepper.

peppermint oil   An oil that gives peppermint its flavor.

pesto   A thick spread or sauce made with fresh basil leaves, garlic, olive oil, pine nuts, and Parmesan cheese. Some newer versions are made with other herbs.

phytochemicals (or **phytonutrients**)   Compounds found in plants that, although not needed for proper body function, provide tremendous benefits to improve health and/or decrease the risk of certain diseases.

phytoestrogens   Substances that come from plants and in the body act similarly to the hormone estrogen, which is involved in the development of sexual characteristics and menstruation as well as reproduction.

pickle   A food, usually a vegetable such as a cucumber, that's been pickled in brine.

pinch   An unscientific measurement term, the amount of an ingredient—typically a dry, granular substance such as an herb or seasoning—you can hold between your finger and thumb.

pine nuts (also **pignoli** or **piñon**)   Nuts grown on pine trees, that are rich (read: high fat), flavorful, and a bit pine-y. Pine nuts are a traditional component of pesto and add a wonderful hearty crunch to many other recipes.

pita bread   A flat, hollow wheat bread often used for sandwiches or sliced, pizza style, into slices. Pita bread is terrific soft with dips or baked or broiled as a vehicle for other ingredients.

plant sterols   Plant-based substances that compete with cholesterol for absorption by the intestines. By doing so, they help lower cholesterol levels.

potassium   A mineral involved in controlling blood pressure and regulating muscle contractions.

prebiotics   Nondigestible substances in foods that encourage the growth of good bacteria in the intestines.

preheat   To turn on an oven, broiler, or other cooking appliance in advance of cooking so the temperature will be at the desired level when the assembled dish is ready for cooking.

proanthocyanidins   Flavonoids that act as antioxidants in the body.

probiotics   Living microscopic organisms that when eaten provide an array of health benefits.

purée   To reduce a food to a thick, creamy texture, usually using a blender or food processor.

quercetin   A major dietary flavonoid. It may help lower risk of asthma, lung cancer, and heart disease.

reduce   To boil or simmer a broth or sauce to remove some of the water content, resulting in more concentrated flavor and color.

reserve   To hold a specified ingredient for another use later in the recipe.

resveratrol   An antioxidant found primarily in red wine, grapes, raspberries, and peanuts.

rice vinegar   Vinegar produced from fermented rice or rice wine, popular in Asian-style dishes.

roast   To cook something uncovered in an oven, usually without additional liquid.

Roquefort   A world-famous (French) creamy but sharp sheep's milk cheese containing blue lines of mold.

rosemary   A pungent, sweet herb used with chicken, pork, fish, and especially lamb. A little of it goes a long way.

rosmarinic acid   A phytochemical that works as an anti-inflammatory and antioxidant.

salsa   A style of mixing fresh vegetables and/or fresh fruit in a coarse chop. Salsa can be spicy or not, fruit-based or not, and served as a starter on its own (with chips, for example) or as a companion to a main course.

saponin   Any of many of a group of substances found in plants. Several affect the heart.

sauté   To pan-cook over lower heat with less fat than used for frying.

savory   A popular herb with a fresh, woody taste.

serotonin   A nervous system transmitter that helps regulate sleep as well as appetite and mood.

sesame oil   An oil, made from pressing sesame seeds, that's tasteless if clear and aromatic and flavorful if brown.

shred   To cut into many long, thin slices.

simmer   To boil gently so the liquid barely bubbles.

skillet (also **frying pan**)   A generally heavy, flat-bottomed metal pan with a handle designed to cook food over heat on a stovetop or campfire.

skim   To remove fat or other material from the top of liquid.

slice   To cut into thin pieces.

soluble fiber   The part of plant-based foods that the body can digest that slow the rate of food going through the intestines. It's found in oats, beans, fruits, and vegetables.

steam   To suspend a food over boiling water and allow the heat of the steam (water vapor) to cook the food. A quick cooking method, steaming preserves the flavor and texture of a food.

stearic acid   A saturated fat found in animal products as well as some plant products, such as chocolate. Unlike most saturated fats, it has little to no effect on blood cholesterol levels.

steep   To let sit in hot water, as in steeping tea in hot water for 10 minutes.

stew   To slowly cook pieces of food submerged in a liquid. *Stew* can also mean a dish that has been prepared by this method.

stir-fry   To cook small pieces of food in a wok or skillet over high heat, moving and turning the food quickly to cook all sides.

stock   A flavorful broth made by cooking meats and/or vegetables with seasonings until the liquid absorbs these flavors. This liquid is then strained and the solids discarded. Stock can be eaten alone or used as a base for soups, stews, etc.

sulforaphane   An isothiocyanate found in broccoli and broccoli sprouts that acts as an antioxidant.

thyme   A minty, zesty herb.

toast   To heat something, usually bread, so it's browned and crisp.

tofu   A cheeselike substance made from soybeans and soy milk.

tryptophan   An essential amino acid the body uses for building protein and essential neurotransmitters.

varietal   The type of grape used to make a wine, such as Cabernet Sauvignon, Merlot, or Chardonnay.

vegetable steamer   An insert for a large saucepan or a special pot with tiny holes in the bottom designed to fit on another pot to hold food to be steamed above boiling water. *See also* steam.

vinegar   An acidic liquid widely used as dressing and seasoning, often made from fermented grapes, apples, or rice. *See also* balsamic vinegar; cider vinegar; rice vinegar; white vinegar; wine vinegar.

vintage   The year in which the grapes were harvested and, usually, in which the wine was produced.

vitamin A   A fat-soluble vitamin essential for the body to function. Because it is fat-soluble, the body can store it and, therefore, it is possible to overdose.

vitamin C   A water-soluble vitamin the body needs to work properly. It's involved in tissue growth and repair as well as wound healing. It is not stored by the body.

vitamin E   An essential fat-soluble vitamin involved in red blood cell development. It also protects the body from free radical damage. It's stored in the body; therefore, an overdose, which would most likely only occur with supplement use, is possible.

vitamin K   An essential fat-soluble vitamin involved in blood clotting.

walnuts   A rich, slightly woody-flavored nut.

whisk   To rapidly mix, introducing air to the mixture.

white mushrooms   Button mushrooms. When fresh, they have an earthy smell and an appealing soft crunch.

white vinegar   The most common type of vinegar, produced from grain.

whole-wheat flour   Wheat flour that contains the entire grain.

wild rice   Actually a grass with a rich, nutty flavor, popular as an unusual and nutritious side dish.

wine vinegar   Vinegar produced from red or white wine.

wok   A pan for quick-cooking.

Worcestershire sauce   Originally developed in India and containing tamarind, this spicy sauce is used as a seasoning for many meats and other dishes.

zeaxanthin   A carotenoid that works as an antioxidant protecting the eye and preventing certain cancers. It's found in green leafy vegetables and orange fruits and vegetables.

zest   Small slivers of peel, usually from a citrus fruit such as lemon, lime, or orange.

zester   A kitchen tool used to scrape zest off a fruit. A small grater also works well.

zinc   One of the minerals essential for the body to function correctly.

B

Superfoods Cheat Sheet

All the superfoods in this book pack quite the nutritional punch. Sometimes it can be hard to keep straight what benefits the different foods provide. Here's a quick list you can refer to at a glance to get an idea of what each food offers. This list is not all-inclusive; it simply lists the most abundant or unique nutrients found in each food. More detailed information is provided in the beginning of each chapter, as well as in *The Pocket Idiot's Guide to Superfoods* (Alpha Books, 2007).

Keep in mind, as with all science, research is on-going, and in some cases is in the preliminary stages. Also, it's best to obtain these potential benefits from the whole foods themselves, not simply buy loading up on pills and other supplements where there could be a risk of overdosing.

almonds Vitamin E (protects against free radical damage), kaempferol (protects against age-related diseases), quercetin (promotes lung and heart health), catechin (protects against cardiovascular disease), magnesium (helps maintain healthy blood vessels).

beans Prebiotics (improves colon health), plant sterols (lowers cholesterol), fiber (lowers cholesterol, prevents constipation).

blueberries Fiber (lowers cholesterol, prevents constipation), anthocyanidins (helps with memory loss), myricetin (fights inflammation).

broccoli   Quercetin (promotes lung and heart health), sulforaphane (possibly protects against cancer), beta-carotene (promotes healthy eyes and skin), lutein (promotes eye health), vitamin K (helps blood clot), vitamin C (boots the immune system), vitamin A (promotes healthy skin, bones, and mucous membranes).

carrots   Beta-cryptoxanthin (promotes eye health), vitamin A (promotes healthy skin, bones, and mucous membranes), alpha-carotene (promotes healthy skin and bones), beta-carotene (promotes healthy eyes and skin).

cayenne   Capsaicin (clears respiratory congestion), vitamin A (promotes healthy skin, bones, and mucous membranes).

cherries   Fiber (lowers cholesterol, prevents constipation), melatonin (aids sleep regulation), anthocyanidins (helps with memory loss).

chocolate   Epicathechin (improves blood flow), catechin (protects against cardiovascular disease), cocoa (reduces blood clotting).

cinnamon   Cinnamaldehyde (decreases blood clotting), fiber (lowers cholesterol, prevents constipation).

cranberries   Fiber (lowers cholesterol, prevents constipation), proanthocyanidins (helps prevent bacteria from sticking).

flax   Omega-3 fatty acids (promotes heart health), lignans (promotes women's health).

grape juice   Proanthocyanidins (helps prevent bacteria from sticking), myricetin (fights inflammation).

honey   Carbohydrates (provides energy).

oats   Beta-glucan (lowers cholesterol).

oranges   Vitamin C (boots the immune system), hesperetin (potentially helps with blood pressure, inflammation, and heart disease), naringenin (potentially helps with blood pressure, inflammation, and heart disease).

peanuts   Vitamin E (protects against free radical damage), folate (promotes heart health), resveratrol (promotes heart health).

peppermint   Peppermint oil (aids digestion), rosmarinic acid (helps with asthma).

pumpkin   Alpha-carotene (promotes healthy skin and bones), beta-cryptoxanthin (promotes healthy eyes), vitamin A (promotes healthy skin, bones, and mucous membranes).

red bell peppers   Vitamin C (boosts the immune system), vitamin A (promotes healthy skin, bones, and mucous membranes), beta-carotene (promotes healthy eyes and skin).

red wine   Resveratrol (promotes heart health), saponin (lowers cholesterol).

salmon   Omega-3 fatty acids (promotes heart health).

soy   Isoflavones (helps with heart disease).

spinach   Beta-carotene (promotes healthy eyes and skin), lutein (promotes eye health), vitamin K (helps blood clot), vitamin A (promotes healthy skin, bones, and mucous membranes), zeaxanthin (promotes eye health), myricetin (fights inflammation).

strawberries   Fiber (lowers cholesterol, prevents constipation), anthocyanidins (helps with memory loss), proanthocyanidins (helps prevent bacteria from sticking), quercetin (promotes lung and heart health), ellagic acid (may lower cancer risk), vitamin C (boosts the immune system), folate (protects against heart disease), potassium (regulates blood pressure).

sweet potato   Beta-carotene (promotes healthy eyes and skin), vitamin A (promotes healthy skin, bones, and mucous membranes), vitamin C (boosts the immune system).

tea   Catechins (protects against cardiovascular disease), quercetin (promotes lung and heart health), myricetin (fights inflammation).

tomatoes   Vitamin C (boosts the immune system), vitamin A (promotes healthy skin, bones, and mucous membranes), lycopene (fights cancer).

turkey   Niacin (aids energy and metabolism), tryptophan (helps with sleep and relaxation), zinc (regulates gene activity).

walnuts   Melatonin (aids sleep regulation), omega-3 fatty acids (promotes heart health).

yogurt   Probiotics (helps digestion).

Resources

To learn more about the superfoods in this book, you can peruse these websites, among others you're sure to find online. We've also included several websites about healthful eating in general.

Websites

Almond Board of California

www.almondsarein.com

Check here for more information about—you guessed it—almonds. You'll find research and nutritional information as well as tips and recipes.

American Dietetic Association

www.eatright.org

At this website, the national association of registered dietitians, you'll find food and nutrition information, learn how to find a registered dietitian in your area, and more.

Beans for Health Alliance

www.beansforhealth.com

Here you'll find more research and nutritional information as well as additional recipes.

California Strawberry Commission
www.calstrawberry.com
Log on here for nutritional information about strawberries, recipes, and more.

California Walnuts
www.walnuts.org
Check out this site for nutrition and health information plus walnut recipes.

Cherry Marketing Institute
www.choosecherries.com
Here you'll find tips, recipes, and more information about the health benefits cherries provide.

Cranberry Institute
www.cranberryinstitute.com
Turn here for the latest news and research about cranberries.

Department of Health and Human Services
www.healthierus.gov/dietaryguidelines
Here you can find the complete copy of the Dietary Guidelines for Americans 2005 (the latest recommendations until 2010) and related articles.

Federal Citizen Information Center
www.pueblo.gsa.gov
Free publication offers.

Flax Council of Canada
www.flaxcouncil.ca
Log on here for nutrition, recipes, and more information about flax.

Flax RD
www.flaxrd.com
This site provides more flax information.

Lipton Tea
www.lipton.com
Lipton offers a cupful of information about tea and its health benefits here.

McCormick
www.mccormick.com
Want more information about cooking with spices? McCormick has you covered.

My Pyramid (U.S. Department of Agriculture)

www.mypyramid.gov

Log on here for more information about My Pyramid and to personalize it for you and your family.

National Agricultural Library

www.nutrition.gov

Information on nutrition, healthy eating, and food safety.

National Dairy Council

www.nationaldairycouncil.org

The National Dairy Council offers information about dairy foods such as low-fat milks, yogurts, and cheeses and their health benefits.

National Fisheries Institute

www.aboutseafood.com

If you're a seafood lover, go here for recipes, tips, health information, and more.

National Honey Board

www.honey.com

Turn to the National Honey Board for the latest research and health information about honey.

National Turkey Federation

www.eatturkey.com

Want to learn more about turkey? Who doesn't?! Check out this site for tips, recipes, nutrition, and more about turkey.

Nutrition.gov

www.nutrition.gov

Check out this site for nutrition and health guidelines, resources, and more from the U.S. government.

NutritionData.com

www.nutritiondata.com

This site enables you to calculate nutrition information for specific foods and recipes.

Peanut Institute

www.peanut-institute.org

Log on here for scientific research, recipes, and more on peanuts and peanut butter.

Produce for Better Health Foundation

www.fruitsandveggiesmorematters.org

Check out this site for health benefits, serving size information, as well as tips and recipes for fruits and vegetables.

PubMed (National Library of Medicine Search Engine)

www.pubmed.gov

This site houses information about research studies and articles published in health and medical journals.

Quaker Oatmeal

www.quakeroatmeal.com

Quaker's site offers recipes, healthy living tips, product information, and more about oats.

Salada

www.greentea.com

At its website, Salada offers more information about the health benefits of tea.

Soy Information Clearinghouse

www.soybean.org

Turn here for health benefit information, recipes, and more about soy.

Supermarket Savvy

www.supermarketsavvy.com

For information on how to grocery shop healthier, check out what Supermarket Savvy has to say.

United Soybean Board

www.unitedsoybean.org

Check here for information about soy and soy foods.

United States Department of Agriculture

www.usda.gov

The USDA offers a variety of health and nutrition information, fact sheets, and more at its website.

Welch's

www.welchs.com

For research, nutrition information, and recipes for Concord grapes, Welch's is the spot.

Wild Blueberries
www.wildblueberries.com
To learn more about blueberries' health benefits and recipes as well as news and information on wild blueberries, turn here.

World's Healthiest Food
www.whfoods.org
Log on here for health information, recipes, and much more on many foods and nutrients.

Books

Dunford, Marie. *Nutrition Logic: Food First, Supplements Second.* Kingsburg, CA: Pink Robin Publishing, 2003.

Duyff, Roberta Larsen. *The American Dietetic Association's Complete Food and Nutrition Guide, Third Edition.* New York: John Wiley and Sons, 2006.

Heroux, Cindy. *The Manual That Should Have Come with Your Body.* Oviedo, FL: Speaking of Wellness, 2003.

Institute of Medicine. *Dietary Reference Intakes: The Essential Guide to Nutrient Requirements.* Washington, DC: The National Academies Press, 2006.

McIndoo, Heidi Reichenberger. *The Pocket Idiot's Guide to Superfoods.* Indianapolis: Alpha Books, 2007.

Melina, Vesanto, Dina Aronson, and Jo Stepaniak. *Food Allergy Survival Guide: Surviving and Thriving with Food Allergies and Sensitivities.* Summertown, TN: Healthy Living Publications, 2004.

Office of Disease Prevention and Health Promotion. *A Healthier You: Based on the Dietary Guidelines for Americans.* Rockville, MD: Office of Disease Prevention and Health, 2005.

Sass, Cynthia, and Denise Maher. *Your Diet is Driving Me Crazy: When Food Conflicts Get in the Way of Your Love Life.* New York: Marlowe & Company, 2004.

Shield, Jodie, and Mary Catherine Mullen. *American Dietetic Association Guide to Healthy Eating for Kids: How Your Children Can Eat Smart from 5 to 12.* Hoboken: John Wiley & Sons, 2002.

Ward, Elizabeth M. *The Pocket Idiot's Guide to the New Food Pyramids*. Indianapolis: Alpha Books, 2005.

Zied, Elisa, and Ruth Winter. *So What Can I Eat?!: How to Make Sense of the New Dietary Guidelines for Americans and Make Them Your Own*. Hoboken: Wiley, 2006.

Newsletters

Nutrition Action Health Letter
Center for Science in the Public Interest
1875 Connecticut Avenue, N.W., Suite 300
Washington, DC 20009
www.cspinet.org

Tufts University Health and Nutrition Letter
PO Box 420235
Palm Coast, FL 32142-0235
www.healthletter.tufts.edu

Index

C

Q

R

W–X

Y–Z

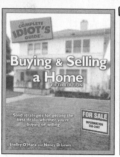
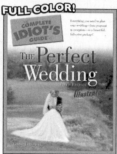
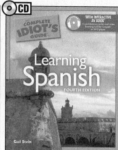

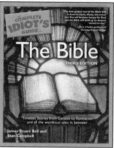
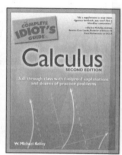

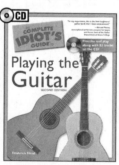